Bombs, IEDs, and Explosives

Identification, Investigation, and Disposal Techniques

Bombs, IEDs, and Explosives

Identification, Investigation, and Disposal Techniques

Bombs, IEDs, and Explosives

Identification, Investigation, and Disposal Techniques

Paul R. Laska

Paul R. Laska Forensic Consulting, Inc.
Palm City, Florida, USA

CRC Press
Taylor & Francis Group
Boca Raton London New York

CRC Press is an imprint of the
Taylor & Francis Group, an **informa** business

CRC Press
Taylor & Francis Group
6000 Broken Sound Parkway NW, Suite 300
Boca Raton, FL 33487-2742

Printed on acid-free paper
Version Date: 20150521

International Standard Book Number-13: 978-1-4987-1449-5 (Hardback)

Visit the Taylor & Francis Web site at
http://www.taylorandfrancis.com

and the CRC Press Web site at
http://www.crcpress.com

Personnel and trucks representing some of the bomb disposal and investigative agencies of South Florida gathered at the memorial service for Thomas Brodie in 2009 to honor his memory and legacy. (Courtesy of Miami-Dade Police Department.)

This work is dedicated to two related personages.

Thomas G. Brodie, MBE, joined the then Dade County Sheriff's Office (now Miami-Dade Police Department) in 1953. He soon gravitated to the Crime Scene Bureau of the Crime Lab. He was attracted to the bomb squad within that bureau, was trained by their lead bomb technician, and then undertook his own education, traveling to places such as New York, London, and West Germany to learn methods in use in those locations. Capt. Brodie was one of those who met to establish the International Association of Bomb Technicians and Investigators in 1971, and worked tirelessly as a member of that organization thereafter. He also gave back many times more than he took; he was always willing to mentor, taught tirelessly, and designed various tools and techniques for the bomb disposal community. His crowning achievement, designed in cooperation with his fellow criminalist and friend, Bob Worsham, was the open top bomb transport device, which continues to this day to be manufactured and used by bomb techs to transport devices to safe locations for disposal. Although Capt. Brodie passed away in 2009, his impact and influence on bomb disposal lives on.

The second personage is a group—the bomb disposal community of South Florida. The 12 active units of this region have long been in the forefront of bomb disposal training and research. The makeup of South Florida—international commerce, tourist mecca, criminal/terrorist magnet, and other such attributes—ensures that it remains active in bomb response, and thus cutting edge. These units, despite being military, federal, county, and municipal, maintain close relations, working and cooperating as one. They also bear a significant honor—the county and city bomb squads of South Florida are all progeny of Thomas Brodie; each squad had some degree of impetus from Tom Brodie in its founding and training.

CONTENTS

PREFACE

Bomb disposal is one of the least understood facets of the public safety function. To the public, bomb technicians consist of the fearless who know to cut the green wire. To their fellow firefighters and police officers, they are insane fools confronting certain death. To the administrator, it is an expensive function that is rarely seen to produce, especially regarding the public relations that administrations thrive on. The realities are far different from these expectations.

As an organized function, bomb disposal only dates to the early twentieth century. However, it has roots that can be traced through several hundred years of prior events. Its evolution has been that of a technical field, with logically minded practitioners developing tools and techniques to safely address devices designed to kill and destroy.

The field also addresses a much wider range of issues than just disassembly of bombs. Bomb technicians' experience has made them the experts in pre-planning for potential targets. They have developed techniques for responding to threats, from proper recording to safe and efficient searching. Their knowledge of explosives, bomb design, and explosive effects makes the bomb squad a central figure in the investigation of explosions and bombings. Because of their training in the safe and proper disposal of explosive materials, bomb technicians are the lead component in the destruction of a wide variety of reactive materials—from ammunition surrendered to agencies or collected from evidence rooms and firearms training units to various pyrotechnic materials turned into local solid waste management agencies, to deteriorating shock-sensitive industrial chemicals that present significant dangers to a community.

While civilian bomb technicians are not trained to do the work of military explosive ordnance disposal (EOD) specialists, they will often be the first knowledgeable responders to a recovery of military munitions in the community. Their training will, at the least, permit them to establish correct safety actions pending the arrival of military EOD assets; in many situations, they will be able to recognize certain common and simple devices and they may be in the position of safely collecting until the military can respond or even conducting appropriate render-safe actions.

As explosives are a form of hazardous chemicals, there is a strong relationship between them and hazardous materials (hazmat) response personnel. Explosive, shock-sensitive, or explosively reactive chemicals may be referred to the bomb squad to safely mitigate. Some situations may require the use of explosives to breach a container and release or destroy a material threatening an area. With the growing specter of chemical, biological, and radiological terrorism, the alliance of bomb disposal and hazardous materials response teams provides a strong, technically competent approach to such incidents and threats.

Finally, the bomb squad brings an assortment of tools and techniques that may be used by other public safety practitioners. Tactical teams may benefit from robotics, disposal of misfired munitions, or other knowledge of the bomb technician. Crime scene investigators may utilize x-ray viewing, endoscopy, and other equipment that is part of the hazardous device technician's stock in trade.

This work is not intended to guide one to the manufacture of explosives, construction of IEDs, or to train the budding bomb technician. With regard to the former two subjects, while there are many publications and Internet pages dedicated to just those subjects, they are also fraught with mistakes, sloppiness, and hazards. As to the latter, one must undertake the serious study of the field through attendance at an appropriate training site; the field requires both knowledge and skills to ensure safety and success.

Throughout this work, I have inserted short historical incidents relevant to the section. What we deal with is not new; we must always remember the events of the past, learn from history, and let what has passed help us improve for today and the future.

The following pages attempt to introduce the concepts, basic knowledge, and a variety of skill sets of the hazardous device technician. It is hoped to be of value to the incoming technician, administrators, and even the experienced technician and commander. While it reflects the American experience, it should be seen by others as a potential source of ideas to possibly inject into other programs.

Throughout public safety and the military, it is well noted that the only constant is change. Whether verbiage, acronyms, policies/procedures, equipment, or nature of threats, change will be constant. Even as this book goes to print, no doubt there will be changes already occurring. However, the meat of this remains also a constant; it may still be applied to new events, and new verbiage merely used to replace the old.

Meanwhile, to my brothers and sisters worldwide, I will repeat the words of my friend and occasional boss, Jerry Dennis—"Always remember the first rule—be safe..."

Paul R. Laska

ACKNOWLEDGMENTS

Over the past 40 years, I learned much from many; most of their names will not appear here, but I value their insight and shared knowledge. The following are folks who directly aided me in the preparation of this work.

Ralf Kreling (Lt., Palm Beach County Sheriff's Office, FL, Ret.), longtime friend, was very helpful in obtaining information of cases from PBSO.

Paul Koinig (Cpl., Palm Beach County Sheriff's Office, FL, Ret.) retired from the bomb squad where he had served many years, spent many years before that in their canine unit, where he was the lead explosives dog handler. His knowledge of explosive detection canine operations, training, and research was very significant in preparing that section. As commander of the squad just prior to his retirement, his and indeed the PBSO's bomb squad's cooperation often provided me photos, information access, etc., that went into the preparation of this book.

Frank Cornetta and Geroge Sujah (both Sgt., Broward Sheriff's Office, FL, Ret.) assisted me in researching incidents that occurred in Broward County and that came to be included in this work.

Roy McClain (MSgt. USAF, Ret., and currently DHS EOD), for his extensive knowledge on explosive canine operations.

John Murray (Miami-Dade Police Dept., FL, Ret.), for his extensive knowledge of tools, techniques, and cases.

J.R. Hansen (Cpl., Brevard County Sheriff's Office, FL, Ret.), a longtime close friend, provided much information, and was always an ear to turn to during the preparation.

Larry Hostetler (Lt., St. Lucie County Sheriff's Office, FL) and the entire SLSO bomb squad. Whenever I needed photos of equipment, techniques, etc., they were there.

Joe Dempsey (Arapahoe County Sheriff's Office, CO, Ret.), who provided me insight into the confusion surrounding the Columbine High School shooting.

Tony Villa, Jorge Arroyo, Dave Shatzer, and other retired members of the US Army EOD, whose minds I often picked to fill out gaps in my knowledge of DoD policy and procedure.

Steve Barborini (ATF, Ret.), for his friendship and help over 25 years, and specifically in helping fill in aspects of one case study.

L.A. Bykowsky (ATF, Ret.), for her assistance in filling in details on a case study.

The team with whom I teach for the ATA Program—Jerry Dennis, Dale Beam, Phil Kersey (all ATF Ret.), George Jackson (Capt., US Army, Ret. and ATF Ret.), and Kent Harris (Chief, Olathe Kansas Fire Dept., Ret.), for sharing knowledge and assisting me in photo preparation of this work.

Bill Bobridge (Philadelphia PD, Ret.), for assisting me in collecting examples of improvisation by technicians over the years.

Tom Gersbeck (CWO, USMC, Ret.), first, for assistance in identifying various ordnance and EOD items for this work. Second, and more valuable, for putting me in contact with CRC, through whose cooperation this book came to be.

Dean Scoville (Sgt., Los Angeles Sheriff's Office, Ret.), a fellow police writer, who undertook to review the draft and made relevant comments.

Mark Listewnik, senior editor, CRC/Taylor & Francis. Mark calmed me, guided me, illuminated me, and made this adventure painless.

And all the hundreds of civilian and military bomb technicians whom I have had the honor of knowing and often working with these many years; their knowledge that rubbed off is reflected throughout these pages.

AUTHOR

Paul R. Laska earned a BS in criminology from the Florida State University. He served with the police department of Belle Glade, FL, as an identification officer until moving to the Martin County Sheriff's Office as a detective with the crime scene unit. In 1979, he attended the Hazardous Devices School and then established the bomb disposal function for MCSO. After a four-month break, when he joined the Florida Division of State Fire Marshall, he returned to MCSO. In his 25-year career at Martin County, he was a crime scene investigator and fingerprint specialist, bomb technician and bomb squad commander, supervisor of the forensic science and records units, and environmental investigator.

Since his retirement, Laska has been active as an instructor in the US Department of State Anti-Terrorism Assistance Program, specifically in the postblast investigation and explosives incident countermeasures classes. He has also participated in a variety of other training programs. Further, he enjoys writing, having produced a growing number of articles for a variety of law enforcement and other public safety periodicals.

1

Bomb Disposal and Investigation within the Public Safety Field

A SHORT HISTORY OF BOMB DISPOSAL

The history of bomb disposal is relatively short, marred by many tragedies, yet speaks volumes about the persons from both public safety and the military who would voluntarily undertake this task. Although someone dealt with explosive bombs ever since Guy Fawkes planted the first under Parliament in 1605's Gunpowder Plot, it was not until 1903 that individuals specialized in it. In that year Lieutenant Giuseppe Petrosino of the New York City Police Department (NYPD) established the Black Hand Squad, tasked with combating immigrant Italian organized crime, which would undertake disposing of infernal devices as part of their routine assignment. Although Black Hand operatives would assassinate Lieutenant Petrosino, his squad evolved into the NYPD Bomb Squad, which over the next 60 years became the model for a variety of bomb squads in major cities across the United States.

In 1940, London was pummeled by Nazi Germany's blitz. Not all the aerial bombs dropped by the Luftwaffe detonated; many were duds, others had time delays, and yet others were booby-trapped for anti-handling. With the intent on keeping London and other civilian centers as operational as possible, the British military developed the concept of explosive ordnance disposal (EOD). It was a severe learning curve; the Army's ammunition technical officers (ATOs) were, to a large extent, writing the textbooks as they went, often in blood, cataloguing the variety of ordnance encountered, establishing procedures to render each safe, and developing specialized tools to attack the variety of ordnance they dealt with. Their success would become the model for EOD operations worldwide, first in the United States in 1941, and eventually in most militaries.

Postwar, the United States, experiencing an unparalleled surge in economic growth, saw an increase in criminal activity also. Organized crime spread from the few megacities to all major cities. Labor unions, earlier beset by violence strikes and organizing, now found some shared aspects with organized crime. A segment of returning veterans became the 1% motorcycle gangs. South Florida became first the home to anti-Batista Cuban militias, and then after the revolution to anti-Castro organizations.

International politics of the late 1960s and 1970s also altered bombings. The Cold War found itself often fought by surrogates. Many were socialist and communist products of academia, who sought to establish a utopian society, while destroying what they saw as a corrupt capitalistic system. The United States found itself facing domestic unrest from three fronts. One was among groups who found the civil rights movement frustratingly slow, and turned to violence to force their view of equality. The second was opposition, especially among college students, to the United States' increasing role in counter insurgency in Southeast Asia. The third was due to a burgeoning radical leftist agenda seeking imposition of a radically progressive socialist agenda on the American way of life. Often, the three found mutual ground and cooperated in violent, terroristic attempts to sway American opinion.

Across Europe, a variety of violent leftists groups attacked the establishment. As a result, many police agencies established bomb disposal operations, to complement the military EOD of most of these nations. Across the United States many police agencies, and even some fire agencies, established bomb disposal units to ensure rapid response to bombs and other explosive incidents that were increasing in frequency. Even Canada found itself confronting a leftist separatist movement in Québec, plus a growing, violent organized crime network among competing outlaws motorcycle clubs.

Responding to these growing sources of bombs, public safety enlarged its role in bomb disposal, as noted above. Police and fire agencies established bomb disposal functions to ensure rapid access to services, and to provide services designed to meet the needs of criminal justice systems. In furtherance of this growth, many nations established national training centers for public safety bomb disposal, providing quality and uniform training plus a deeper pocket for establishment and support of training.

In recognition of the need to exchange intelligence and technical knowledge, two important developments occur. Great Britain, beset by the resurgence of Irish Republican Army (IRA) terrorism in 1970, established the first Bomb Data Center (BDC) to collect technical information on bombs and on evolving procedures to confront them and distributed the information among military and police bomb disposal forces. This was soon emulated by West Germany, Canada, Australia, the United States, and an ever-growing number of other nations. These BDCs soon began to exchange information, in recognition that terrorists export and exchange information, and of the lifesaving benefits of sharing techniques rather than reinventing procedures.

The second development began with a meeting in 1971 of the majority of functional American bomb squads, Royal Canadian Mounted Police (RCMP), Great Britain, the FBI, and Bureau of Alcohol, Tobacco, and Firearms (ATF). This initial meeting germinated into the development of the International Association of Bomb Technicians and Investigators (IABTI), a professional organization dedicated to furthering the exchange of information and education among bomb technicians. Since its birth, the IABTI has grown to about 5000 members, representing military and civilian bomb disposal in over 70 nations.

The United States, with its three-tiered law-enforcement system, faced serious impediments to train bomb squads. The US Navy EOD School was open only to military members; further, much of its program trains technicians to handle a wide range of military ordnance, which was of little value to public safety. Most police bomb squads had obtained some training from the NYPD Bomb Squad, and then established their own, often on the job, training programs. However, this resulted in cost ineffective, redundant, and sometimes less than well-designed programs.

In 1970, commanders met to discuss establishment of a national bomb disposal training center. As a result, the Hazardous Devices School (HDS) was established at the US Army's Redstone Arsenal in Huntsville, Alabama. The Department of Justices' Law Enforcement Assistance Administration administered the school in its early years; in 1982, upon dissolution of this office, HDS was transferred to the FBI. The US Army was contracted to provide logistical and training support. In the early days this meant a civilian cadre of about 15 instructors reinforced by about a dozen active-duty Army EOD techs. As will be seen later, this has grown, as the school has established itself in the American system and has continued to evolve in response to growth in the field, to meet changing demands brought about by the use of the bomb, and by introspective follow-up to tragic incidents. In 1987, following the deaths of two technicians on a device, a meeting of senior bomb technicians, working in conjunction with the FBI BDC developed a document entitled STB 87-4, National Guidelines for Bomb Disposal Technicians. These were basic guidelines for technicians and squads, addressing for the first time minimum response staffing, minimum equipment lists, basic and continuing training, and other technician life safety considerations.

In 1995, in response to President William Clinton's issuance of PDD 39, which established the FBI as the lead federal agency for crisis management in weapon of mass distraction incidents, the FBI established that it would depend upon the American public safety bomb disposal community as its local response force. In response, HDS first established a 40-h weapon of mass destruction (WMD) course for existing technicians, which was also incorporated into its basic training class. It also added the requirement for bomb technicians to meet OSHA's hazardous materials technician training standards, and eventually added this training to its basic technician curriculum.

Then in the late 1990s, in response to calls for technician certification and bomb squad accreditation, the FBI hosted a meeting of bombs squad commanders from across the nation. As a result, the National Bomb Squad Commanders Advisory Board (NABSCAB) was established. This organization, made up of elected representatives from bomb squad commanders on a regional basis, and augmented by nonvoting members from the FBI, ATF, and IABTI, established bomb technician certification standards, bomb squad accreditation standards, and basic procedures to be adhered to by certified technicians and accredited squads.

The FBI and ATF are key components in American bomb disposal. Under federal law, ATF has primary jurisdiction for federal bomb and explosive laws, and is responsible for regulation of the explosives industry. The FBI has been assigned primary responsibility of investigating the acts of terrorism, and also of response to use of WMD.

The FBI maintains a multifaceted bomb response program. Each field office has at least one, and usually several, Special Agent Bomb Technicians (SABT). These HDS trained technicians will provide operational bomb tech support to FBI investigations. They also provide liaison with local public safety bomb teams and are a resource to provide support to local teams.

The Hazardous Devices Response Unit (HDRU) is headquartered at the FBI's training, forensic science, and research facility at the Quantico

Marine Corps Base in Virginia. HDRU is composed of experienced public safety bomb technicians, who are tasked with conducting research, major special events support, and major incident response.

Although not a bomb resource, the Hazardous Materials Response Unit (HMRU) is designed to dovetail into bomb incidents. Also located at Quantico, HMRU is comprised of a wide variety of hazardous materials experts—experienced fire rescue hazardous materials technicians, chemists, biologists, and others whose expertise in dealing with chemical, biological, and nuclear/radiological issues may be needed. Like HDRU, HMRU is deeply involved in research, special events support, and support for FBI cases involving any potential for WMD.

The FBI is also the administrative home for the HDS located at the Redstone Arsenal in Alabama. This program will be examined in greater detail further in this book.

ATF, as the federal regulatory agency for the explosives industry, has significant responsibility in that area. All explosive products produced for use in the United States are submitted to ATF, which then maintains extensive reference files for physical and laboratory identification. All sales and transfers of regulated explosives must be reported, and those records are available to ATF for use in investigative tracing. Federal licensing of manufacturers, dealers, and users of related explosives is conducted by ATF, and its inspectors are responsible for inspection of the physical storage magazines and records of those licensees.

Tasked with enforcement of federal laws relating to criminal possession and use of explosives and bombs, ATF has trained a selective cadre of Special Agent's as Certified Explosives Specialists (CESs). These CESs are not especially HDS trained bomb technicians; however, they are extensively trained in demolition techniques, specialized investigative techniques relating to explosives, and postblast investigations (PBI). Most commonly, explosives and bomb investigations will be assigned to these agents, ensuring that a highly trained specialist will be the lead in the case. ATF does maintain a growing cadre of HDS-certified bomb technicians, who generally serve as CES agents.

For major explosion and fire responses, ATF developed its National Response Teams (NRT). These teams, when activated, will see a variety of agents, including CES, certified fire investigators, nonspecialist special agents, Explosive Enforcement Officers (EEOs, bomb technicians functioning in a purely technical role for ATF), laboratory chemists, detection of detection examiners, and supervisors, sent to a scene, along with a specially equipped response truck towing a small skid steer-type loader.

An NRT is designed to provide the manpower to ensure adequate scene investigative activity plus immediate access to laboratories services. The NRT may be activated to support an actual ATF case, or to provide support services to a local investigation.

ATF and the FBI have explosive analytical capabilities in their labs. The FBI lab, at Quantico, includes bomb techs capable of reconstructing devices, plus incorporates the capabilities of chemists and toolmark examiners from the lab. The ATF maintains a number of labs located regionally across the United States. Because of ATF's relationship with the explosives industry, it also maintains a cadre of chemists who only analyze explosives and their residues. Further, ATF maintains the Explosives Technology Branch, which uses former EOD technicians as subject matter experts, assigned to each of the ATF labs for their capabilities.

The roles and capabilities of the FBI and ATF have become complementary. Today, the two agencies are each able to conduct significant explosive-related investigations, which encompass a wide aspect of related services for national and local investigations.

In the shadow of the 9/11 attacks and the global war on terror, a growing support infrastructure has been established to address improvised explosive devices (IEDs). In addition to FBI and ATF initiatives, several Department of Defense (DOD) programs that not only support their EOD but also share with public safety. Leading at the exchange level has been the Technical Support Working Group (TSWG). However, the Joint Improvised Explosive Devices Defeat Organization (JIEDDO), which especially involves research for IED detection and defeat, has also developed technologies that have been shared with the public safety world by the military.

The Department of Homeland Security (DHS), established by President George W. Bush to bring agencies most concerned with internal security under one umbrella, has also affected the bomb disposal community. DHS oversees a variety of research programs into IEDs, especially through the Transportation Safety Administration and the Federal Air Marshals. It also is the primary funding source for monies earmarked for local administration for antiterrorism.

As can be seen, in just over 100 years, bomb disposal field has become an important aspect of public safety responsibility. It is not large; of about 18,000 law-enforcement agencies in the United States, only about 450 provide bomb disposal services. Of some 800,000 law-enforcement officers in the United States, less than 2500 are active as bomb technicians. However, their responsibilities are very significant to the public safety system.

WHAT IS BOMB DISPOSAL?

But what is bomb disposal? Depending upon the agency, it is much more complex than the obvious. At its core is a highly trained technician tasked with rendering safe improvised explosive devices. For many years this meant either explosive destruction of the item, or the highly dangerous hand disassembly of the device. Especially since the 1950s, and through the efforts of pioneers such as NYPD, Thomas Brodie in Dade County, Florida, Chicago PD, and both the United States and British militaries, diagnostic procedures have been introduced and remote techniques developed.

Explosives disposal is also part of the bomb tech field. Every year thousands of pounds of explosives are recovered, often after lengthy periods or improper storage, resulting in significant, dangerous, deterioration. The technician brings knowledge and skill to their safe disposal.

Military ordnance also comes to the bomb technician's attention. Because there are literally tens of thousands of different designs of ordnance, military EOD is the primary resource for their disposal. However, public safety bomb squads are often the first responders, establishing safety zones and gathering information for EOD to study. Often, when ordnance is being used for criminal purpose, bomb squads become involved for evidential purposes. Currently, with military EOD resources stretched thin with the demands of a war on multiple fronts, public safety finds itself dealing with ordnance that can be identified as having less complex fuzing that permits its removal, transportation, and render safe without advanced knowledge.

VIP support generally involves bomb disposal units. While military EOD assets will accompany national leaders, their role will be to ensure the immediate safety of the principle. Much in the way of safety sweeps falls to local bomb technicians, and all render safe will fall to them.

Bomb squads are finding a growing role in tactical operations. Explosive breaching is an entry methodology being studied by a growing number of tactical teams, and they often use bomb technicians for storage, manufacture, safety oversight, and even placement and function of charges. Bomb squad robot assets often support SWAT entries—the robot is capable of rescue of downed personnel, reconnaissance, and acting as a conduit for negotiation. Finally, bomb squads are often brought the scenes to stand by during use of chemical agents and distraction devices, available to dispose of any such munitions that fail to properly function.

Because of their expanded role in the response to WMD, bomb squads are involved in the preparation and response to such incidents. This often entails their close interface with hazardous materials teams. In a number of jurisdictions, a WMD response team operates under the bomb squad, providing tools, techniques, and technical knowledge aimed specifically at response to an incident involving chemical, biological, or radiological components.

Most bomb squads also are a key component in PBIs. A bomb tech brings many capabilities to a scene—safety consciousness for secondary devices, an understanding of the physics of different types of explosions, an ability to recognize explosive effects and device componentry. The bomb tech also is valuable in helping medical providers recognize and safeguard explosive debris from victims. During subsequent searches the technician is much more aware of potential dangers lurking in a bomb shop, plus is much more cognizant of components and related tools that should be seized as evidence.

In many jurisdictions the bomb squad assumes the lead for most bomb explosive-related investigations. This may include bomb threats, bombings, recoveries of bombs, explosives and ordnance, possibly collection and dissemination of related intelligence, and as a point of contact for other agencies regarding explosives, such as the FBI, ATF, Postal Inspectors, or the Secret Service.

In many jurisdictions, the bomb squad is also assigned regulatory responsibilities. These may include oversight of consumer fireworks sales, licensing or inspection of commercial fireworks pyrotechnics, and regulation of local explosives industry rules, licensure, inspection, and complaint review.

Finally, most bomb disposal units are heavily involved with outreach programs. Many participate in academy training for police and fire recruits. Many provide outreach to the business community on bomb incident response. Most find themselves consulted by local media for fireworks safety information. Finally, they may find their service is called upon to aid in the development and review of plans, both governmental and in the business/industrial community, for bomb-related response.

In the multifaceted American public safety system, the role assigned to a bomb disposal unit will usually be dictated by the needs of the agency and community it serves. Major agencies such as the Los Angeles and NYPDs, characterized by high demands for disposal only, employ a bomb squad for render safe, technically knowledgeable for investigations, and special event support. Conversely, many smaller agencies may find it most efficient to task their bomb squads with a wide variety, or even all, of the above missions, feeling secure in having a core unit with knowledge and capabilities to be used in a highly flexible manner.

2

Bomb Disposal Organization

Within the American model, bomb disposal will be located in a variety of places on agency organizational charts. As the overwhelming majority of bomb squads in the United States are part-time units, and assignment is a secondary assignment for the bomb technician, many squads are located for convenience where the senior or supervisory technician is assigned.

Within the fire services, bomb disposal usually falls under one of two specialty areas. Most commonly, bomb squads appear to be a component of the hazardous materials function of a fire agency. This is a very logical placement. First, bomb disposal—explosives disposal—is a specialized area of hazardous materials response. It is heavily technical and equipment-oriented. Much like hazmat and very unlike fire suppression, it is generally a slow, carefully orchestrated approach to a hazardous situation, as opposed to the dynamic attack usually necessitated by fire suppression or rescue operations.

The other location where the fire service commonly locates bomb disposal is within its investigative services. In this model, the fire investigators are often cross certified as law enforcement officers. Because of the destructive nature of both fire and explosives, their physical investigations require technical understanding beyond that of other investigative fields. Further, since most bomb responses will involve criminal incidents, their investigative expertise ensures a more understanding approach to the collection of information, and gathering and handling of evidence.

Within law enforcement agencies, functional placement of bomb squads will usually be found within four locations. Many agencies have situated their bomb disposal function within the investigative services area, often under a "lesser" field such as auto theft. This is often a reflection of the demands of the primary assignment. Although an important function, an investigative unit such as auto theft can suspend its routine flow while the emergency demands of bomb incidents are dealt with.

Traditionally, many bomb squads have been assigned within the criminalistics services of an agency. This is been highly successful placement for a number of reasons. First, the bomb is an item of physical evidence; once rendered safe it may well be a treasure trove of forensic clues. Like a crime scene investigation, a bomb disposal response is less a race with time (although "beat the clock" is a serious consideration) and much more a well thought-out, procedural approach to a problem. Finally, bomb technicians, like practitioners of various criminalistics fields, are technically oriented problem solvers; administratively, it makes their supervision easier by keeping like minds within the same branches of the organizational tree.

Some teams have long been located under units responsible for organized crime or intelligence organizations; currently, with the enlarging arena of terror, this is seen more placed here. This has ensured squads of close investigative support of their operations, a consideration often shorted or overlooked by many agencies. It also ensures that bomb technicians are in the downstream for sharing of intelligence either developed by or shared with the agency. It also aids in ensuring a team is supported, financially and in manpower, as its immediate chain is very cognizant of the outside threats and capabilities the unit brings to the issue.

A recent trend has been to situate bomb disposal under the tactical operations of an agency. In this placement, it is important for the structure above bomb disposal to understand one major difference between bomb response and tactical response; in that bomb response must be a slow, methodical approach, as opposed to tactical operations which, while often based upon carefully gathered intelligence and well planned out, must proceed dynamically to ensure safety and success through surprise. However, this mating is also very beneficial to both sides of the marriage. Bomb disposal is almost always responsible for maintenance of explosive K-9 training aids, storage and sometimes employment of explosive breaching materials, robotic support for many tactical teams, and oversight for safety and disposal of chemical and distraction agents. Conversely, special weapons and tactics (SWAT) especially comes to a better understanding of bomb disposal's unique security needs, and can come to design and implement security procedures to complement bomb squad responses. Both benefit from the closer relations as they may train together on incorporating bomb technicians into tactical operations, where a bomb tech may be an integral part of the entry team, tasked with identifying IED's and booby-traps and establishing safe routes for the SWAT members mounting an entry.

Every agency employing a bomb disposal unit should develop at least three agency procedural guidelines regarding bomb-related response. The first protocol should deal with guidance for an officer responding to any bomb-related incident—bomb threat, suspicious items, recovery of explosives or military ordnance, and postblast response. This should outline bomb threat responses, in conjunction with applicable laws, to provide guidance as to behavior on the scene (who decides on evacuation, where responsibility for search falls, use of explosive K-9 support, mandatory written reports, etc.). Additionally, it should set forth safety protocols such as limitations on radio and cell phone use, establishment of open hardline communications, guidelines for safe evacuation procedures, etc.

A second protocol should establish procedures for requesting and supporting bomb squad response. This should include guidance for when bomb disposal should be requested—suspicious devices, military ordnance, or explosives. It should also establish what actions an officer should take while awaiting the bomb squads arrival—evacuation and sheltering considerations, securing the scene, notification of agency superiors, request of support agencies (fire rescue, FBI, ATF), documentation and reporting of as much as is possible, and establishing a secure working environment for the bomb squad.

The third area of protocol should describe the bomb squad. Is it a full-time work or corollary assignment? What are the minimum training requirements necessary before an officer may be called a bomb technician? What constitutes a response while national guidelines require two certified technicians, a growing number of agencies are using three or four technician responses. It should also set out other bomb squad responsibilities—VIP support, technical support, hazmat support, investigative assignments, equipment maintenance, training requirement, etc. It should also set forth selection protocols to be used in selecting new members of the team, possibly to include a period of apprenticeship. Basically, this procedural guideline should lay out the overall organization, competencies, and requirements of the bomb squad and its members.

Development of these standard operating procedures (SOPs) should include input and review by the bomb squad. Trained, experienced bomb technicians have considerable exposure to policy, whether in their HDS training, through other training such as that offered by the DHS National Consortium, or through attendance at national bomb squad commanders' conferences.

In addition to agency level SOPs, a bomb squad should maintain internal operating guidelines. These may require approval from administrative hierarchy, but should only be posted at the unit level. These protocols will deal with the guidelines for technicians as to their operations on incidents, maintenance issues, training, including internal training, etc.

Americans especially bristle at the imposition of rules. However, a framework provides guidance and protection for all involved. At the same time, they should be guidelines, not strict policy statements, giving the technician the leeway to address situations that deviate from the routine, or to respond to new challenges in an intelligent and safe manner.

3

Training and Training Resources

Currently, there are about 3000 bomb disposal technicians in the United States. Were they under a single agency, training would be easily accomplished. However, they represent about 450 different agencies, supporting ~18,000 law-enforcement agencies in the United States. Were each of these agencies to attempt their own training, the result would be a haphazard, inefficient, and potentially unsafe situation.

As previously noted, events of the latter 1960s saw a significant increase in bombs in the United States. While a few major jurisdictions, notably NYPD, Los Angeles Police and Sheriffs, Chicago Police, Milwaukee PD, and Dade County Public Safety Department, already had organized bomb squads, the increase in incidents required more assets. A number of other major jurisdictions soon formed squads, using a combination of training from military EOD and extended trips to existing civilian squads. Recognizing that, first, existing teams would require replenishment as members moved on professionally or retired, second that even more teams would need to be organized and trained to meet national needs, and third that uniformity of training and procedures nationally would best benefit populations, a variety of agencies worked together with the United States Department of Justice Law Enforcement Assistance Administration to establish a national training center. In 1970, the first class attended the HDS, conducted at the US Army's Redstone Arsenal in Huntsville, Alabama. Initially, HDS was a three-week program. However, a one-week refresher was added, with a recommended attendance of every three years. Upon the dissolution of LEAA in 1982, the FBI, already home to the BDC, became the administrative home to HDS, continuing to contract the US Army for logistical and instructional support through its facilities at Redstone Arsenal.

Over the 40-year history of HDS, there have been significant improvements in its program and facilities. Initially, it was housed in an old military training building on main base, with range facilities being just an open field among the arsenal's many miles of ranges. Over the years, the Army provided additional facilities to the program. In the early 2000, based upon the Army providing a large area of land to HDS, the FBI constructed a state-of-the-art facility, consisting of classrooms, offices, and maintenance facilities plus a response city incorporating a variety of structures and props that provide a dedicated scenario and site built to withstand the abuse of rendering safe operations. At that time response trucks were placed into operation, permitting each student team to function in training as in a real-world operation.

The programs have also expanded to meet the evolving needs of the field. Early HDS consisted of the three-week Hazardous Devices Course, and a one-week refresher. The Hazardous Devices Course has expanded, currently consisting of five weeks attendance at HDS, plus one week attending the hazardous materials technicians' certification program at the FEMA Center for Domestic Preparedness in Anniston, Alabama. To maintain hazardous device certification, the refresher program was reformatted into a one-week recertification program, which incorporates two days of intensive recertification testing with three days of update training. HDS also offers a one-week robotics course, designed as a program for advanced operation training, plus training and maintenance skills. A one-week advanced diagnostics and disablement class provides training on high-tech skills and techniques. Finally, HDS offers a three-day administrative officers course, which is designed to provide intense introduction to bomb disposal for nontechnician administrators who oversee bomb disposal teams.

The staff at HDS has also grown significantly from the early days, when a team of about a dozen Army EOD techs augmented a civilian staff of about dozen instructors, primarily all retired military EOD techs. Currently, while the Army continues to provide about a dozen technicians in the program, some 60 civilian instructors form the core of the program. These instructors include retired military and public safety personnel, representing a wide variety of local agencies. In early 2015 the FBI took over all HDS operations, with the Army withdrawing its active duty EOD techs and transferring its civilian instructors to the FBI.

The HDS personnel also support other FBI activities. These include field programs taught regionally by the FBI for bomb squads nationally. Also,

HDS instructors deploy in support of major special events planning, often providing programs for local teams in reparation for events such as Super Bowl, political conventions, etc. Finally, HDS supports IABTI training by often supplying instructors as speakers at many IABTI training functions.

As noted above, HDS provides support to other FBI training programs. Annually, FBI field offices scheduled one-week classes popularly known as roadshows among a variety of locations. Using an instructional team of HDS personnel and senior FBI SABT, the roadshows include a mix of refresher training in common skills with the introduction to new techniques and current intelligence briefings.

Helping local bomb squads to prepare for special events is a major concern of the FBI. In addition to HDS instructors and SABT working with local technicians to update skills and knowledge, the FBI brings in subject matter experts on subjects considered especially relevant to the planned event, providing the most current response research and latest intelligence for use to the bomb disposal community.

Because of the growing threat of large vehicle bombs (LVBs), and in recognition that these pose unique postblast investigation challenges, the FBI offers its LVB course. This program is most often offered in the Western United States, at large military bases, where LVB may be set off safely and without causing local disruption. Classes consisting of public safety bomb technicians and military EOD study the procedures for such an investigation, recognition, and analysis of evidential materials, and undertake an actual LVB postblast in this one-week program.

The ATF is very active in providing bomb and explosives training. The ATF has long offered the Advanced Explosives Investigation Training Program. This two-week program combines explosive and bomb technology, investigative procedures as applied to explosive scene investigations, criminalistics at both the field and laboratory level, and in-depth practical exercises to provide its diverse audience of bomb technicians, investigators, and criminalistics practitioners a valuable training experience.

Since ATF is the primary federal agency with jurisdiction over both criminal investigation and commercial regulation of explosives, it has considerable experience in the destruction of explosives. Disposal of explosive materials is the single greatest area of danger to the bomb technician. In response, ATF has developed the Advanced Explosives Destruction Training Course. In this program, technicians learn safe handling of deteriorated explosive materials, regulatory and environmental concerns related to explosives disposal, and appropriate procedures towards the handling of different families of explosive materials.

Both of these programs are conducted at ATF's new National Training Center, located at Redstone Arsenal in Huntsville, Alabama. Location of the facility so near the FBI's HDS is not a coincidence; first, Huntsville is ideal for 12-month training operations. Second, and more importantly, this provides the two cadres the opportunity to easily communicate and cooperate, to the benefit of the bomb disposal community.

Both the FBI and ATF are offering home-made explosives (HME) training. While HME has long been used by bombers, the rise of peroxide-based explosives has made the situation much more critical. Thus both agencies work to ensure the field practitioners in the United States are intimately familiar with improvised explosives, their chemistry, manufacturing methods, and safe disposal.

The US DHS provides a variety of training in WMD-related areas through the National Domestic Preparedness Consortium. DHS has identified leading providers of knowledge in a variety of areas; for explosives they tap the Energetic Materials Research and Training Center (EMRTC) at New Mexico Tech, the leading academic site for explosives research and education in the United States.

EMRTC offers two programs. The first is the Incident Response to Terrorist Bombings (IRTB) program. This four-day class, held in Socorro, New Mexico, the home to New Mexico Tech, is aimed at all first responders, including bomb technicians. It combines training on bomb and explosive technology, preventative and protective measures, threat, incident, and postblast response, and the importance of inter-agency cooperation through intelligence and incident command system (ICS) principles. The students also have three trips to New Mexico Tech's 43 square miles of explosives ranges, where they are introduced to a wide variety of explosive effects.

The second program, Prevention and Response to Suicide Bombing Incidents (PRSBI), is especially tailored for attendance by bomb technicians, SWAT personnel, and law enforcement and fire administrators. This four-day program exposes its students to bomb and explosives technology, theory and tactics of suicide bombers, range demonstrations of suicide bombing techniques, and a variety of current response protocols. Its aim is to give its attendees tools to return to their jurisdictions to develop policies that are appropriate to their local needs.

Other National Consortium programs of value to the bomb tech include nuclear/radiological programs at the Nevada Test Site, a wide variety of chemical agent training programs at the FEMA Center for Domestic Preparedness in Anniston, Alabama, and biological programs offered by Louisiana State University.

The DHS Transportation Safety Administration (TSA), whose jurisdiction has been enlarged to cover all aspects of transportation, often works to offer local training. Such training often includes local programs on aircraft operations, rail operations, bus operations, and pipeline response.

DHS is also home to the Federal Law Enforcement Training Center (FLETC). The International Law Enforcement Academies (ILEA) have been operated by FLETC for many years. Located in Roswell, New Mexico, Bangkok, Thailand, Budapest, Hungary, Gaborone, Botswana, and San Salvador, El Salvador, the academies provide executive and advanced operational training to a wide variety of foreign national agencies. Among the programs offered is PBI, providing investigators intense training in the techniques necessary for successful information and evidence collection and analysis at bomb scenes.

The United States Department of State (DOS) conducts the Antiterrorism Assistance Program (ATAP). ATAP is especially designed to provide training for smaller, less advanced nations that lack the domestic capabilities to prepare for terroristic activities. Programs are delivered both at training sites in the United States, where students are brought in for the classes, and in home countries, with instructional staff and training materials transported to appropriate sites for the training to be conducted.

Two of the programs are of specific focus for bomb technicians. The Explosive Incident Countermeasure (EIC) program is a six-week program designed to produce bomb disposal technicians. Many times these graduates have returned to their home nations to establish bomb response programs and provide training for their police agencies.

The PBIs course takes a ground-up approach to the subject. Over three weeks, students are exposed to a wide variety of training on explosives technology, investigative techniques, and the application of forensic science to bombings. It is also structured so that participants conduct many hands-on blast investigations, permitting them to apply the techniques they have been taught and observe the actual effects of a variety of explosives and devices.

In 1973, a first annual explosive ordnance disposal conference was sponsored by California's Sacramento County Sheriff's office. A follow-up conference the next year, attended by technicians and investigators from the United States, Canada, and Great Britain, resulted in the organization of the IABTI. Currently listing more than 5000 members from more than 70 nations, IABTI's motivating factors are training, education, and information exchange among those in the bomb disposal and investigative field.

The IABTI is organized within the limits of a membership-based organization. Annually it holds an international educational conference, usually attended by 700 or more members. Each of its seven regions conduct one-week conferences annually, providing a somewhat more accessible venue for members within the geographic area. Finally, each chapter, organized along state, provincial, or national borders, provides at least annual, and some chapters more frequent, opportunities for training. At the international level, many leading figures provide briefings on current technical research, evolving intelligence, and recent cases, plus major suppliers of equipment showcase their products. While regional and chapter meetings cannot attract some of the speakers or exhibitors, they often are able to more conveniently offer hands-on training sessions.

The IABTI also provides support to other training projects. This is especially true of ATF's, AEITP, and AEDT programs, where generally one instructor is provided through the IABTI, bringing in experienced state or local bomb technicians and knowledge to the podium, providing a different aspect to that of federal investigators.

Also, the IABTI publishes The Detonator, a bimonthly magazine that has expanded to also incorporate an ever-growing number of technical presentations.

Since the bomb disposal field has close relations with explosive detection canine and tactical breaching operations, the IABTI has reached out to welcome those specialists into it and to provide a significant source of information exchange among these specialists. As often training explosives for dogs are provided by bomb squads, and explosive breaching supplies are maintained, constructed, and even emplaced by bomb techs on missions for tactical teams, this helps build a stronger bond among these fields which may otherwise not communicate as well as is practical.

As in any technical field, training, education, and information exchange is crucial to the bomb specialists. In a field as life-threatening as this, highly trained professionals maintain the edge to increase their survivability while also providing the best services to their fellow professionals and the communities they serve.

4

Legal Aspects of Bomb Disposal

Bomb disposal and investigations are deeply enmeshed in a multilevel web of laws and governmental regulations. This book will not attempt to address specific laws and rules to recognize the wide variety of jurisdictions involved in this field; to do so would fill a multi-volume treatment alone. Instead, this chapter will review variety of legal guides and constraints that exist, and permit the practitioner to research the law as it applies in any set jurisdiction.

It is also important to recognize that in the multitiered American system of federalism, an agency may have authority under, and also be bound by, local, state, and federal laws and rules. It is crucial for each agency to independently determine where it stands in the legal system.

As in any police endeavor, procedural law plays an important role. While rules applying to interview and interrogation come into play, bombs and components are physical evidence; all involved in this field should stay abreast of current procedural law and changes in case law affecting search and seizure issues and the collection and preservation of evidence.

Most commonly, technicians and investigators will be familiar with criminal laws relating to both explosives and bombs. In a multi-tiered legal system such as the United States, they should maintain their familiarity with all applicable laws. For example, under federal laws, chemical reaction bombs, commonly referred to as soda bottle bombs, do not fall within the definition of a destructive device. However, a number of states have modified their laws, which previously had often been a clone of federal law, to incorporate sanctions for possession and use of these very commonly encountered devices.

It is important to understand what the terms in the law mean, yet very often law itself does not define them. Definition may be found in a variety of locations. Sometimes it may be other laws. Often government rules and regulations contain detailed definition. Professional references such as the International Society of Explosive Engineers (ISEE) Blaster's Handbook, Picatinny Encyclopedia of Explosives, other textbooks, and military manuals will provide definition and guidance. Unfortunately, most criminal attorneys are not familiar with this field; however, criminal prosecution offices in major jurisdictions often have some staff who are conversant in the field, as do most US Attorneys offices. Also, major agencies such as ATF and the FBI employ legal counsel.

Generally, when considering statutory law, law enforcement concerns itself with only procedural and criminal laws. However, a field such as explosives will be affected by a variety of other, noncriminal, laws and it is important for the bomb technician to become familiar with them and capable of researching them. This will accomplish several ends—possibly provide definition for terms appearing in the criminal laws, possibly provide suitable regulatory avenues for either circumstances not covered by criminal law, or possibly not rising to the level of criminal prosecution, and, very importantly, makes technicians aware of legalities which cover various aspects of bomb disposal.

The bomb disposal field encompasses a variety of behavior, including numerous jurisdictions that are subject to governmental control. Most obvious are purchase, possession, transportation, storage, use, and disposal of explosives. Some jurisdictions require any user of explosives to be licensed, while others exempt public safety personnel who were involved with explosives within their professional operations. For transportation, commercial operators are required to obtain a commercial license with an endorsement for hazardous materials; again some states exempt public safety from such provisions. Also regarding transportation, do public safety vehicles transporting explosives need to bear placards?

Environmental laws may seriously impact operations. To what extent are public safety operations exempt? In dealing with clandestine drug labs, many agencies have run afoul of laws regarding cleanup of chemically contaminated locations.

The primary tool of the bomb squad is the x-ray. In the United States, every state has laws overseeing the use of x-ray equipment. Usually this will encompass a license or registration for each machine in use, promulgation of a local safety protocol, routine inspection by a state authority, and personal monitoring (dosimetric) and record keeping. The specifications will vary, as well as the complexity of the program, but it is assured that failure to comply will expose the agency, and possibly individuals, to sanctions in the form of civil liability.

In the United States, the federal government and all states provide for individual agencies to promulgate procedural rules, with many of these rules being given criminal as well as regulatory sanctions. Their names vary; the federal level promulgates the Code of Federal Regulations (CFR), while states may call them regulations, rules, administrative codes, or other names.

Since rules are developed by those agencies responsible for regulation of a specific field, technically they are often the most complete source of information for defining laws. If for no other reason, reference to them provides the investigator valuable guidance in determining if a material is covered under the law, or whether a behavior is illegal.

As with the civil sections of statutory law, regulations impact bomb squad operations. Here is the meat, the detailed direction of how governmentally regulated operations may proceed in the jurisdiction. The rules will detail how to store explosives, safe waiting times for a misfire, equipment which may exempt a public safety vehicle from some hazmat transportation rules, etc. Indeed, it may provide rules applying specifically to bomb squads. For example, under the rules of the Florida Department of Environmental Protection, public safety bomb squads are provided an "emergency permit" provision alleviating them of much cumbersome regulation when conducting emergency disposal of shock-sensitive materials.

As criminal investigators, it is important to recognize that some regulations are provided criminal sanction. Nationally, many components of the CFRs contain criminal as well as regulatory sanctions. Each state has a different approach; in Florida, it requires statutory authority to be criminalized. For example, Florida's Rules of the Insurance Commissioner (State Fire Marshal) regulate the explosives industry and provide definition and direction in applying the criminal law, but are not themselves criminalized. However, Florida's statutes provide that a willful and knowing violation of the Rules of the Florida Department of Environmental Protection is a criminal act. Thus these rules may provide an investigator another avenue of enforcement when conducting an investigation.

It is also important to recognize that violations of rules, even when not criminalized, may permit the referral of a case to regulatory authorities. This will vary, depending on the nature of the rules. Many only regulate licensed individuals; however, they may provide an option in pursuing closure to an incident.

A final aspect of the law to be cognizant of is the case law. Case law refers to the decisions by court that interpret or even dismiss the applicability of the law. Most often, police look at the impact of case law on procedural law—search and seizure, self-incrimination, due process, and so on. However, all statutory law is subject to review by the courts. Thus many criminal laws have been either deemed unenforceable, or have had its applicability constrained upon review of a court. This case review may occur at any level of court; the lowest court with jurisdiction may rule on a law, with that case law applicable within its legal jurisdiction until either overturned by a higher court, affirmed by a higher court at which time the ruling extends across that level of jurisdiction, or until the law is either repealed or modified by the legislative process.

How may this apply? In one case, a county established a local ordinance outlawing sale of consumer fireworks. However, when promulgating the ordinance, insufficient research had been conducted; state courts had previously ruled that state law preempted local legal action. When enforcement of the new ordinance was attempted, corporate counsel pointed out the conflict to local authorities, who found themselves armed with an unenforceable law.

Bomb disposal is one of a few areas of law enforcement that finds itself involved with a wider than normal aspect of law. The bomb tech will find many tools within the various parts of the law to help in enforcement activity. However, the bomb technician should also maintain familiarity with the various aspects of the law that may impact an agency's bomb disposal function, and protect the technician and agency from civil or even criminal liability arising from ignorance.

5

Bomb Incident Responses

It is important that technicians and administrators recognize and understand the variety of responses that may face a bomb squad. It should also be recognized that some of these might not fall to every squad, depending upon the needs and organization of the agency.

BOMB THREATS

First, it should be noted that it is rarely justifiable for a bomb technician to respond to a bomb threat. A bomb technician is a highly trained and skilled asset, whose role should primarily be in response to items determined to be potentially explosive. The activity in a threat operation may deplete personal energy, tiring, and losing mental sharpness necessary for safe functioning when conducting render-safe operations.

However, threat response is important to the technician. First, for those teams that also conduct bomb threat follow-up investigations, a proper response helps in ensuring that all so important information trail is preserved. Second, although less than 1% of bomb threats result in suspicious items for a team to handle, the actions leading up to a bomb squad's arrival will affect the steps to be taken by the technicians.

Threats are made in several forms. Most commonly thought of is the telephone threat. However, threats are also made in writing, electronically such as e-mail and in-person. Indeed the face-to-face threat, long dismissed as a foolish attempt to frighten or extort, has gained a much greater level of gravity as the public sees suicide bombers and surrogate bombers.

On a typical bomb threat, a response should consist of a single patrol unit that will have two objectives, assisting the target in safely responding to the threat and to gather information to begin a criminal investigation. Unfortunately, many agencies, especially those without the benefit of a bomb squad in-house to aid in proper development of protocol, overreact to a bomb threat, without justification for the employment of resources, and often to the satisfaction of the bomb threat maker.

Overwhelmingly, bomb threats are made with the intent to harass, intimidate, disrupt, or extort. For a simple assault, an agency would not respond with multiple units, paramedics, the medical examiner, and homicide detectives; yet for a bomb threat many will send an equivalent response. Especially when the threat was intended to harass, intimidate, or disrupt, public safety has served the criminal, not the victim, by such a response.

A successful bomb threat response begins, as do most investigations, with dispatch. Collecting detailed information helps determine how units should respond. Is it a mailed letter, an internet threat, a phone threat, or an in-person threat? Is it just a threat, or is there a suspicious item involved, which completely alters the response? Of course if the threat is made directly into public safety dispatch (as a significant number are), the dispatch personnel need to be trained to ask appropriate questions, record all details of the call, institute recording and track/trace if available, and themselves prepare written reports (Figure 5.1).

The responsible officer's role begins prior to physical arrival. About 100 yards before arriving at the address, the officer should declare arrival and then turn off radios and cell phones. Upon entering the premises, the officer should identify the phone involved (if a telephone threat), protect it from use, and establish a hard line telephone link from another phone to the communications center.

At the target, the officer should make contact with the individual who received the threat, and the person in charge of the site. The officer should obtain detailed information right from the first:

- Phone number/line if telephone threat.
- If written note, package it to protect it for physical evidence such as fingerprints, DNA, and document evidence.
- Obtain detailed voice description.
- Obtain any detail on background noises overheard on the phone.
- Obtain detailed description of the threat, recording as exactly as possible the words.

International Association of Bomb Technicians and Investigators

IABTI ®

PLACE THIS CARD UNDER YOUR TELEPHONE

QUESTIONS TO ASK:

1. When is bomb going to explode?
2. Where is it right now?
3. What does it look like?
4. What kind of bomb is it?
5. What will cause it to explode?
6. Did you place the bomb?
7. Why?
8. What is your address?
9. What is your name?

EXACT WORDING OF THE THREAT:

____

____

____

____

____

____

____

Sex of Caller: _______ Race: ____________

Age: ____________ Length of Call: ________

Number at which call was received:

____

Time: __________ Date: ____/____/____

BOMB THREAT

CALLER'S VOICE:

______ Calm	______ Nasal
______ Angry	______ Stutter
______ Excited	______ Lisp
______ Slow	______ Raspy
______ Rapid	______ Deep
______ Soft	______ Raggy
______ Loud	______ Clearing Throat
______ Laughter	______ Deep Breathing
______ Crying	______ Cracking Voice
______ Normal	______ Disguised
______ Distinct	______ Accent
______ Slurred	______ Familiar

If voice is familiar, who does it sound like?

____

____

BACKGROUND SOUNDS:

______ Street Noises	______ Factory Machinery
______ Crockery	______ Animal Noises
______ Voices	______ Clear
______ PA System	______ Static
______ Music	______ Local
______ House Noises	______ Long Distance
______ Motor	______ Booth
______ Office Machinery	______ Other ________

THREAT LANGUAGE:

______ Irrational	______ Incoherent
______ Foul	______ Taped
______ Well Spoken (educated)	______ Message read by threat maker

REMARKS: ______________________________

____

____

____

Report call immediately to:

____

Phone Number ___________________________

Date ___________________________________

Name __________________________________

Position ________________________________

Phone Number ___________________________

Printed as a Public Service by the IABTI
www.iabti.org

Figure 5.1 The bomb threat recording form, recommended for use at any call-taking location. (Courtesy of IABTI.)

- If an internet threat, a copy of the e-mail, including a full header, should be printed, plus information on the ISP, e-mail service, etc.
- If an in-person threat, detailed physical description of the threat maker, and name if known.
- If an in-person threat and the responsible party is present, the responding officer(s) need to think tactically of safe response, to determine if the individual presents the hazard of a person borne device, and then a method to safely take the person into custody.

Both individuals should be queried for any apparent motives behind the threat. Commonly they may involve disgruntled employees or ex-employees, disgruntled customers, labor disputes, chronically absent personnel, or personal disputes that may spill over to the business environment.

Questions often surface about evacuations. First, most jurisdictions do not have legal provision for public safety to evacuate a location based upon a mere threat; to do so exposes the agency to civil liability for lost payroll, overhead, and income. If law permits to order an evacuation for public safety, it may be considered but still is not especially the best response.

Second consideration must be the conditions. In the height of summer, in heavy rain, or the cold of winter to evacuate to open ground exposes the evacuees to these extremes and health threats. Some facilities are also almost impossible to evacuate, such as a hospital. Others may have processes underway that cannot be stopped nor left unmonitored. Again, consideration must be given to successfully completing the threat maker's ends by conducting an evacuation.

In most jurisdictions, the decision to evacuate must be left to the individual in charge of the site. This may be the manager/clerk at a convenience store, the director of security for major office building, the principal of a school, or the CEO of the corporation. The officer should be able to provide guidance, but generally leave decisions on evacuation and search to the site manager.

One important consideration is to what extent evacuation and other reactive procedures should be incorporated into written, formalized plans. While the plans need to establish policies regarding evacuation, a plan that sets forth specific plans for evacuation ("floor marshals will ensure all personnel will proceed in a safe and orderly fashion out the rear of the building to the loading parking zone") may provide an actual bomber direction on using a threat to herd victims to a specific location for targeting. As in many other aspects of security, guidelines rather than hard and fast, directions are often the best.

Search is a function for which public safety personnel are poorly suited, unless it is their facilities. Efficient search requires knowledge of a location, the ability to rapidly scan items present, and determine whether they belong. Fire and police personnel lack that knowledge; to them many items would be suspicious which site personnel will know to be innocuous. Bomb technicians are even a worse choice, as their training directs them to considering any such item a threat.

Thus, the regular occupants of the target are best suited to conduct the search. This must be a policy decision of that location, on determining how they may undertake a search.

Many bomb squads provide outreach to business organizations by providing guidance on policy development and training to personnel. Usually, this will include presenting policymakers a variety of approaches that are already in general use. They will also review the policy and ensure it does not conflict with local public safety policies. Training programs usually include threat reception and response, search principles, considerations for determining suspicious items, principles of evacuation, safety considerations for evacuation activity, and consideration of secondary devices. The training will also include handling of a suspicious item and postblast activity.

From an investigative aspect, it should be recognized that 50% or more of bomb threats can be solved. To do so requires that responding officers treat the call as a serious crime, gathering information and evidence that can then be followed up on. It is also earmarked by outreach to the community, offering consultations and training to potential victims, that is, the business and government communities.

Most threats leave a trail that can be followed through investigation. Written threats may yield fingerprints, DNA, document evidence, or traceable postage materials. The internet provides an electronic trail that, unless dealing with a knowledgeable cyber-criminal, provides a roadmap. Telephones, both hardline and cellular, leave wide paths that may end at a payphone or disposable phone, but otherwise provide viable investigative leads.

With the rise of suicide and surrogate bombers, the in-person threat takes on new, very serious dimensions. They are often the targets of a fast takedown. With today's threats, the potential of it being a suicide or surrogate is increased. Therefore, relevant consideration of response will be included as part of the section dealing with suicide bombers.

SUSPICIOUS ITEM RESPONSE

It looked like a big dinner pail and innocent enough.

In the early twentieth century, Milwaukee, WI, was home to a great deal of anarchist and radical socialist activity. While most often directed at industry or the state, any foe of "progress" could find itself a target. Thus Rev. August Giuliana, pastor of the Italian Evangelical Church on Van Buren St., had earned the distaste of local radicals for his patriotic support of the United States.

On November 24, 1917, while her mother attended to her duties cleaning the church facilities, 10-year old Josie Spicciatti found an item in the alley alongside the church. Dragging it inside, it sat unattended until later, when another worker at the church, told of the item, disassembled it, moved it, and then reassembled it. That evening the church janitor was directed to take the unknown item to the nearby Central Police Station. Some at the station, which had just undergone a shift change, feared it, while others poked fun at it. When taken into the shift commander's office, Lt. Flood directed: "Get that thing out of here. Don't fool around with anything like that!" Taken to the squad assembly room, several detectives began to examine the unknown item, when it exploded. Nine police officers and a civilian reporting an offense were killed. This loss would be the nation's greatest loss of officers in a single event until September 11, 2001. The 20-pound device of black powder would, many years later, be attributed to Mario Buda, whose vehicle-borne bomb of September 16, 1920 would literally as well as figuratively shake Wall Street to its core.

If there is one concept that is accepted across the board in the bomb field is that any item that makes any party suspicious enough, report it as a potential explosive or explosive device, and should be treated as such until qualified bomb disposal personnel evaluate and either determine it as misidentified or take steps to render it safe. It is not, and should never be, the first responder's role to interact with a potential device. Two salient points:

1. Always move the people from the bomb; never the bomb away from the people.
2. Not my bomb; not my building. Buildings can be rebuilt—people cannot.

The first responding officers should act in evacuating to an adequate safe area, secure witnesses, and request appropriate support.

Recent research by ATF and DOD has resulted in publication of charts showing safe distances for both sheltered and open evacuation

Bomb disposal support should be first requested. If the jurisdiction must reach out (as over 17,000 must), response may be quite time intensive. Teams that support regions of the state, state law-enforcement units, and even more so military units may require hours to respond; some may have air support for initial evaluations, but the bulk of the movement must be by highway. Consideration should be given to notification of ATF, the FBI, and Joint Terrorism Task Force (JTTF) resources. The sooner the investigation can commence, the better the potential of solution.

With federal mandate for incident management being put into effect, a jurisdictional emergency operations center may be activated. These incidents quickly attract the press, also public information resources need to be activated.

Finally, especially in smaller jurisdictions, consideration must be made of mutual aid response. Scene security is intense and lengthy; the incident may also be designed to draw off local police resources to permit another criminal act to be conducted. Bringing in additional support, especially state law enforcement, which is often traffic-oriented and highly adapted for the control needs of such an incident, ensures adequate manpower on the scene that helps for the overall safety of the community.

Upon arrival of the bomb squad, the scene from the cold zone perimeter to the innermost hot zone should be turned over to the bomb squad, with them being in complete control of that area. They may determine whether the perimeter needs to be expanded, or see fit to decrease it. They should also obtain a complete briefing by the first responding officer, incident command, and any witnesses of value.

Once the bomb squad has the opportunity to evaluate the situation, they will begin to conduct their operation. Circumstances dictate procedures; the team will continuously evaluate the existing intelligence and developing knowledge to determine how they will proceed. Options available to the technicians include further diagnostics (photography, x-rays, hazmat monitoring), remote operations via robot, removal of an item to a safer location for render-safe, render-safe *in situ*, or even hand entry, if the item determined presents an immediate threat to life that cannot be otherwise mitigated. Bomb technicians appreciate as much complete information on conditions, the situation, and intelligence as possible; however, it must be recognized that the decisions of the bomb squad are based upon training and national guidelines, and no attempts should be made to influence their decisions. For the bomb tech, public safety, responder safety, and tech safety are of paramount importance.

No mention has been made of using explosive detection canines or electronic monitors to evaluate the item for explosive hazard. Once someone has determined an item to be suspicious and potential explosive, it should be treated as a life-threatening item. If K9 does not alert, or electronic monitor does not react, it does not indicate that the item is inert; not all dogs are trained for all explosive materials, dogs do tire and have bad days, and monitors may not include the item in their library. It is too dangerous to expose a valuable resource like a canine team, or an individual with a monitor, to an item that will still require technicians to determine its actual hazard.

Upon conclusion of render-safe operations, if the item was found to be either an explosive device or a hoax, it must be treated as evidence. Many bomb squads, when working within their jurisdictions, will handle this aspect. Some handle no evidential matters, and refer this aspect to either agency resources (criminalistics or an investigative unit) or an outside agency (ATF or the FBI, depending upon case circumstances). When outside of jurisdiction, bomb teams may sometimes handle evidence; most often them turn this aspect over to local or federal authorities. However, the bomb squad will maintain safe custody of recovered explosive materials, providing an adequate lab sample for investigators, and storing remaining explosives as evidence in an explosives magazine.

POSTBLAST RESPONSE

From Horseshoes and Staves (le machine infernale)

Christmas Eve, 1800. The emperor, Napoleon Bonaparte, argued with the Empress Josephine, he then ordered his driver to speed off in his carriage to the opera. Josephine and their daughter, Hortense, followed the carriage, with their driver racing to catch the far-in-the-lead emperor.

Meanwhile, conspirators had set a vehicle-borne IED along the path they knew the emperor's entourage would follow. A rented, horse drawn carriage was weighed down with one or more barrels of black powder, themselves hidden under a pile of nails and iron trash. The leader of the team paid a teenage girl to hold his horse and carriage while he "attended to some business." As the royal entourage approached, a member of the assassination team lit the fuse extending from a barrel. Moments after Josephine's carriage passed, the infernal device exploded; the child attending the horse died, as did the horse, and estimates of up to 50 others were injured or killed. Hortense, Napoleon's daughter, was slightly injured by fragmentation.

Emperor Napoleon immediately laid blame on the Jacobins, his former allies and extremist democrats of the Revolution. However, his Minister of Police, Joseph Fouche, did not take the easy way of agreeing, despite Napoleon's rush to arrest and punish many Jacobins. Rather, Fouche and his investigators first conducted a true PBI. Despite the extensive damage to the cart and horse, they reconstructed the device and, from remains of tack and horseshoe hardware, were able to identify the farrier; based upon this, they were able to locate the man who had rented the horse and wagon, and then began following the trail of the bombers. When completed, Fouche would bring to justice a cabal of Royalists, who had in collusion with British supporters hatched the plot, which had so devastated a neighborhood of Paris and barely missed killing its intended target.

It is an unfortunate fact that many bombings are never investigated, or not properly investigated. Relatively minor incidents such as mailboxes, port-a-potties, newspaper boxes, and toilet bombings are classified as vandalism, attributed to juvenile pranks, and forgotten. If nothing else, a proper investigation provides personnel the opportunity to learn and hone their skills for the day they face a more serious bombing or explosion. Also, while these incidents are often pranks, they may have darker intentions, such as a message of intimidation, or may be a testing by a bomber preparing to carry out a more significant bombing.

PBIs are not limited to bombings. Accidental and even natural explosions will be investigated. It is much like the concept of death investigation; a proper investigation will determine the cause—if accidental or natural, perhaps engineering controls may be later derived to increase safety. If criminal, the investigation may continue and expand.

In the United States, the concept used and taught by the FBI, ATF, Postal Inspection Service, and the Department of State Anti-Terrorism Assistance Program is based upon the following six skills:

- Leader
- Investigator
- Photographer
- Schematic artist
- Evidence custodian
- Bomb technician

The makeup of a team that would be working small explosions may only have one or two investigators; they will share duties, and there may not be a bomb technician involved. In major investigations, many teams, each composed of multiple members, may comb debris.

It is also important to recognize that circumstances have also affected blast investigations. In areas beset by terroristic bombings, local officials have often acted to document the scene and then collect all debris, transporting it to a sterile area, and permitting a return to normality on city streets. In the combat theaters of Iraq and Afghanistan, where the IED has become a weapon of choice, mixed teams of military personnel and law enforcement investigators have learned to conduct a comprehensive scene documentation and evidence search in less than one half hour, minimizing their exposure as targets. Exigent circumstances, especially weather conditions, may force the investigation to take steps in protecting the site from the elements, or even move the evidence from the location of the occurrence to a location better suited for preserving the evidence.

Postblast response should always incorporate certain factors. First is scene security. Law enforcement must act to secure an area greater than the anticipated evidential debris field. Investigators use the 50% rule—locate the furthest piece of identifiable evidence from the seat of the blast, add 50% greater distance as a radius, and this becomes the basic search perimeter. Now add to this an adequate buffer zone to be used for staging various working components, and a security perimeter can then be established outside of this (Figure 5.4).

Identification of the perimeter needs to be established early to provide scene control for personnel and eventual security. During rescue, it is important that fire rescue personnel are unimpeded, plus recognize that untrained, unequipped responders attempting to help are in fact potential victims. Limiting scene access lessens the degradation or destruction of evidence, much of which is minute or microscopic.

Secondary device searches are often the province of bomb technicians, but all first responders must be alert for suspicious items. Internationally, secondary devices, usually aimed at the response community, have become commonplace. Domestically, they have been encountered, most notably in the case of serial bomber Eric Rudolph, who planted secondary devices at two of his bombings. Bomb technicians are a very finite resource; it is imperative that every responder be responsible for individual safety, maintaining vigilance for secondaries, especially when arriving and staging outside of the blast perimeter.

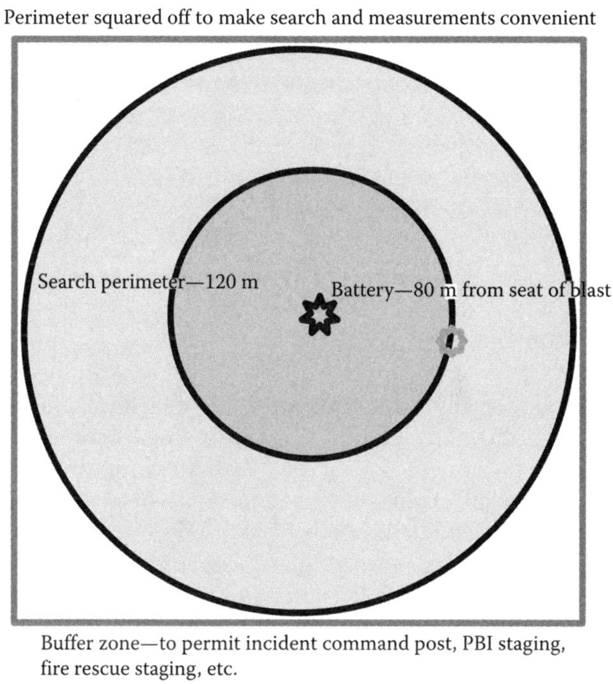

Figure 5.4 Generalized sketch of application of 50% rule and overall set-up of postblast crime scene.

This initial response often results in first responders driving into the blast perimeter. Further, rescue requires manual activity in that zone. Thus, it may become important to inspect tires of first-in vehicles and footwear of all on-scene personnel for fragmentary evidence so that it is not lost.

While investigation begins parallel with rescue, it takes over in earnest once rescue is complete and the scene can be sealed off completely. After the scene being sealed, access must be controlled through one entry—egress point. This point should act as a choke point for access to the actual investigative area, including contamination control.

The bomb technician enjoys a multifaceted role in the PBI. Because of the potential of secondary devices, the technician will be actively inspecting the site for suspicious items, analyzing them and conducting render-safe operations. During the initial examination of the scene, the technician will join with the team leader and photographer, as the scene is documented prior to search, as the perimeter of the search zone is determined, and as crime scene tactics are developed. The tech is especially valuable in identifying that crucial, furthest identifiable piece of evidence. During scene operations, examination of the seat of the blast (crater) is often assigned to the technician, due to the tech's ability to recognize potential evidence from that area.

At the hospital where victims are being treated, the technician's knowledge is valuable in identifying device components from among fragmentations recovered. Later, the technician can serve the same purpose as forensic autopsies are conducted on fatalities.

It is crucial that a technician be involved in any searches; suspect's residence, workshop, or any other location or vehicle associated with the suspect. This is for both safety as well as evidence identification. A bomber may take protective measures—booby-traps—to prevent unwanted entry. While many commercial explosives are engineered for stability, poorly stored materials, deteriorated explosives, and HMEs may be highly unstable. Further, the technician's knowledge of the evidence recovered on a scene may aid in identifying components and equipment located during searches.

A technician's knowledge often provides reasonable leads long before laboratory analyses can provide definite answers. Damage to device containers or objects immediately adjacent to a device may give the technician an indication of the type of explosive used. Depending upon the condition of device debris recovered, the technician may be able to determine the design and function of a device.

Very often, technicians will rebuild the device, if adequate information can be gleaned from the debris. Nonfunctioning models are valuable for investigators following up on a case, and for use in the courtroom. Often a functional device will be built, taken to an explosives range, and functioned while being photographed and videotaped. This documentation of the effect of the device is then a powerful evidence to illustrate the potential of the device, both to educate investigators and prosecutors and to educate the members of the court.

Finally, the bomb squad functions as a part of the evidence custody program. Live explosives must be stored in appropriate explosive storage magazines. Thus bomb squads will become evidence custodians of this material, whether for their cases or to store evidence generated by other agencies such as the ATF and FBI. Since explosive magazines require limited access and demonstrable security, the bomb squad can usually adopt an evidence handling protocol similar to that of the agency's evidence custody program with ease.

TACTICAL SUPPORT

The role of bomb squads in tactical support has been a slowly evolving process for well over 30 years. The latest requirements interface diametrically different functioning fields.

Probably the first tactical role filled by bomb technicians was in explosive entry. Reinforced doors or other obstacles to entry often confront tactical teams. Various tools are used to overcome these barriers—rams, sledges, jacks, pneumatic tools, etc. Military tactical units, often tasked with counterterrorist operations, developed explosive breaching to take advantage of several simultaneous benefits—surprise, instant results, and significant distractive effect. As these techniques were adapted for civilian law enforcement use, it was a natural fit for bomb technicians to be the handlers. Obviously, there are many agencies preparing for explosive breaching without benefit of a bomb squad. Among those that do, most integrate the bomb squad partly or wholly into explosive entry operations.

The role of bomb squads varies. At the least, they provide explosive materials and standby for disposal of failed entry materials. Many teams conduct local research and development of entry devices and construct many devices used for training and operations. Finally, a considerable number of teams handle all aspects of the process, embedding a technician into tactical entry teams to employ and initiate the explosive breach.

To prepare, most bomb squads that support explosive entry have technicians attend one of the nationally recognized explosive breaching training programs. They also train on a regular basis, combining R&D with training to ensure prowess and an understanding of needs regarding local architecture. This will also incorporate training with tactical teams; it is important that entry teams are trained under live explosive fire in order to prepare their members for actual implementation.

A natural outgrowth of this relationship was for bomb squads to support tactical teams with disposal of malfunctioning distraction devices and chemical agents. When these devices fail to function they pose a safety threat to any approaching. Further, as they are now waste and hazardous material, they must be disposed of in a manner consistent with legal requirements.

To prepare bomb squads for this role, it is not unusual to send technicians to instructor training for both distraction devices and chemical agents. The tech may not be used as an instructor; however the knowledge they receive aids them in safe disposal of failed munitions. Indeed, some agencies utilize their bomb squads as safety officers, observing from a nontactical view the use of these items, pointing out potential hazards, or supporting alternate delivery methods.

Robots or unmanned ground vehicles (UGV) have become a major safety tool of the bomb squad, mandated since 2009 for national accreditation. Soon after their implementation, their advantages to a tactical situation were recognized. First, the full-size robots have the heft and power to drag an unconscious individual out of harm's way for rescue. Mounting microphones and multiple cameras are excellent platforms to conduct surveillance and building clearance without unnecessarily exposing officers to hazards. In barricaded suspect situations they may act as negotiation platforms, and may be used to deliver food, water, phones, etc.

Robots may also provide other services. Most are capable of turning doorknobs to open the door and gain safe access. Either their disruptor or an attached semiautomatic shotgun may be utilized to remove locks that otherwise deny access. They may be used to deliver chemical agents or distraction devices.

Indeed, robots have shown their value in several incidents where a bomb robot, supporting a SWAT operation, found itself the target of a criminal's bullets—instead of an officer. In at least one incident, a robot, climbing stairs that provided the barricaded suspect tactical superiority, was shot multiple times. The robot was blinded, but was able to retreat; the criminal, realizing that his plan to execute officers had been foiled, maintained his cover but committed suicide.

Review of the 1998 Columbine High School massacre resulted in law enforcement adopting active shooter tactics. No longer would officers secure a perimeter and await for the arrival of SWAT; with an active shooter, whatever officers are quickly available form an entry team to flush and control the shooters. However, Columbine also presented a second hazard, that of almost 100 explosive devices, some functioned, some malfunctioned, and some intact.

Technicians may be seconded onto entry teams, whether improvised active shooter teams or SWAT entry teams. Here is where opposing philosophies must be intermixed. SWAT and active shooter tactics are built upon the surprise element of a dynamic entry and search technique. Bomb disposal is built upon a time consumptive, methodical, diagnostic approach.

Cognizant of the necessity for dynamics in a tactical setting, many bomb teams are currently developing procedures to provide embedded support that will not hinder the tactical function, while looking to ensure safety for entry teams, rescues, and follow-up personnel.

The rapid recon and rapid rescue systems developed in Hillsborough County, Florida need to be mentioned here. Originally developed in consideration of WMD incidents, they also lend themselves to modification for an active shooter scenario.

In rapid recon, a diamond-shaped entry team, dressed out to the highest level of chemical PPE safely practical for this scenario, will move through a scene. The diamond will include one bomb technician, two SWAT entry officers, a hazmat technician, and a medic. Their role is to quickly sweep through a scene, directing all ambulatory individuals a path for escape, while marking a safe route and detailing rescue, bomb disposal, and hazmat mitigation needs.

In rapid rescue, the bomb technician is replaced with a second medic. The team sweeps the scene to triage and remove any ambulatory victims. A major benefit of these systems is their flexibility—with adequate intelligence, positions may be dropped and replaced with additional, necessary positions.

Bomb squad support of active shooter responses is requiring the field to adapt to a major deviation from its traditional techniques. Bomb squads are rising to this challenge, establishing new procedures, researching new tools, and training with their tactical counterparts to ensure safety and success.

Although bomb disposal and tactical police operations are philosophically 180° apart, they are finding a broad area where they may interface for the benefit of tactical operations and the citizens they serve. Originated by bomb squads providing support services to the SWAT field, it is evolving into an adaptation of the bomb squad to provide embedded support to the tactical team.

6

Explosives and Bomb Technology

The bomb technician must have a well-founded understanding of explosives and explosive effects. Most devices will utilize an explosive; knowledge of explosives will aid the technician in selecting the most appropriate render-safe procedure (RSP) as well as establishing adequate safety. An understanding of explosive effects aids in confronting those devices that do not use an explosive. Knowledge of explosives and their effects aids in understanding PBI. The technician also uses explosives, as a render-safe tool, as a method of tactical entry, and in support of other functions; knowledge of explosives is necessary to safely use them as tools and to select an appropriate explosive for the situation encountered.

TECHNICAL ASPECTS OF EXPLOSIVES

Many years ago, Tom Brodie tongue-in-cheek described an explosion as a sudden movement from one place to another, accompanied by noise, heat, and pressure. Simplistic and lighthearted, it also accurately describes an explosion.

An explosion may be due to one of three causes. The first is a mechanical explosion. This is as a result of an item's inherent strength being overcome by pressure. In the winter, especially in northern latitudes, it is not uncommon to hear of boiler explosions. Usually it is due to metal fatigue or improper use, resulting in excessive pressure that causes boilers used for heating to fail, thereby resulting in explosions of sometimes tragic magnitude.

Another example is found by the fire service. This is the boiling liquid expanding vapor explosion, or BLEVE. Here, a pressurized container is exposed to a fire source, often because of some incident such as a rail or truck accident. Fire from whatever source heats the container. The combination of weakened container and often increasing internal pressure results in a compromise of the container; even if it is a nonflammable material, it is still highly dangerous as the container may torpedo out of control. In case of a flammable material (e.g., liquefied petroleum or vinyl acetate), the escaping contents will ignite, increasing the hazard and damage.

Because of adolescents and young adults emulating a television show, bomb technicians very commonly encounter a mechanical explosion in the form of chemical pressure bombs, often called soda bottle or dry ice bombs. These devices use carbonated beverage containers with any variety of materials that will react to produce extensive vapors, much in excess of the strength of the container.

Nuclear explosions, whether known as atomic bombs, hydrogen bombs, thermonuclear explosions, neutron bombs, or nuclear bombs, are examples of the tremendous releases energy when an atom is altered. Whether using a gun-type or implosion-type system, the effect of the nuclear explosion is universally feared.

Current technology requires a conventional, chemical explosive to be used as a trigger for the nuclear explosion. However, when dealing with military devices, the safety systems may include both failsafe/self-destruct and/or booby-trap systems, making the rendering safe of nuclear devices an intense, delicate operation for a select cadre of military EOD technicians.

The meat and potatoes for the bomb technician will be chemical explosives. These are chemical mixtures and compounds that are highly unstable. Given an appropriate impetus of energy, these chemicals will convert rapidly into by-products, releasing significant amounts of energy, heat, pressure, and sound.

Chemical explosives are classified as either low or high explosives; the differences are significant to their uses and effects. A low explosive is a chemical that deflagrates, or burns at a very high rate of speed. This deflagration releases tremendous amounts of gas; if contained, it will build up until the container's inherent strength is overcome and the gas is released with tremendous force.

Without containment, or with insufficient containment, the gaseous by-products of burning merely dissipate as a cloud of smoke. The heavier and stronger the container, the greater the explosive effect.

High explosives (HE) do not burn; rather they detonate and disintegrate at the molecular level as a shockwave travels through them. Except primary explosives, high explosives require a shock to initiate their detonations; only primary explosives are so sensitive to heat that they may be initiated by either heat or shock.

High explosives are also classified as primary, secondary, and tertiary. Primary high explosives are considered very shock-sensitive; a spark or flash of a match will detonate them. Due to sensitivity, they are only used in minute amounts, most often as the first level of explosives in a detonator, which then initiate the more powerful, less sensitive base charge of the detonator.

Secondary explosives require a more sufficient shock to detonate, that is, a detonator. Dynamite, tri-nitro toluene (TNT), RDX-based explosives (C-4), etc., are all secondary explosives. Some explosives, classified as tertiary, are so insensitive that a detonator cannot initiate them. Also called blasting agents, these materials such as ammonium nitrate and fuel oil (ANFO) require a booster of a secondary explosive for effective initiation.

As detonation effect releases so much energy, a high explosive does not need any containment to achieve explosive effect. The use of a container is usually either to provide concealment, or to add shrapnel (engineered fragmentation) to the effect of the blast.

A low explosive will burn at a rate of less than 3000 feet per second (fps) (1500 m/s), while high explosives will detonate at a velocity greater than that. Low-velocity high explosives are generally used industrially for their ability to break without shattering material such as rock. Higher velocity materials are selected for their greater shattering power, or brisance. Thus slower explosives, such as dynamite, can permeate materials such as steel, but only by gross tearing of the material. Therefore, a high-velocity explosive such as C-4 is used for cutting of steel and similar materials, because the higher velocity and brisance shatters the molecular makeup of the steel, resulting in much cleaner cuts. For public-safety personnel, especially when faced with special applications such as breaching, an understanding of this is crucial.

As public safety use of explosives has moved into more tactical applications, the net explosive weight (NEW) of a charge becomes crucial. Where use of explosives to countercharge, or explosively destroy, a bomb merely requires an adequate amount, a tactical operation requires an amount suitable for the need, without so much that it becomes deadly. Thus, NEW is closely adhered to in tactical use of explosives.

One set of terms is often confusing, especially to new initiates of blasting. These terms are of high and low order. These have nothing to do with the classification of the explosive, but rather refer to the efficiency of the explosion. In a high-order explosion, all the explosive materials are consumed in the ensuing explosion, and the expected effect is achieved. In a low-order explosion, the explosives are not fully consumed, and the explosive effect is not of the power it should be. Low orders may be due to improper priming of the explosive charge or degradation of the explosive materials. Investigatively, a low-order explosion also presents a very dangerous situation, as the partially consumed explosives may be much more sensitive than when intact (see Figure 6.1).

The explosive firing train refers to the stages necessary for an explosive to be initiated. Low explosives and primary high explosives require only a heat source; the match, burning fuse, and so on will initiate them. A secondary high explosive requires a shock source; its train will consist of a heat source, a primary explosive, and the secondary explosive. Due to their insensitivity, tertiary explosives require the heat source, primary, and secondary explosives in their train to initiate them.

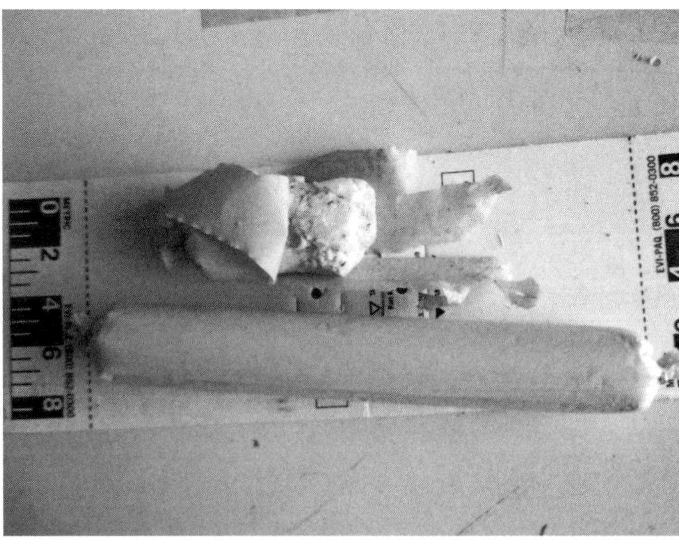

Figure 6.1 Top: remains of the low-order explosion of a cartridge of emulsion dynamite; below: a complete, unfired cartridge for comparison.

The bomb technician needs to understand a variety of explosive effects. This is of more value during the investigations and while planning for safety.

As stated previously, an explosion is accompanied by a release of pressure, heat, and noise. Pressure is the single greatest component of the explosion. The first phase is a positive pressure phase, caused by the rapidly expanding gases of the explosion. This is the single greatest hazard of the explosion; the overpressure alone at the scene of the blast may be well over the fatal limits for the human body, as well as its destructive effect on structures. Additionally, this force may pick up smaller items, or break apart and propel fragments of larger items as dangerous projectiles.

While the overpressure is a serious hazard to humans, it also decreases exponentially with distance from the seat of the blast. Recent research has established charts for various NEW of TNT overpressure at various distances. Especially for a technician in a bomb suit, a scant few feet may spell the difference between severe/fatal injuries and even total safety. The use of a telescopic manipulator (Figure 6.2) may provide a technician in a suit with sufficient distance to prevent any injury when forced to handle a device.

The second pressure effect is known as the negative pressure phase. The initial, positive pressure phase evacuates the scene of the blast at such

Figure 6.2 An officer photographed here using a telescopic manipulator. (Courtesy of Palm Beach County Sheriff's Office.)

a high velocity that a partial vacuum forms. As a result, the negative pressure phase sees a reverse action, with some material being sucked back towards the blast location. This has two effects—first, the victims may be pummeled or lacerated by this return of fragmentation, and, secondly, debris and evidence will not be deposited in any logical order.

Explosive reflection is an effect of great concern to the bomb technician. While the positive pressure phase has tremendous concussive power, it is also affected by solid objects it encounters, especially at right angles. These encounters will produce reflected waves of pressure, which will be considerably enhanced during their reflection.

A most tragic example occurred in Moscow, when a security officer encountered a bomber carrying a device in a bag. The bomber was taken into custody and the bag was left on the sidewalk, adjacent to a building wall. When the bomb disposal robot broke down, an experienced, respected bomb technician made an approach in a bomb suit. As he approached the device, it detonated. Due to multiple reflections of pressure off the ground and the wall, and his proximity to the device, what would have been a survivable and potentially injury-free incident in the open, resulted in fatal injuries.

An understanding of the heat generated in an explosion has benefits and safety considerations as well as potential investigative ones. All explosives generate heat; the higher the velocity of the explosive, the higher the heat generated. A low explosive such as black powder may generate a heat impulse approaching 1000°F, whereas high-velocity high explosives such as C-4 generates a temperature impulse in the thousands of degrees. However, that velocity also affects the time of the heat impulse—C-4 may be measured in milliseconds, where black powder is measured in a much longer fraction of a second. Thus black powder's heat impulse has a much better potential of igniting materials, where the C-4's impulse is so short that only highly volatile fuels are likely to ignite.

Distraction devices use low explosives, often either black powder or a perchlorate/chlorate-based pyrotechnic mixture. They must be carefully used, choosing to toss them into areas void of loose paper, fabric, etc., that could be ignited by the long heat impulse of the low explosives. Explosive breaching uses high explosives, often PETN, RDX, or TNT-based explosives, to ensure appropriate power and brisance is employed to penetrate the wall or door material. Caution needs to be taken if there are volatile flammables such as natural gas, propane, or gasoline immediately adjacent to the area of employment; however, fuels such as wood are of minimal risk, due to the extremely short time pulse of the high temperature.

Technicians must be aware of the sound generated by explosions. Unlike the shooting range, where the noise is constant, even in training the pace of the explosions is such that participants overlook the hazard. However, the impulse of the explosions, especially from high-velocity high explosives such as detonating cord and C-4, is very harmful to hearing. During training, and whenever possible in operations, technicians should use protection when detonating explosives.

Investigatively, sound is also of value. Again, the velocity of the shot is integral to the effect. The effect of low explosives, such as black or smokeless powder, will generally be described as a bang or boom sound. As the velocity increases, the sound will be described in sharper values. High-velocity high explosives will especially be noticeable in their sharp, distinctive crack noise signature.

Finally, the smoke effect should be understood. In tactical use of explosives, it is important that smoke does not obscure the vision of officers. The manufacturers of destruction devices carefully select explosives that will provide sharp sound, flash, and pressure effects, while producing smoke that rapidly rises, not obstructing the view.

Smoke is also a clue in determining explosive in PBI. Where black powder produces billowing clouds of white smoke, smokeless powder produces thin clouds of grayish smoke. Heavily carbonaceous explosives such as TNT and C-4 produce dense clouds of dark brown or black smoke. Gathering witness descriptions of smoke color and noise permits investigators to often determine the class of explosives used long in advance of obtaining laboratory reports.

MANUFACTURED EXPLOSIVE MATERIALS

Initiation

All explosives require some energy to initiate. In the case of low explosives, this will be a heat source; for high explosives it will incorporate a source of detonation velocity shock.

Safety fuse is a core-like material, ~1/4-inch (6 mm) in diameter, consisting of a center core of black powder, wrapped with several layers of waterproofing, strong thread, and either a wax or plastic exterior (Figure 6.3). It is designed to carry a spit of flame at approximately 8 inches per minute. It may be used directly to initiate low explosives (black powder being used for some quarry operations) or to deliver the heat to a blasting cap to initiate high explosives.

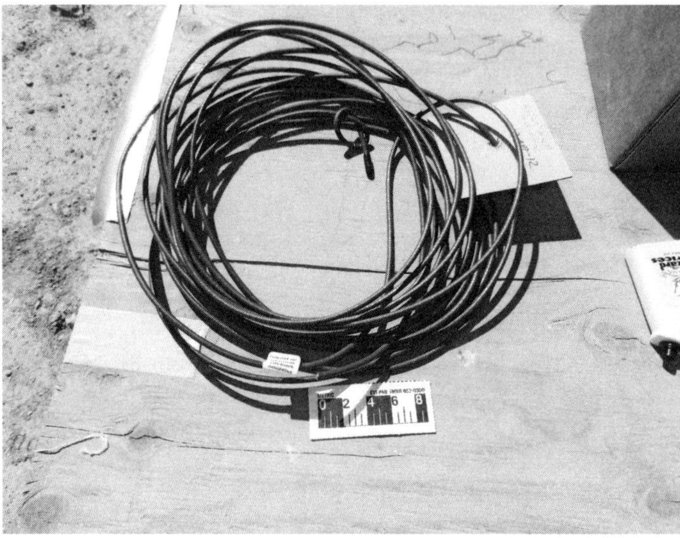

Figure 6.3 Mixed Kinestik. The ammonium nitrate was originally white. When mixed and sensitized with the nitromethane, which is red in color, it becomes a pink, which indicates to the user it is sensitized and now a high explosive.

Although fuse is still extensively used, it is found much less commonly than in previous days. First, it is inexact. Fuse may absorb humidity, which will alter the burn rate of the black powder. Blasters will always test a length of fuse to determine its current burn rate. Also, while rare, a section of fuse may not be fully packed with black powder; when the burn reaches this point it will skip along the remaining powder, rather than burn at normal rate, and shorten the expected burn period. This inexactitude limits its usefulness in many operations where multiple shots need to be either simultaneous or require precise delays. Fuse cannot be cut to ensure fractional second precision, thus precise jobs cannot be undertaken with it.

Second, once ignited, the blaster loses control of charge's initiation. The blaster ignites the fuse, and retreats to a safe area. Should something occur to require the abortion of the shot, it cannot be done.

To address this problem, the explosives industry developed electric initiation. With low explosives, this will be an electric match or a squib. An electric match consists of lead wires, used to connect to the electric lines laid back to the safe area, and a head consisting of an igniter, and a

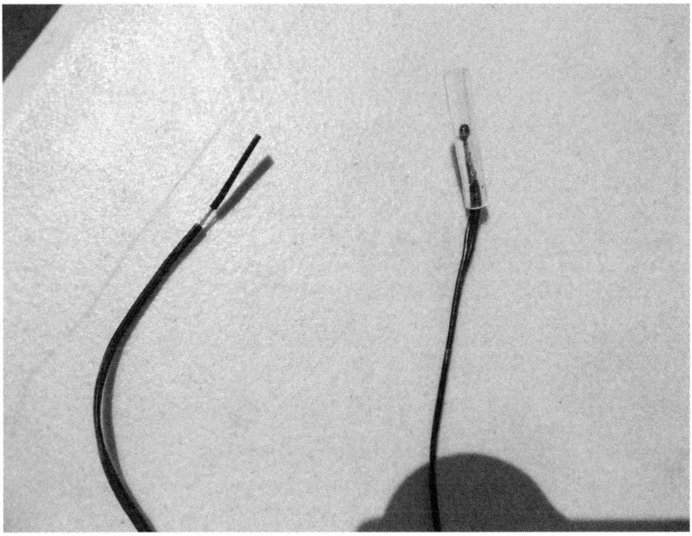

Figure 6.4 An example of an electric match; the plastic sleeve over the match element protects it from damage.

high resistance piece of wire (Figure 6.4). When current is introduced to the firing circuit, the head instantaneously develops high heat, capable of initiating low explosives.

A squib consists of an electric match that is housed in a very small metal container. Within this container there will be a small amount of black powder. When energized, the match ignites the black powder, which will then be either used to give an effect, or be used to initiate a main charge of low explosive. Squibs are especially used in theatrical and motion picture effects.

To initiate high explosives requires a sufficiently strong shock to detonate secondary high explosives. Thus the blasting cap was developed. Fuse or nonelectric blasting caps (EBCs) consist of a thin metal, usually aluminum, container. The first part of this container is open and empty, designed to fit over a piece of safety fuse. A small amount of very sensitive primary explosive forms a first, heat sensitive layer. There is then a second layer of less sensitive but more powerful, explosive, and finally a main charge of RDX or PETN, high velocity secondary explosives (Figure 6.5). Commercial blasting caps (also referred to as detonators) are usually referred to as a number six strength, and contain a base charge of 15

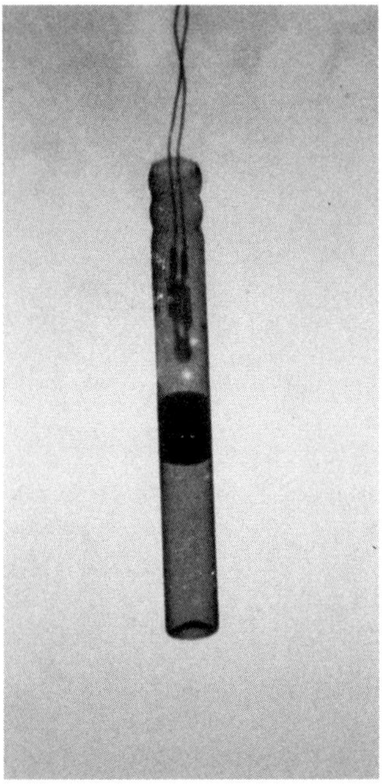

Figure 6.5 X-ray of an inert electrical detonator: void below match would contain primary explosive, while lower void would contain secondary, main charge explosive.

grains of explosive. Military blasting caps, often referred to as number eight engineer special caps, contain twice the base charge, to ensure initiation of C-4, which is especially insensitive.

The fuse caps face the same shortcomings as fuse. Thus the electric blasting cap (EBC) was introduced. The EBC basically mates the fuse cap with the electric match; at the base a rubberlike plug is seated and heavily crimped in, both holding the parts in close alignment and providing a waterproof closure. Additionally, a time delay could be included, inserted between the igniter and charge, which could be increments from milliseconds to several seconds in length. In commercial applications, a series of shots may be connected, with time delays separating each; in many mining operations this is used to promote efficiency in rock breakage, or to minimize production of vibrations, often a source of complaints from neighbors of blasting operations (Figure 6.6).

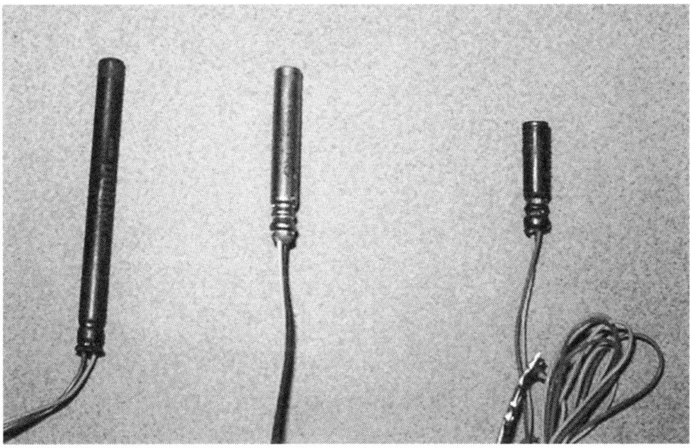

Figure 6.6 Three electrical detonators; difference in length represents delay elements, which are used to provide delays of between 250 and 1000 ms.

Electrical initiation provides the blaster absolute control over the shock, and provides the opportunity for delay blasting. However, it also has a significant hazard. As it comes from the factory, the wires of the electric cap are short-circuited by being tied together (shunted) by a metal or plastic object called a shunt (Figure 6.7). Once the shunt is removed, and the wires are loose, the wires become an antenna, open to any source of extraneous electrical energy. This may be static electricity (such as in dry atmospheres, or as is produced from walking across a carpeted floor), lightning discharges, or radiofrequency (RF) waves. Blasters handling electrical detonators ensure they are grounded to dissipate any static charge. Blasting operations are suspended upon advance of any thunderstorms. However, RF presents the greatest hazard, and one that is growing.

Depending upon the frequency and power of an energy source, an RF hazard may extend a few feet to several hundred feet. For this reason no radio equipment is permitted on blasting sites. For public safety, this translates to turning off all radio equipments, including cell phones and two-way pagers, within 100 yards of a device. On a threat response, or when the location of a device is unknown, it means switching off all communication equipments as one approaches the target location. The communication systems such as trunked radios and cell phones, while on high frequencies and low powered, are especially hazardous because

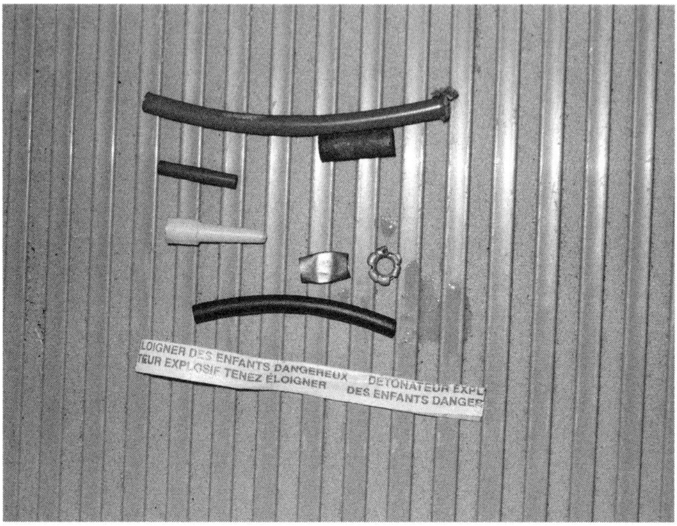

Figure 6.7 A variety of shunts; all act to short-circuit the lead wires of the detonator and prevent extraneous electrical flow.

they are constantly transmitting information to their control station. Many bomb squads have invested in communication systems for robots and bomb suits that are designed to safely operate in proximity to electrical detonators.

Manufacturers of explosives are constantly striving to improve their products safety, efficiency, and cost. Thus shock tube initiation, sometimes referred to as Nonel® or nonelectric, was developed. In this system, a detonator (Figure 6.8), which may be instantaneous or include a delay element, is crimped to a length of approximately 3/16 inch diameter plastic tubing. The inside walls of the tubing are coated with a thin dusting of a mixture of finely powdered aluminum and HMX, which is an extremely high velocity explosive. In this configuration, the HMX–aluminum mixture is not capable of detonation; however, it can transmit a spark at 6500 fps. A variety of tools are available to initiate the spark; these include electrical generation and devices firing a shotgun primer. The system permits absolute control, and safety in electrically hazardous environments. Indeed, most bomb squads use shock tube initiation as their primary initiation technique (Figure 6.9).

It has been mentioned that the shell metal of detonators usually being was made of aluminum. Other metals have been and are used. However,

Figure 6.8 The effect of a single detonator on a watermelon.

some metals, in combination with the chemicals of the primary explosive used in detonators, may produce extremely sensitive, highly dangerous explosive compounds. This was especially true in the use of copper as a shell when lead azide was used as the priming element. The copper and the lead azide would react to form copper azide, an extremely sensitive and unstable explosive material. Tragic incidents have occurred, including for bomb technicians involved with disposal operations, when copper azides, formed within detonators, have self-initiated from otherwise normal or delicate movement.

Low Explosives

For over 1000 years, black powder was the only explosive known. The earliest black powder was a loose mixture of saltpeter, charcoal, and sulfur. As science, specifically chemistry, improved, and as methods of true manufacture were instituted, black powder evolved to a compounded

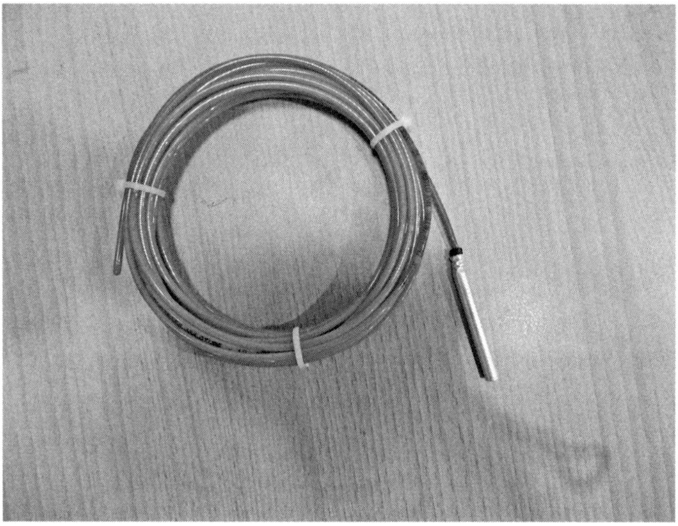

Figure 6.9 Short length of inert shock tube. This is found attached to detonators and also used in this form to deliver pressure energy to firing pins of disruptors.

material, making it much more reliable and consistent as an explosive. Until the late 1800s, it was the only propellant in use, powering all firearms from pistols to artillery.

Although it is largely obsolete, black powder remains a common explosive. Especially in the United States, sportsman shoot black powder firearms, replicas of the original flintlock and percussion firearms, for hunting and shooting sports. Additionally, because of its relatively low velocity and gentle heaving effect, it is used in the quarry of materials like marble, where the miners are attempting to separate large sheets of rock for use in construction and sculpture.

Black powder is most commonly encountered in relatively fine granulation's, for use in firearms. It is classified by a code system, where Fg refers to a large, coarse grain, most often used in cannon propellant, and an increasing number of Fs indicates smaller, finer grains, with FFFFg being the finest granulation, used for small caliber firearms and priming the locks of flintlock firearms. Other classification systems are used for black powders designed for fireworks, quarry and mining, fuse manufacture, and military applications.

Figure 6.10 Initiation of a one-pound can of black powder; typical thick, white smoke from its combustion.

Upon initiation, black powder (Figure 6.10) produces copious amounts of thick, white smoke. It produces a lower sound than most other explosives, indicative of its lower velocity. It also produces a very distinctive odor due to its high sulfur content.

Black powder is highly sensitive to heat, friction, and shock. While all explosives should be handled carefully and respectfully, this is especially true of black powder. Most jurisdictions require the use of storage magazines for possession over a relatively small amount as a safety measure.

Black powder is also hygroscopic; when moist it becomes unreliable or even inert. However, when it dries out, the evaporation of water also removes some chemical components making it more sensitive than in its original condition. Any black powder suspected of having been wet and dried should be handled with utmost care, especially from friction or shock.

Due to both the hazards and storage requirements, the sporting industry developed black powder substitutes. A variety of powders are available. Some, like Pyrodex, are a modified black powder, having chemical additives to greatly lower their sensitivities. Others, such as Black Mag Three, American Pioneer, and GOEX Pinnacle are ascorbic acid based, while some such as Hodgson's TripleSeven, are gluconic acid-based. All are designed to give results and effects similar to black powder in firearms. From investigative aspect, each will produce similar effects to black powder, although their laboratory analyses will vary significantly.

In the latter part of the nineteenth century a new explosive propellant, smokeless powder, was introduced. What is now known as single-based smokeless powder was a finely granulated nitrocellulose. Nitrocellulose permitted much higher velocities; this also resulted in the capability of using smaller projectiles.

A significant improvement in this technology was the combination of nitrocellulose with nitroglycerin, which itself is a primary high explosive, to produce a family known as double-based smokeless powders. Rocket research resulted in the development of triple-based smokeless powders, which added nitroguanidine to double-based smokeless powder.

In addition to providing meaningful improvements to ballistic science, smokeless powders also improved the safety and handling of gunpowder (Figure 6.11). While still sensitive to heat, friction, shock, and static, they are much less so than black powder. They are also much less hygroscopic than black powder. Further, they are not made more sensitive to initiation when wet and dried out.

From the aspect of the bomb technician, it is most important to understand that a single-based smokeless powder will only function as a low explosive. However, double and triple-based smokeless powders may function as a high explosive, by initiating them with a detonator rather than a heat source. If used in this manner, then may achieve velocity of detonation (VOD) of approximately 15,000 ft/s, similar to dynamite.

Pyrotechnic powders are generally mixtures of potassium chlorate or perchlorate with finely ground aluminum powder. They are most commonly used in fireworks production. Depending upon local laws, bomb squads may seize consumer fireworks during the holidays, and face disposal of these stocks. Also, illegal explosive devices known as an M-80s, cherry bombs, blockbusters, or other names may be encountered. Under

Figure 6.11 Low explosive burn trail; here, a segment of smokeless powder is burning. It burns with yellow flame, but puts off very thin, gray smoke.

federal law, a consumer fireworks is defined as containing two grains or less of explosive materials. Any item containing a greater amount is no longer classified as a consumer firework, and is instead a regulated explosive. While the devices themselves pose significant hazards, the clandestine manufacturing sites pose even greater hazards to investigators and the communities in which they are located.

Pyrotechnic mixtures are far more susceptible to heat, friction, shock, and static discharge than black powder. This is especially dangerous in clandestine factories, where industrial hygiene is rarely practiced. Floors, walls, counter surfaces, etc., are likely to be heavily coated with a heavy dusting of the mixture; an exposed flame, dropped tool, scuffed shoe, or electrical spark may initiate for a building-wide explosion.

High Explosives

The development of nitroglycerin (NG) in the mid-nineteenth century altered forever the field of explosives. NG, as a high explosive, provided much improved potential over black powder. Now there was an explosive that could literally shatter rock, rather than push it around. However, NG is a highly shock-sensitive primary explosive and an extremely hazardous tool to transport or use.

Alfred Nobel's research changed that. By absorbing the NG into Kielsguhr, a form of diatomaceous earth, he found that its shock sensitivity was greatly reduced, permitting it to be safely transported and handled with reasonable care. Further, packaged into sticks or cartridges, it could be used in a wide variety of situations.

Dynamite was not perfect, and improvements were constant. To increase its water resistance, it would be gelatinized by the addition of nitrocellulose. To provide better reliability in cold temperatures, it was mixed with ethylene glycol dinitrate (EGDN). Since it produced toxic asphyxiating fumes, permissible dynamites were developed for use in underground mining.

Dynamite remains the most hazardous of commercial high explosives (Figure 6.12). Straight dynamite is susceptible to freezing; while melting it is more sensitive to shock. If ignited, it is highly sensitive to shock; no efforts should be made to extinguish a dynamite fire (nor any other burning explosive) and the area should be evacuated. However, its greatest hazard, for any dynamite containing NG, is separation of NG from the absorbent.

Figure 6.12 A tractor barn where a case of deteriorated dynamite, estimated as abandoned for 25 years, was found.

Figure 6.13 Damaged case sets on upper shelf; plastic liner was full of liquefied nitroglycerine.

Since NG is absorbed and suspended by the dynamites filler, gravity will act to percolate the NG from the filler. In storage, cases of dynamite will be routinely turned, permitting the NG to be moved to the top and maintain its saturation of the cartridges. If not properly maintained, the dynamite will eventually bleed off the NG, which will usually collect in the liner of the case. This now presents a serious hazard, one that many bomb squads have been called upon to mitigate as a public safety danger (Figures 6.13 and 6.14).

Ammonia dynamite was developed to meet some of these shortcomings. For this product, ammonium nitrate replaces part of the NG; the result is an explosive with less fume production, less shock and friction sensitivity, and less deterioration hazard. This should not be confused with US military dynamite, which is a NG-free, sensitized ammonium nitrate material for use by military engineers.

Technicians should also be aware of a physiological effect of NG on the human body. NG acts to open the blood vessels, permitting greater blood flow. This is why NG is used medically, to alleviate some heart conditions. In the gross quantities encountered in the explosives industry, the result can be serious headaches. To whatever extent possible the technician should be prophylactically protected by using suitable, nonpermeable

Figure 6.14 From different angle; cartridges of dynamite still have a familiar shape. After tractors and various farm chemicals were removed, the barn was burned to destroy the deteriorated explosives.

gloves to prevent absorption of NG through the skin, and avoid eating, drinking, or smoking until after thoroughly washing. While the most common effect of NG is to cause headaches, overdosage may have other toxic effects. A common field expedient relief to NG exposure is use of caffeine products, such as coffee or cola drinks.

Sensitized ammonium nitrate explosives have been developed to provide safer, cheaper explosives otherwise comparable to dynamites. Water gel explosives consist of ammonium nitrate, water, finely ground aluminum, and other components. They are most commonly encountered as plastic-wrapped cartridges, similar to sausage from the deli. Water gels have very similar effects to dynamite, but being NG-free, do not have the hazards associated with it.

The most common ammonium nitrate explosive is ANFO. This is found packaged in cartridges, 50-pound bags, and also delivered to the site by pump truck. ANFO is not detonator-sensitive; an additional step in the explosive firing train, a booster, is required to ensure initiation. Because of this insensitivity, ANFO is classified as a blasting agent, with lesser control over transportation and storage.

A wide group of ammonium nitrate-based explosives, known as emulsions, have been developed for commercial use (Figure 6.15). Depending

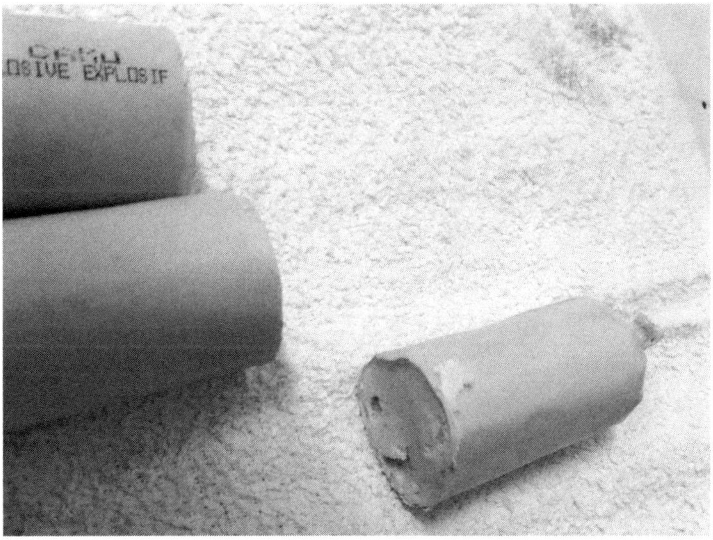

Figure 6.15 Sectioned cartridge of an emulsion; note the thick consistency of the explosive.

upon their chemical components, some are blasting agents, others are high explosives. They are encountered in sausage like cartridges, bags, and pump trucks—the latter not being classified as explosive until pumping, as the truck mixes the different, nonexplosive components as it pumps them into the ground.

Noncap-sensitive materials, such as ammonium nitrate and many emulsions, require an intermediate initiation force. These explosives, referred to as boosters, may be manufactured from several explosives. At least one line of boosters has used a plastic cylinder of about 1 pint (500 mL) capacity, filled with dynamite and then sealed to prevent much NG separation.

The vast majority of boosters are referred to as cast boosters. These are manufactured from TNT, PETN, RDX, or a combination of these, such as pentolite, a mixture of PETN and TNT (Figure 6.16). These explosives are quite similar in appearance—hard-like plaster with an off-white coloration and some slight crystalline appearance. They are melted and poured into forms, usually cylindrical cardboard tubes. These cast boosters are very stable and insensitive, with excellent shelf lives. They are also powerful, with VOD between 20,000 and 24,000 fps. Indeed, because of these

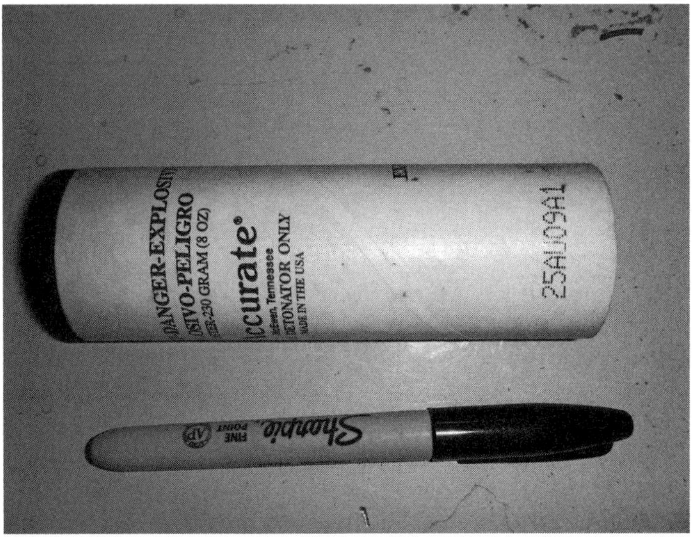

Figure 6.16 A one-half pound (230 g) pentolite cast booster.

factors and also their availability and relatively low cost, cast boosters are often the choice of bomb squads as a material for use in explosive destruction of devices.

Another variety of booster, which is often used to boost smaller shots, is called a slip-on booster (SOB). This consists of PETN explosive mixed with a flexible plasticizer, cast into small, thin-walled cylinders usually 1–3 inches long, about 3/4-inch in diameter with a 1/4-inch center hole. SOBs are also popular with bomb teams for a variety of tasks where smaller explosive charges are appropriate.

A very common explosive product is detonating cord (or detcord), sometimes referred to by a commercial term, Primacord®. This product consists of either RDX or PETN contained in a fiber or plastic spun exterior cord varying in diameter from about 3/16-inch to over 1/2-inch, depending upon the NEW per foot of the cord. Detonating cord is designed to transmit explosive energy over a distance, usually to connect and initiate a variety of shots (such as multiple holes in a quarry operation).

As noted above, RDX and PETN are very high VOD explosives. The detonation of a length of detcord above ground makes an unmistakable cracking sound, and leaves a trail on open ground where it had lain.

Figure 6.17 A length of 50 grain-per-foot detonating cord surrounding a length of 25 grain detonating cord.

Detcord is a very common bomb squad tool. It is used in a number of disposal and breaching techniques, and is used to initiate buried shots, to avoid placing a blasting cap below ground (Figure 6.17).

TNT is a castable explosive material that is extensively used as a military explosive. This is due to a number of properties. First, TNT has a high VOD, approximately 22,000 fps. As noted before, it is relatively insensitive. An important sensitivity test is the bullet impact test, where a sample of explosive is subjected to the impact of a bullet from a 30-06 (7.62 × 63 mm) cartridge at relatively short range. TNT will not detonate in such a test. Further, it is extremely stable in storage, with an almost indefinite shelf life if properly stored.

TNT is also the standard material against which all other explosives are compared for power (Figures 6.18 and 6.19). Assigned a value of one, explosives such as dynamite rate at 0.74, while C-4 rates at 1.35. This provides a quick method for users, needing to relate explosive power or to quickly determine NEW to substitute on a project.

The US military has developed a wide range of explosives for military application. Beginning with Composition A, it has developed a number of explosives designed to provide malleable materials. The most

Figure 6.18 The cardboard container for a US military, one-pound block of TNT.

well-known, Composition C-4, consists of RDX and a plasticizer, resulting in an off-white colored material with, at room temperature, a consistency slightly harder than modeling clay. C-4 is also a high VOD explosive, about 25,000 fps, highly brisant, especially valuable for its ability to cut dense metals such as steel. With its plasticity, it may be formed to fit into the shape of a target, or be loaded into a shaped charge container (either cylindrical or linear), which use the Munroe effect to produce an explosively formed cutting jet, capable of defeating a considerable thickness of steel (Figure 6.20).

Although limited in availability, C-4 is a popular explosive in the bomb disposal community, where its utility in either cutting or destroying thick metal is appreciated. It has been adapted to a number of techniques designed especially for bomb disposal, and is used with a shaped charge containers for breaching of metal objects.

Sheet explosives consist of RDX or PETN in a rubberlike plasticizer. Available in a variety of thicknesses, sheet explosives are used in industrial operations for cutting and welding of steel. The military uses sheet explosives for many functions, including cutting steel and demolition charges. They are also used in public safety bomb disposal, where they have been adapted to provide explosive propulsion to a number

Figure 6.19 A case of Soviet TNT, recovered washed ashore on a beach. Each block is wrapped in a wax paper material. When recovered, the entire case had been primed by the placement of an electrical blasting cap in the topmost block of TNT. No explanation was ever determined for either its washing ashore or its being primed.

of render-safe techniques. A confusing aspect when dealing with sheet explosives are their naming protocols; differentiated by thickness, the sizes are called C-1 through C-6, which sometimes causes confusion with Composition C-4, more commonly referred to as C-4.

Binary explosives are materials designed to provide a material that is not explosive until mixed (Figure 6.21). The most common binary

Figure 6.20 Three M-112 blocks of Composition C-4 were recovered from the crawl space beneath a mobile home.

explosives are based upon ammonium nitrate, which is then mixed with a sensitive fuel, making it cap sensitive (Figures 6.22 and 6.23). The two most common products are packaged in plastic packages similar in size, shape, and explosive output to dynamite. While binaries were especially designed for agricultural and construction use where the user has minimal need for explosives and can thus store them without magazine, they have found favor in the bomb disposal community as well.

Figure 6.21 Kinestick, a commonly used binary explosive. The plastic "stick" contains ammonium nitrate, the plastic tube contains nitromethane fuel; when mixed they form a cap-sensitive high explosive.

Figure 6.22 Ammonium nitrate prills removed from the Kinestik.

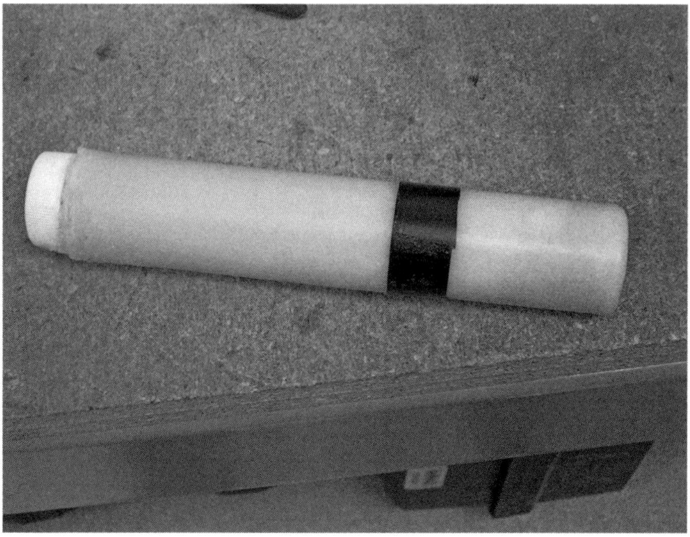

Figure 6.23 Mixed Kinestik. A pink coloration indicates it is mixed and now a high-explosive material.

This has been a very brief introduction to commercially manufactured explosives, especially those most commonly encountered or used by the bomb disposal field. Explosives perform many valuable functions in applications such as manufacturing, mining, and demolition. They are also valuable tools to the bomb technician. However, when permitted to deteriorate or in the possession of persons with evil intent, they present significant hazards to the community.

IMPROVISED EXPLOSIVES

Improvised or HME have long been a public safety concern. A variety of HME, from black powder to NG to "poor man's C-4" have been encountered. Most recently has been the emergence of peroxide-based explosives, which have found favor with a variety of international terrorist groups.

Bomb technicians encounter HME in response to clandestine labs, recoveries of HME, HME-based IEDs, and in PBIs. Improvised explosives are encountered in clandestine manufacturing of illegal devices such as M-80s, burglars producing NG to attack safe doors, and terrorists improvising a variety of explosives.

Commercially manufactured explosives are produced under highly controlled conditions, with explosive engineers and chemists intimately involved in their preparation and production. Improvised explosives are usually produced by individuals working off a recipe, in less than desirable facilities, usually with kitchen or other household materials substituting for laboratory grade equipment. Industrial hygiene is not practiced; for example, improvised manufacturing facilities for illegal devices such as M-80s are usually covered with a silver gray dust from the flash powder mixture being permitted to float about in the facility. Dealing with HME, especially clandestine labs, is one of the most dangerous assignments a technician mission will face.

Although a number of books, internet articles, and videos provide instruction on making a variety of HMEs, the list of commonly encountered materials includes the following:

- Black powder
- Pyrotechnic (flash) powder
- NG
- ANFO
- ANIS (ammonium nitrate and icing sugar)
- ANAL (ammonium nitrate and aluminum powder)
- Urea nitrate
- Poor man's C-4 (potassium chlorate and petroleum jelly mixtures)
- Peroxide explosives

The bomb technician must first recognize the danger in manufacturing any of these materials. It should only be conducted under the guidance of experienced explosive chemists, and under the auspices of the FBI or ATF. Some are physically sensitive; others use highly corrosive and toxic chemicals in manufacturing; some are highly reactive in manufacturing; if not properly combined, heated, or cooled, then they are capable of self-detonation. Generally, it is only acceptable for public safety agencies to manufacture HME when preparing exhibits to test in regards to a case.

Any response involving HME should be treated with greatest caution. Any improvised explosive should be treated as highly sensitive to any energy source. Static, friction, heat sources are all potential initiators

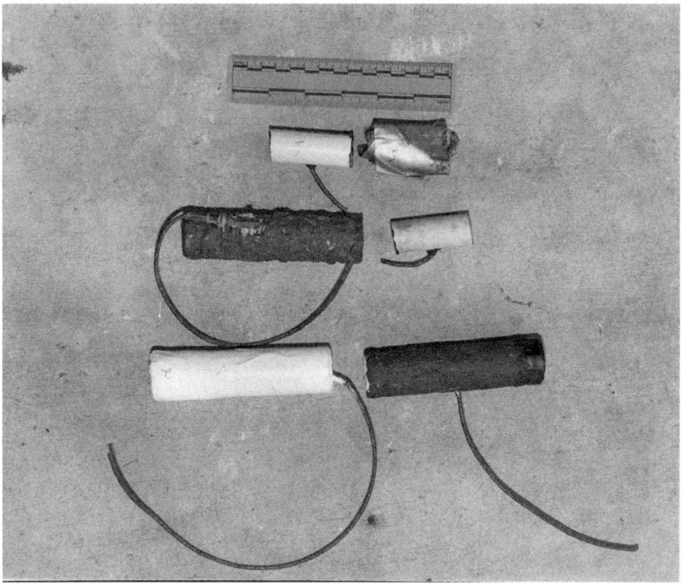

Figure 6.24 A variety of HME devices, incorporating black powder and improvised pyrotechnic powder.

of improvised explosives; all prudent steps should be taken to prevent them (Figure 6.24). All cotton clothes and rubber sole shoes should be the dress code. All radio equipments should be secured safely outside the scene. All lighting equipment must meet all explosion proof standards. Photographic flash equipment should not be used for photography unless the flash is certified as intrinsically safe.

Manufacturing sites are especially dangerous. A manufacturing facility in a residential or otherwise occupied area should not be entered until an adequate area has been evacuated. Fire and EMS must stage safely, if available hazmat personnel, and if at all possible an explosive chemist to consult with regarding the processes and handling of materials. Without the chemist, no process should be interrupted or any material handled directly; instead, remote operations should be conducted to safely accomplish such ends.

While HME present significant hazards to the technician, it presents even greater dangers to first responders. It is important to establish agency procedures for response to either caches or laboratories (Figures 6.25 and 6.26). Many items of HME appear similar to many drugs; clandestine drug

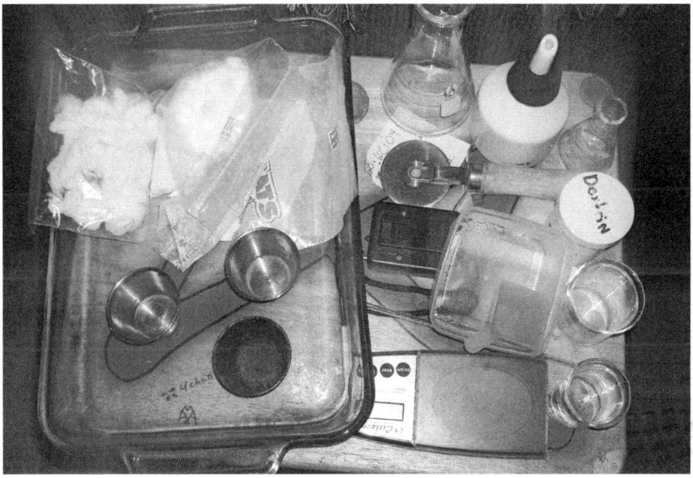

Figure 6.25 "Lab" materials in use at a HME factory where a variety of explosives, including TATP, were being manufactured. (Courtesy of Brevard County Sheriff's Office.)

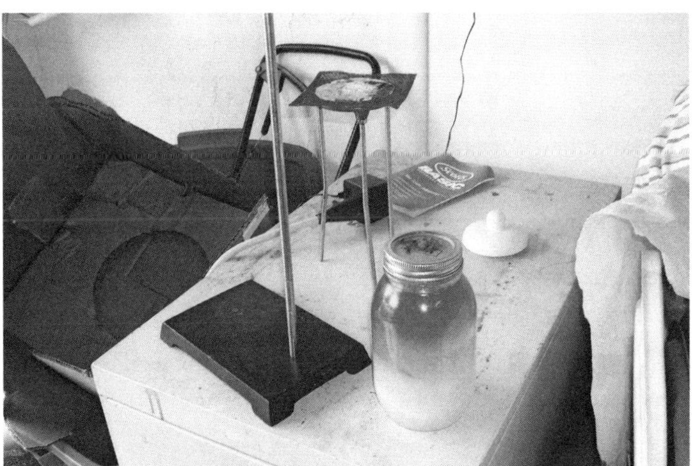

Figure 6.26 Additional lab materials found at this location. (Courtesy of Brevard County Sheriff's Office.)

and HME labs will share a similar appearance. It is crucial that patrol officers and investigators understand the hazards of using drug field test kits on unknown materials; most explosive materials are highly reactive to the acids used in most narcotic field test. It is valuable for patrol and investigative personnel to have reference material describing HME precursors, which will aid them in determining if they are dealing with a drug or explosives incident.

When preparing to work in a clandestine lab, a bomb disposal team is wise to reach out to appropriate environmental regulators. The clan lab is a hazardous waste site; by incorporating environmental response, the public safety agency can protect itself from inheriting liability for cleanup, which can reach a five- or six-figure expense. Working together, bomb disposal and environmental regulators can ensure public safety is provided for while the appropriate legally responsible party is held financially accountable.

Improvised explosives have been a serious obligation of the bomb's squad since its earliest days. Now, in the second decade of the twenty-first century, popularity is increasing more, as a variety of groups are turning to them as explosive materials. The bomb disposal community must maintain its hazmat skills, keep abreast of changes and additions to the HME arsenal, and upgrade its knowledge of handling and rendering safe improvised explosive incidents.

BOMB TECHNOLOGY

Earlier it was stated that this work will not address the manufacture of explosive devices. However, it is imperative that the technician and investigator understand what a bomb is, what is required for it to function, and aspects that will affect safety and successful investigation.

The current model used to define device construction is the acronym PIES:

- Power source
- Initiator
- Explosive
- Switch

The following shall examine each of these and its role in the construction of devices.

Explosives

Explosives have already been reviewed. Their choice is determined by a number of factors:

Source
Knowledge
Capabilities

Source is the single most important of these factors. In the United States, low explosives are easily obtained. They may be purchased at gun shops, where black powder is stocked for muzzleloading enthusiasts, and smokeless powder is available for cartridge reloading. Ammunition is often disassembled for powder. Consumer fireworks have been used as a source of low explosives, as occurred in the Columbine incident.

High explosives are considerably more difficult to obtain. Since 9/11, all high-explosive transactions require licensing and completion of tracking paperwork. However, the nature of explosives results in most storage being in remote locations, where despite hardened storage magazines, their remoteness exposes them to burglary and theft. It is also not unusual for explosives to be targeted by employee theft; while in use, explosive accountability is required. Bookkeeping "errors" are not difficult to introduce. Even military explosives are far from secure; a member of service can secrete small quantities of energetic materials from legitimate operations and smuggle them off base.

The military actions in Iraq illustrated another source of high explosives (HE)—military ordnance. When the Hussein government fell, terrorists raided unguarded, hidden caches of ordnance. Artillery projectiles especially became favored as readymade pipe bombs; the terrorist would merely place an initiator into the fuse well of the device, which became a ready source of HE and fragmentation.

HMEs not only continue to be a source, but are increasing. Black powder and flash powder may be improvised quite easily with commercially available precursors. A number of "underground" books have provided directions to the manufacture of NG, TNT, RDX, PETN, and other explosive compounds. While highly hazardous and requiring chemical skills, it can be accomplished. Peroxide-based explosives, long discarded by military and industry as too hazardous, have emerged over the past 30 years as relatively easily synthesized HE. Also, a number of tertiary HE are easily manufactured by mixing easily acquired chemicals.

Knowledge and capabilities may be discussed together. Often low explosives provide the less informed bomb maker an easy avenue to construction of a device. The use of high explosives requires greater knowledge and skills, somewhat limiting their application by the bomber. Similarly HMEs require knowledge and skills to both successfully manufacture the material as well as to safely manufacture it.

Initiation becomes dependent upon the nature of the explosive main charge. Low explosives and peroxide explosives are extremely heat sensitive; burning fuse, and electric match, or even a spark may be used to initiate such a charge. A phosphorous-based material, Armstrong's mixture, is sufficiently sensitive to friction that it has been loaded into hollow balls and thrown at targets; impact is sufficient to initiate the mixture. Most HE requires a detonator of sufficient strength for the charge. Commercial detonators, either fuse or electric, may be obtained by theft, often at the same time as the main charge HE. Some military explosives, especially C-4 and its related compounds, are quite insensitive and require more powerful (military) detonators, or a booster charge, to reliably initiate them.

A tertiary explosive, such as ANFO, is very insensitive, and cannot be initiated by a detonator. Instead, a firing train consisting of a detonator and a secondary explosive booster is necessary to provide sufficient shock to achieve detonation. Commercially, explosive boosters are employed. Small boosters, referred to as SOBs, made from extruded plastic explosives, are designed to slide over a blasting cap and initiate smaller quantities. For most large quantities, a commercial product called a cast booster is employed. This is most often a hard cast cylinder of pentolite, a mixture of PETN and TNT, usually available in sizes from 4 ounces through 5 pounds, with the selection being made based upon the quantity of the base charge.

However, a sufficient quantity of any HE may be used as a booster for tertiary explosive initiation. Indeed, it is common for bomb technicians who have supplies of C-4 but lack military detonators to use either an SOB or a "monkey fist" knot of detonating cord to boost the initiating energy into the plastic explosive.

Power Source

Power source is a relative term. While it brings to mind images of batteries, here it refers to any energy source used for a device.

A common source will be a match or similar heat source. Pyrotechnic fuse or safety fuse requires a heat initiation. A match, a mechanical energy source, is a power source frequently encountered.

Mechanical power is also encountered. Many devices depend upon a spring to insert appropriate energy into the function. Rat traps have often been modified to permit the bail to crush a shotshell primer, which then spits flame into a low explosive device. The US military M-60 and M-81 fuse igniters use a spring-powered firing pin to strike a shotshell primer, which spits forth flame to initiate time fuse.

Chemical energy has also been encountered. A variety of systems have been used where a powerful corrosive is placed into a reactive metal, rubber, or plastic container; it corrodes the container and then mixes with a separate, reactive chemical that produces flame to initiate the firing system.

Friction has been used as an initiator. Ammonium tri-iodide is an easily manufactured chemical that explodes with any application of friction. It is commonly encountered in school chemistry labs as a prank; however, during the Vietnam War a small mine called a gravel mine was developed; air delivered to paths used by the enemy in wet form, upon drying it became a powerful, anti-personnel device capable of maiming the unexpecting marcher.

The most common power source is the battery. Almost any battery will power a detonator or electric match; as long as the current is about 1.5 mA, the initiator will function. The small size of most fuzing systems ensures that resistance is low, and thus most voltage will push sufficient amperage to guarantee initiation.

A battery may be of many types. While the AA/AAA/C/D/9volt are most commonly encountered, a wide variety may be used, their choice often being merely based upon the access of the bomb maker. Today's electronic selection has introduced many more designs; some may provide additional advantages in shelf life, meaning a device may have a longer period to sit idle, waiting for triggering.

Automotive and similar wet cell batteries are also used. Most often, they are used to power devices in a vehicle in which the wet cell is already installed. Technicians need to be especially cognizant of the presence of multiple battery systems in some vehicles, which may permit the bomber to use parallel energy sources.

Especially in PBI or post render-safe investigations, techs and investigators need to be aware of the construction of batteries (Figure 6.27). After an explosion, they may be torn apart. Many are very unusual in

Figure 6.27 Cutaways of 9 V batteries, showing the different types of construction.

their make-up. For example, 6 and 12 V lantern batteries are composed of 4 or 8 D cell batteries, in series, in the battery case. Nine-volt batteries consist of either rectangular wafers, about 1 mm thick, stacked within the case, or six AAAA batteries in series inside the case. It is also important to recognize the inner components. Many cylindrical batteries, especially smaller, like AA and AAA, use an anode that, out of the battery, looks like a small nail. During the postblast scene examination, investigators must realize that anything that cannot be accounted for must be collected, until it can be positively identified or eliminated.

Other power sources should be considered. While uncommon, wall power (120 V in North America, 220 V throughout the rest of the world) has been used—either by plugging the device into "shore power" or by building the device into a structure or a component of a structure. Capacitor storage, now used for a tactical flashlight line, may be employed. A solar cell system designed to produce sufficient amperage could be employed. It is important to remain open minded to the advance of technology, especially as it may affect IED construction.

Initiator

Initiation may be accomplished in many manners. Electric matches, squibs, and detonators have been examined under explosives. However,

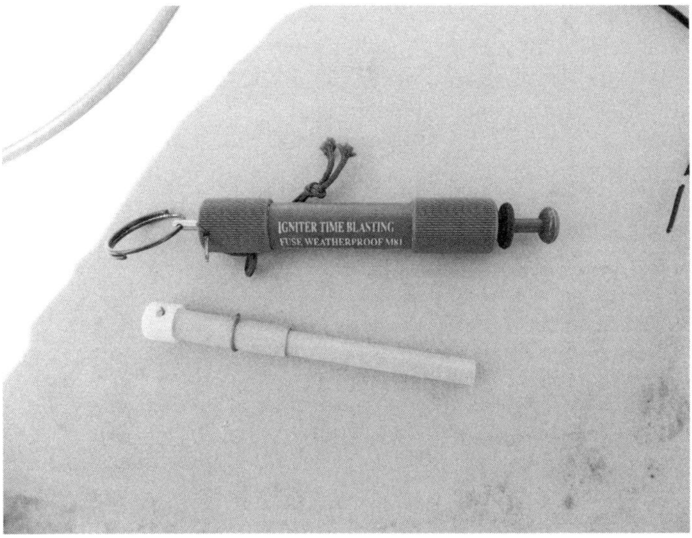

Figure 6.28 Fuse lighters, devices designed to initiate safety fuse. Top is a current, US military M-81 fuse lighter; below is a commercial fuse lighter.

a wide variety of other items may be used to accomplish initiation as well.

Commercially, fuse is ignited predominantly using a fuse lighter (see Figure 6.28). This is a mechanical device designed to impart high heat into the black powder core of safety fuse. Most commonly encountered will be either the military fuse lighter or the commercial fuse lighter. The former varies among militaries, but is generally a plastic grip that contains a spring-powered firing pin, a primer such as a shotshell primer, an arming/firing rod, and a safety pin. The safety fuse is inserted into the open end of the device, which usually has a clamp of some type to hold the fuse tightly against the end of the primer. The safety pin is removed, this pin having prevented the rod from moving and releasing the firing pin. The user then pulls back quickly on the rod; this completes compressing the spring and releases the spring to force the firing pin free from the rod and into the primer, releasing a large energetic spark, which ignites the fuse.

Commercial fuse lighters are less robust than their military counterparts; cost is more important than reliability for commercial purposes. The lighter consists of a cardboard tube slightly greater in diameter than safety fuse. A wire or string extends from the top of the device; it is impregnated with pyrotechnic material that is designed to spark when the pull is used, which then ignites a small pellet of pyrotechnic material, in turn igniting the core of the safety fuse.

Improvised electrical initiation is also encountered. Hobby rocket motor igniters have often been used as initiators for heat-sensitive explosives. Initiators have been improvised from incandescent light bulbs, usually flashlight or small decorative type bulbs, where the glass jacket has been broken to permit the element to ignite a sensitive powder or flammable liquid vapor. While not often encountered today, and generally considered a collectible, photographic flash bulbs have been used to ignite powders; cracking and breaking the glass exterior permits direct access of the high temperature burning filament to explosive powder.

Various field-expedient techniques are also taught for igniting fuse. These include placing a match head into the split end of fuse and igniting the match head to then ignite the black powder core; using a butane lighter to ignite the core; and use a hot item, such as a cauterizer or high temperature soldering gun, to ignite the fuse.

A variety of improvised methods have been encountered for the ignition of heat-sensitive explosives. Reactive chemicals, separated by placing into easily corroded containers, have been used; when the container is corroded through, the chemicals mix, resulting in flame that initiates the device. Common matches have been placed against a friction material; when the material is moved, it acts to ignite the match and initiate the enclosed heat-sensitive explosive.

Mechanical methods have been used to initiate a device. Most commonly has been an improvised firing pin system, which when released impacts a shotshell or cartridge primer; the spit of flame from this then initiates the explosive material. These systems have included rat traps, the bail having a firing pin attached which impacts the primer. Others have utilized a firing pin held under spring tension; when the mechanism holding the spring under tension releases it, the firing pin is released to crush the primer and release its flame.

Switch

In bomb technology, switch refers to much more than the commonly thought of electrical component. The term refers to an action that initiates the firing sequence of the device. It may be extremely simple, or highly complex.

Up to this point, the components are a relatively finite group. However, in considering switches, the field becomes extensive and complicated further on combining various fuzing systems. Another point of terminology: a fuse is a device designed to transmit heat mechanically. Safety fuse is a device consisting of a center core of black powder, wrapped in asphalt impregnated fabric, then either a wax or plastic powder, or water-resistant cover. A fuze is a device designed to initiate an explosive device, incorporating power source, initiator, and switch.

Switches may be mechanical, mechanical/electrical, electrical, electronic, and even chemical. They may be commercial items, modified devices, or improvised. They will range from simplistic and basic, to highly complex designs. Perhaps the simplest switch will be the hand that manually ignites a piece of fuse.

Switches may also be classified by their actions. These include the following:

- Time
- Anti-lift
- Anti-opening
- Light activation
- Pressure
- Pressure release
- Light
- Temperature
- Metal degradation
- Movement
- Any alarm type function

Indeed, this list is far from inclusive; many other actions, limited only by the bombers imagination and mechanical talents, may be utilized.

Many off-the-shelf items may be utilized in the switch function considering the myriad electrical switches—from toggle, to micro switches, ball and mercury switches, to complex devices such as relays. Step up to electronics, and while the knowledge and skill sets needed to employ them increase, so do the variety of applications. Combinations of capacitors, transistors, silicone controlled rectifiers, light sensors, and many other electronic components may achieve a desired switching effect. A knowledge of digital electronics permits construction using a wide variety of integrated circuits and modification of the many electronic devices. Recent applications have included electronic timers, a wide variety of radio systems ranging from simple walkie-talkie systems to computer-controlled devices such as telemetry monitoring and cellular telephone equipment, and electronics adapted from motor vehicle systems.

Improvisational switches range from from simple wire loops to advanced electronics. The loop switch, with two pieces of connection wire, a broad loop stripped at the end of each, and the insulated leads fed through the opposing loops, is a commonly employed switch. Soft wire, wound into a coil, with a separate length of wire hung down the center, has been used as a vibratory or anti-movement switch. Clothespins have been adapted to a variety of configurations. Similarly, mouse and rat traps have been modified to provide a wide variety of mechanical and electrical switches.

Bombers with the appropriate skills have crafted fusing systems using advanced electrical, electronic, and digital circuits. Since these systems are well designed and skillfully built, such as the devices used by Irish Republican terrorists, they can be accurate and dependable weapons in the criminal's arsenal.

While time is most commonly thought of, many other switching applications have been encountered. Thermometers, thermostats, and thermistors have been incorporated to use temperature to cause device function (Figures 6.29 through 6.37). Barometric pressure, usually as a

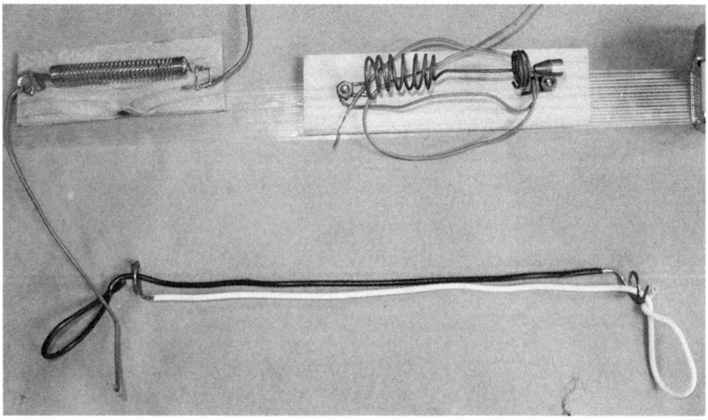

Figure 6.29 Improvised switches. At top, two vibratory switches. At bottom, a loop switch.

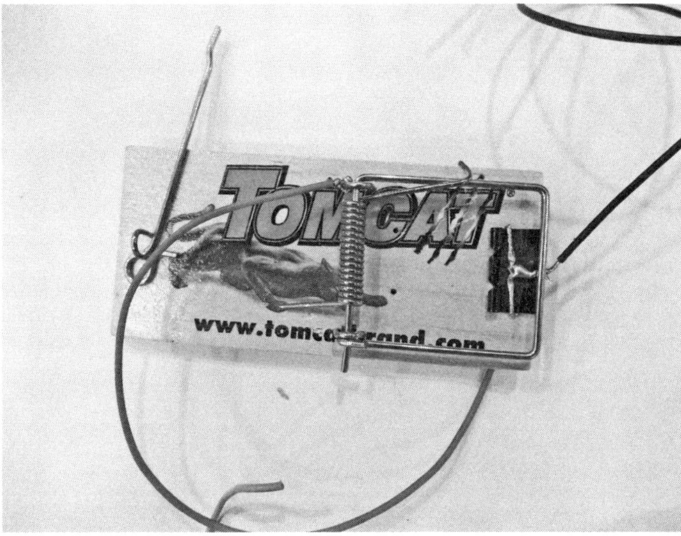

Figure 6.30 Improvised anti-opening switch using modified mouse trap.

result of altitude change, has been designed into devices. Photo resistors have been incorporated to switch a device when lights are switched on or off, or even as a result of dawn/dusk (Figure 6.38). Similarly, infrared sensors have been used with invisible infrared beams for access trip devices. Passive infrared, commonly used for alarm and entry lights, have been

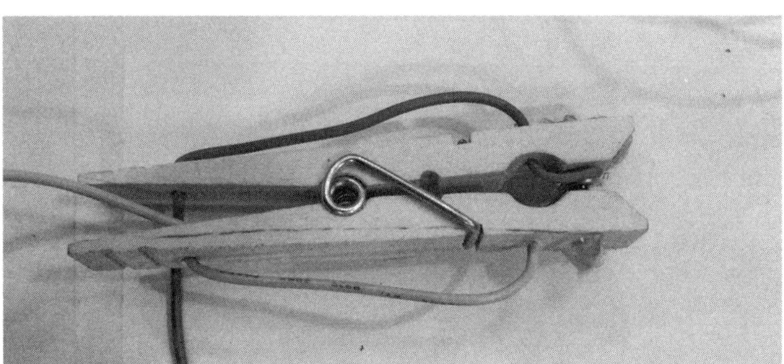

Figure 6.31 Improvised clothespin switch.

Figure 6.32 Clock modified as time switch.

used to detect minute temperature differences as a victim approaches (Figures 6.39 and 6.40).

It is a long known truism in the bomb disposal field that the only limitation on a bomber is his imagination. While many successful bombers stick to the KISS (keep it simple, stupid) principle, many with backgrounds

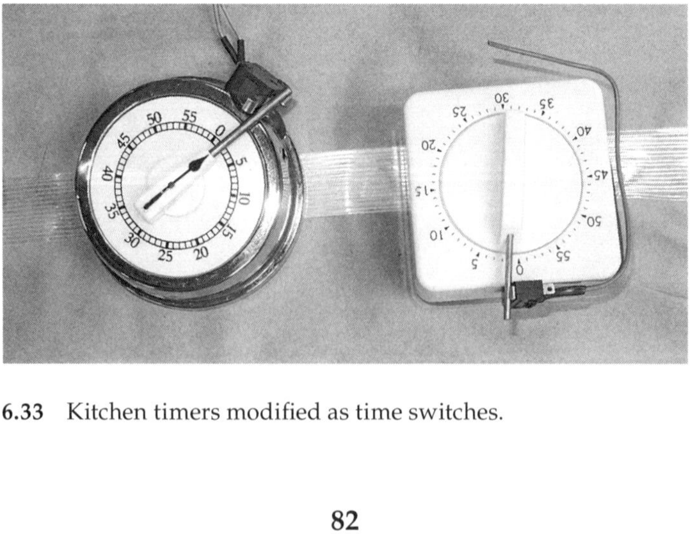

Figure 6.33 Kitchen timers modified as time switches.

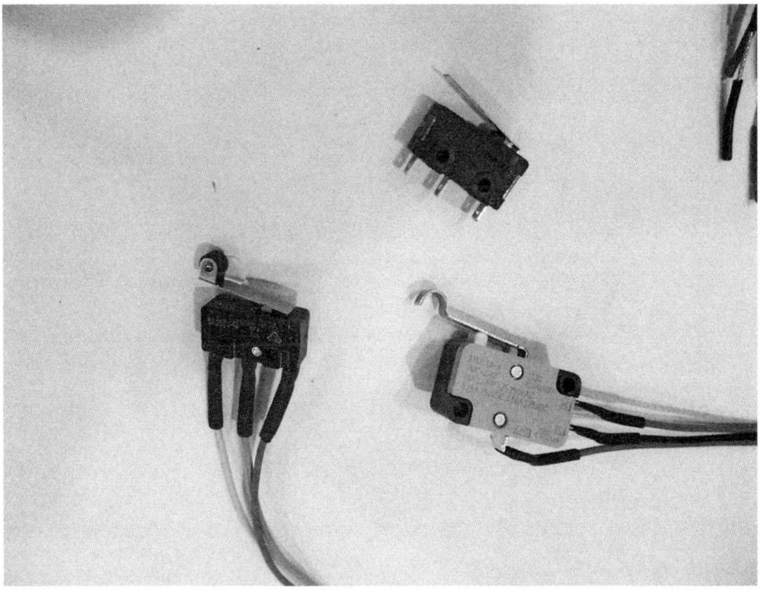

Figure 6.34 A variety of microswitches, a common electrical component.

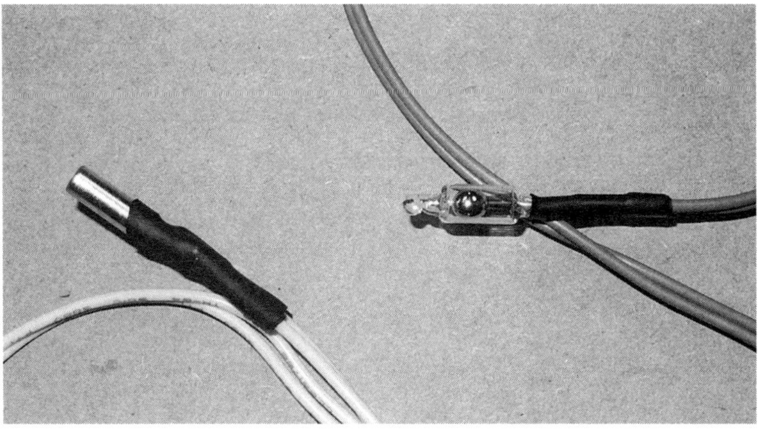

Figure 6.35 On left, a ball switch. On right, a mercury switch. Both are position/movement-sensitive switches.

Figure 6.36 Electrical relay; it is feared for its extreme sensitivity as the control battery wears down.

in mechanics or electronics will opt to design and construct more ambitious devices. Ted Kaczynski, the Unabomber, evolved to constructing devices completely from raw materials; with the combination of research, careful design, and skilled construction, he built devices that were highly functional and devoid of traceable components. Many who attempt such

Figure 6.37 Silicone controlled rectifiers, or SCRs—electronic switches similar in use to relays.

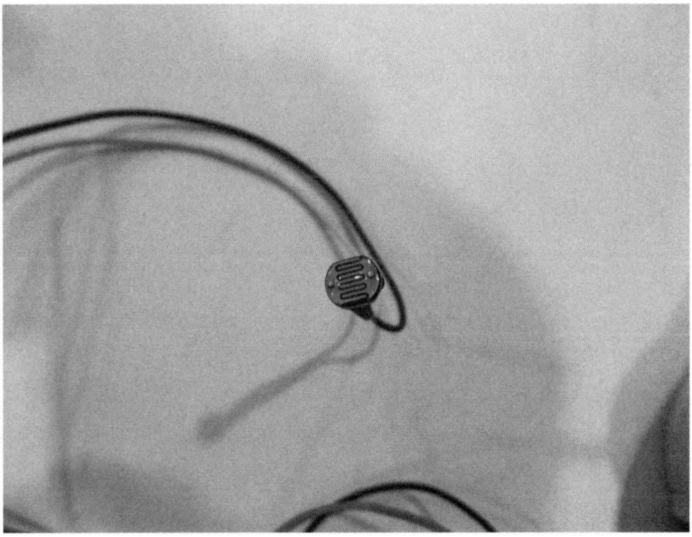

Figure 6.38 Photocell.

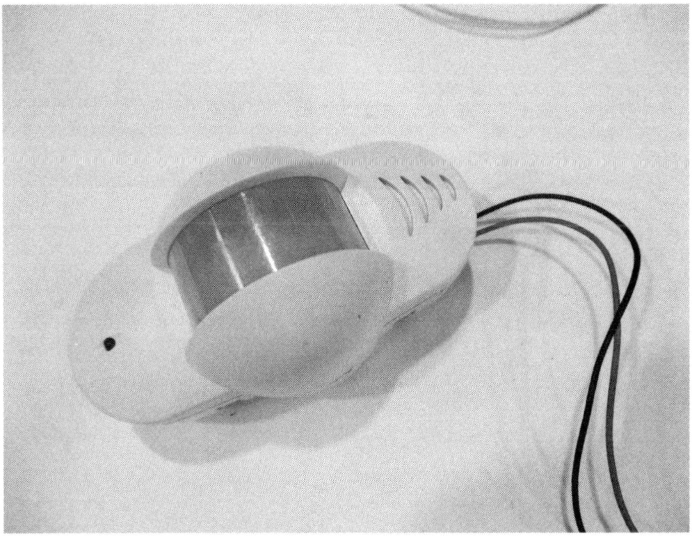

Figure 6.39 Passive infrared (PIR)—movement (heat) sensing switch.

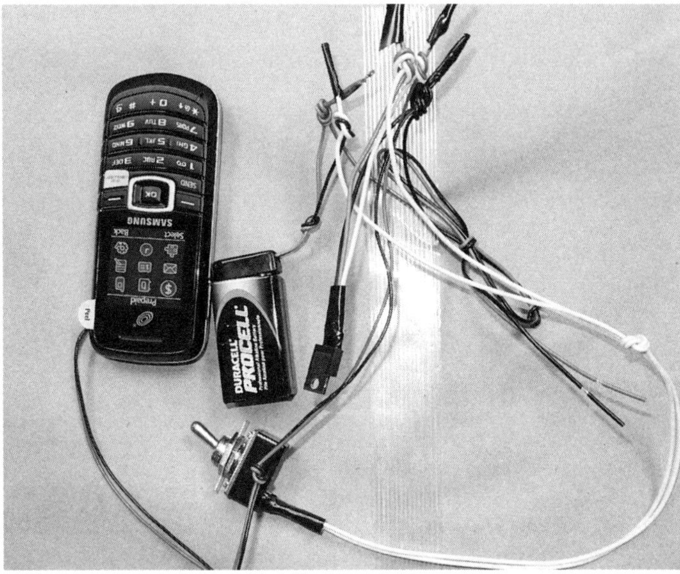

Figure 6.40 Cell phone modified as remote control fuzing system.

devices fail to apply sufficient research or skill, resulting in devices that fail to function. However, for the bomb technician, this is no cause for relaxation. Such a malfunctioned device may actually now be a sensitive hang fire, malfunctioning due to a poor solder point or temporary short-circuit, or contain a highly sensitive explosive which has been low ordered due to incorrect initiation.

7

Bomb Disposal Equipment

Unlike most law-enforcement fields, only criminalistics is equipment dependent than bomb disposal. Even in the earliest days of the field, when most officers needed only a revolver, truncheon, and handcuffs, bomb technician's were equipped with screwdrivers, knives, cutting pliers, and a variety of other tools to permit attacking and disabling infernal devices.

Today, to ensure compliance with STB 87-4 and the NBSCAB accreditation standards, a bomb squad must maintain certain equipment.

- Bomb suit
- X-ray
- Demolition toolkit with explosives
- Hand toolkit
- Robot
- Disruptor
- Explosives storage magazine
- Rigging equipment
- Radiation detection
- Chemical, biological, radiological, nuclear, explosives (CBRNE) personal protective equipment (PPE)

Additionally, there is a wide variety of other equipment and items.

- Bomb transport trailer
- CBRNE monitoring/field testing equipment
- Weather station
- Thermal destruction unit
- Tactical PPE
- Explosive breaching equipment

- Specialized explosively powered disruption tools
- Specialized viewing equipment
- Evidence collection equipment
- Photographic and video equipment
- Dedicated response vehicles

The sources of this equipment will vary. Some is only available commercially. Many items may be obtained locally, or even as items transferred from the evidence room. Bomb squads also had a long history of improvisation—both to save budget monies for necessary purchases, and because many items do not exist in the commercial arena, but may be devised by a skilled craftsman.

COMMERCIAL PRODUCTS

A wide variety of tools and equipment is available. Until the early twenty-first century, there was much less variety among items, indeed there was much less off-the-shelf equipment available.

The bomb suit cannot be effectively improvised. Early suits, such as the Spooner suit, were neither researched nor tested (Figure 7.1). In the Spooner suit, the chest, face, and legs were covered by armor plates of steel and fabric carriers hung on the technician. They may have deflected fragmentation, but provided no protection against overpressure.

Today's bomb suits are the products of extensive research and testing. They are engineered to provide reasonable protection against penetration by fragmentation, absorb and dissipate overpressure, deflect effects, and to protect the wearer from spinal and cranial injuries due to projected, backwards falls (Figure 7.2).

In addition to bomb suits, most teams also have search suits, designed for military unexploded ordnance and humanitarian demining operations, and tactical armor. Although providing less protection than bomb suits, initially they were the only bomb type suits that could be worn in conjunction with chemical PPE for WMD response. Many teams have also found them of value for rapid intervention team (RIT), standby rescue teams supporting bomb technicians downrange. They also provide the technician another choice when faced with conditions where a full bomb suit is impractical due to tight surroundings or other mobility issues.

A key piece of equipment is the x-ray (Figure 7.3). Until the mid-1970s, bomb squads that had x-ray units used surplus medical units and wet

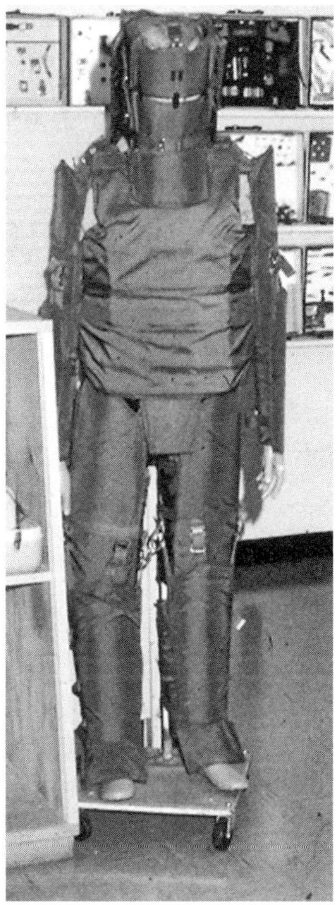

Figure 7.1 Spooner suit—basically a canvas carrier with steel plates inserted; gave some protection from fragmentation, none from concussive effects.

film processing. Then they discovered industrial inspection x-ray. First, the most common, manufactured by Golden Engineering, are very lightweight. Second, they are x-ray generators and do not employ hazardous radiological sources. Third, they are relatively low power, again a significant safety feature.

For about 30 years, these units were primarily used with Polaroid® x-ray films, much more convenient than wet-process films (many old-time technicians tell of shooting film by jumping into a patrol car and driving lights and siren to the nearest hospital to have their film developed). In the

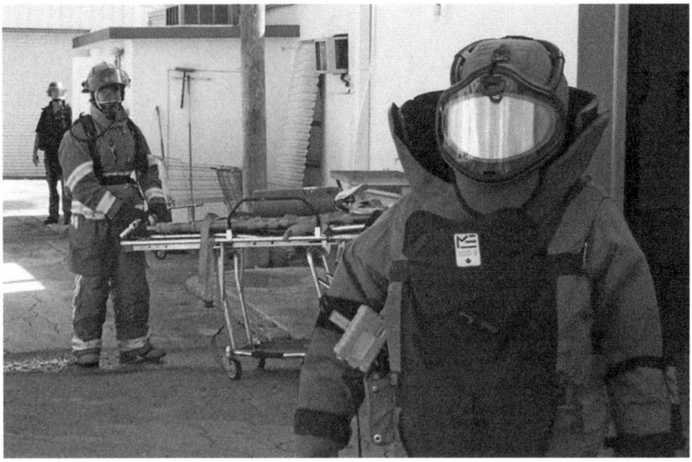

Figure 7.2 Bomb tech in full bomb suit proceeds downrange, with a member of the rescue team trailing to stand-by in safe downrange location.

Figure 7.3 Tech places x-ray generator in place. This shows use of instant film; this has largely been replaced by digital documentation.

latter 1990s, the first digital x-ray systems were available, but the image collectors were bulky and required cables to connect the x-ray source to the screen and then back to a computer. However, newer systems are available that require no connection to either x-ray unit or computer, and use thin screens rather than either film cassettes or bulky collectors. A processor attached to the computer transfers the image onto the computer, where the software permits considerable enhancement of the image to provide the technician a quality image with only one approach downrange (Figures 7.4 and 7.5).

Figure 7.4 Film x-ray image of Mk.2 hand grenade with cocked fuze.

Figure 7.5 Two digital x-ray images, stitched together to provide a single image of the larger device; digital systems permit image manipulation to improve examination.

In addition to standard x-ray equipment, specialized real-time x-ray systems are available (Figure 7.6). These units use an interconnected x-ray source and collection unit, which then transmits its data to a collection point at a computer. On the computer a live image of the target can be viewed. If the target is too large for a single image, it can be used to "scan" the item. If an item has moving parts (such as a clockwork device) they can be observed as they move for valuable information and to determine a clockwork device's function, or if malfunctioned.

Bomb disposal robots (or UGV) have been fielded since the 1970s, when British forces first employed them in the field. Over 40 years, their availability expanded, sophistication increased, and offerings by size and power became more varied. A fully functional robot has certain requirements—a minimum 300 foot operating distance from controller, manipulator, attachment of disruptor, and availability to deliver and deploy general disruption systems or countercharges.

Figure 7.6 Real-time x-ray used to scan a large device; can scan large items, will pick up internal movement such as clockwork. (Photo courtesy of Loel Clements.)

Current robots are controlled by cable tether, fiber optic control line, or radio signal; many provide for a choice of system. Video cameras, from 1 to 5, may be incorporated, providing black and light, color, very low light, or even thermal imaging. The controller, once a large suitcase like a fair, has been significantly shrunk in size providing an ever more versatile and sophisticated control ability.

Large frame UGVs continue to be the workhorse of the field. Their size provides them reach, their weight greater stability, and their larger motors ensure their strength. However, a new breed of small footprint robots has provided new avenues of utility—these units fit down the aisles of their craft and buses, are lower to the ground for getting more access under vehicles or other items, are small enough to easily store and transport in limited confines, and light enough to be man portable (Figures 7.7 through 7.9).

New, specialized UGVs are increasing the versatility of robots. A variety of UGVs, designed around radio control technology for tactical use, are finding bomb disposal applications for surveillance, monitoring, or delivery of single disruptors. Even smaller units, designed for tactical surveillance, are being adapted for bomb response, providing secondary

Figure 7.7 Full-sized robot removes pipe bomb to location capable of withstanding detonation for RSP.

Figure 7.8 Robot just after using disruptor to render safe a device.

Figure 7.9 Robot being used to inspect contents of suspicious, crashed vehicle.

standoff cameras that provide depth view of the main robot (Figures 7.10 through 7.13).

At the other end of the size spectrum are skid steer pieces of equipment that have been equipped with remote operating controls and cameras (Figures 7.14 through 7.16). Originally designed for tactical support, these units also have great value for dealing with threats such as large vehicle bombs. In one incident, a cache of C-4 and military ordnance had been discarded into a major canal; after draining the canal a remotely operated device with backhoe blade extracted the muddy bottom of the canal, protecting technicians from the dangerous job of manually digging it out.

Disruptors are the most commonly used tool in the bomb technicians' render-safe toolbox. They are evolved from the military EOD disarmer, a heavy steel tool using an electrically initiated 0.50-caliber blank, to propel a slug or water at a target (Figure 7.17). In public safety a variety of calibers are used for propulsion, with the most common being based upon the 12-gauge shotgun shell.

Figure 7.10 Small footprint robot equipped with semiautomatic shotgun as disruptor or for door breaching.

Figure 7.11 Small robot with its arm fully extended; permits it to inspect under vehicles, etc.

Figure 7.12 Very small robot, especially useful for use in vehicles, aircraft, etc., where maneuver room is very limited. (Photo courtesy of Loel Clements.)

Figure 7.13 Small robot using improvised stand to deliver disruptor to a target.

Figure 7.14 Miami-Dade Police Department (MDPD) bomb squad remote operated skid steer loader, hooked up to tow vehicle for response.

Figure 7.15 Remote control skid steer loader approaches a target; it is equipped with a 90 mm disruptor. (Courtesy of Palm Beach County Sherriff's Office.)

Figure 7.16 Robotic skid steer loader with scoop shovel during excavation of canal containing dumped munitions. (Courtesy of Palm Beach County Sheriff's Office.)

Initially, most public safety disruptors were improvised, using galvanized water pipe fittings, a locally loaded 12-gauge shot shell hull containing black powder, either fuse or electric match initiation, and waterproof sealant, this being used to propel a load of water, clean sand, or metal slug. However, these disruptors had significant shortcomings—less than optimum projectile velocities, unreliability of initiation due to hygroscopicity, and serious recoil by the pipe due to its light weight (Figure 7.18).

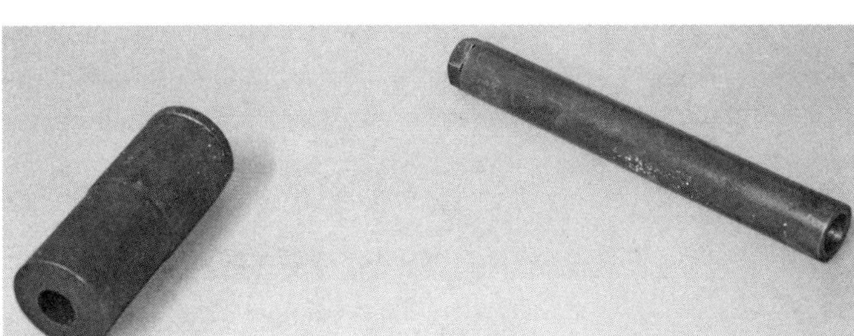

Figure 7.17 Military 0.50 caliber dearmers from which the disruptor has evolved.

A number of bomb squads arranged for locally fabricated steel disruptors, some designed for black powder, but a few for smokeless powder (Figure 7.19). An early commercial unit, the Canadian Neutrex disruptor, using a proprietary 20 mm cartridge, enjoys considerable success in Canada but has found limited acceptance elsewhere.

A US Navy project at the Los Alamos National Labs resulted in the development of the percussion actuated neutralizer (PAN), better known as the PAN disruptor. This unit uses any 12-gauge shot shell, and a line of specialty rounds loaded for bomb disposal. The round is initiated with shock tube used to transmit pressure to its firing pin from a safe firing location. The PAN has been furnished to all American bomb squads by the FBI, and has been adopted by the US military for its anti-IED mission (Figure 7.20).

The Royal Arms disruptor, another 12-gauge tool, can use standard and specialty 12-gauge rounds as well, again using shock tube initiation (Figure 7.21). The Royal Arms can also be had with adapters that permit use of proprietary and locally loaded electrically fired 12-gauge loads, and even locally loaded, fuse-initiated 12-gauge loads.

Other calibers are also available. Ideal Tool, the manufacturer of the PAN disruptor, also manufactures specialized 0.357 and 0.410 disruptors. These units are designed for precise targeting of individual components, as opposed to general disruption techniques. A 90 mm recoilless disruptor

Figure 7.18 A 12-gauge shotgun used as a disruptor, shooting a water-filled test tube. Water has entered the left side, and is about to exit the right side, of target lunch box.

Figure 7.19 Electrically initiated 12-gauge disrupter, manufactured locally according to the specifications of a local bomb squad.

is available from ARA Robotics for use with its robotic skid steer device, especially designed for use against vehicular platforms.

Additionally, several manufacturers have adapted their disruptors for recoilless operation. This is especially important to users of small footprint UGVs, which could be damaged by the recoil of traditional disruptors. Most of these recoilless disruptors direct recoil pressure out at the back of the tool, often through a water-filled chamber that absorbs and deflects the back blast.

Figure 7.20 PAN disruptor at the moment of impact on the target. This primary disruptor is in use in America, and it has been adapted to robots, and has had small caliber, high velocity models introduced to permit pinpoint targeting of components.

Figure 7.21 A Royal Arms disruptor using an improvised, robot-delivered stand at the time of initiation. Without sandbags or a heavy stand, all disruptors will exhibit significant recoil.

In the late 1990s, the FBI distributed a pager-like radiation detection alarm to bomb squads. It has continued to support bomb squads by upgrading the devices with newer technology. In addition, many teams have invested in other radiological monitoring equipment, such as Geiger detectors. The addition of these tools permits a technician, approaching a device or postblast scene, to determine whether a radioactive device, especially a radiological dispersion device, is involved.

Chemical, biological, radiological, and nuclear (CBRN) protection is important to a tech facing a potential WMD device. As noted earlier, search suits have been adapted for use with chem/bio PPE. Also, latest generation bomb suits have evolved with the provision to wear with PPE, although at a much greater weight than the use of search suits (Figure 7.22). Additionally, the bomb squad must have chem/bio protective ensembles to use with these suits.

Many agencies opt to use traditional-level B/C coveralls, often stocking several different materials to permit appropriate choices depending upon the suspected hazard. Others have opted for newer suits, developed specifically for WMD wear. These are more expensive, but designed to provide broad threat protection in a more comfortable and physically functional ensemble (Figure 7.23).

Appropriate PPE includes respiratory protection. This comprises two major categories, self-contained breathing apparatus (SCBA) and air purifier respirators (APR). SCBA is mandatory when entering atmosphere

Figure 7.22 From left, rescue team member in full fire fighting bunker gear, bomb tech in full coverage bomb suit, team member in full bomb suit with SCBA.

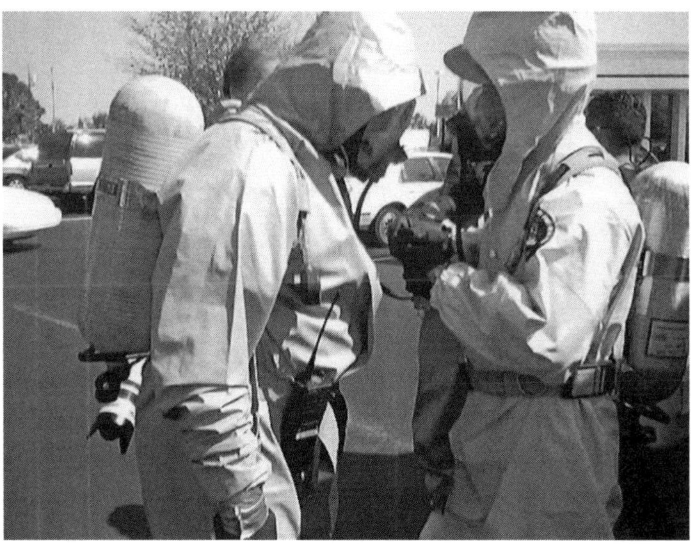

Figure 7.23 Members of combined hazmat bomb squad entry team gearing up for entry into possible chem/bio incident.

without adequate oxygen content, or where a toxic material that cannot be filtered out will be encountered. When first adapted to the CBRN role, the helmets of the bomb suits were found to be only compatible with a very few SCBA masks. Later bomb suit designs, and evolving respirator mask designs, are making this a moot point. What this means is that a team can now acquire the same SCBA as its local fire authority, which has the ability to conduct routine maintenance on equipment. This is a crucial consideration, as OSHA mandates continuing maintenance.

Careful consideration must be made during the selection of APR's. When appropriate, use of an APR is a major weight saving choice, thus relieving stress and fatigue. A gas mask should not be considered as a replacement for an APR; a gas mask is a specialized respirator, only suited for filtering nontoxic materials such as tear gas. An APR can function as a gas mask if appropriate filter may be used.

The most common-type full-face APR uses a removable filter that attaches to the faceplate. For tactical operations, they have a downside that the filter may interfere with vision and mounting a long arm. Also, they inhibit breathing and thus increase fatigue. Powered air purifying respirators (PAPR) have a hose running from the mask to a fan/blower, usually mounted to a waist pack or backpack. While adding some weight, they ease breathing by pushing a positive pressure stream of air at the face, not requiring the wearer to labor by drawing air through the filter manually.

Along with respirator selection, the agency must adopt and practice a respiratory protection policy. OSHA and similar agencies require users to have adequate procedures, testing, medical clearance procedures, and training during the selection and use of respirators prior to their use by the employee. Often an agency may tail board on their local fire authority, sharing their procedures, to ensure not only conformity but also access to trained professionals who everyday depend upon respiratory protection for their job.

Many people did not understand the important role of explosives and demolition techniques to the bomb squad. Disruptors, whether shock tube, electrical, or fuse based, are functioned using explosive initiation procedures. Explosive initiation techniques are used in open thermal disposal of explosive materials. Bomb technicians are often called upon to conduct explosive breaching support to tactical teams. Finally, bomb squads routinely use explosives to destroy by countercharging IEDs, military ordnance, and decomposed explosives when it is the safest, most appropriate method.

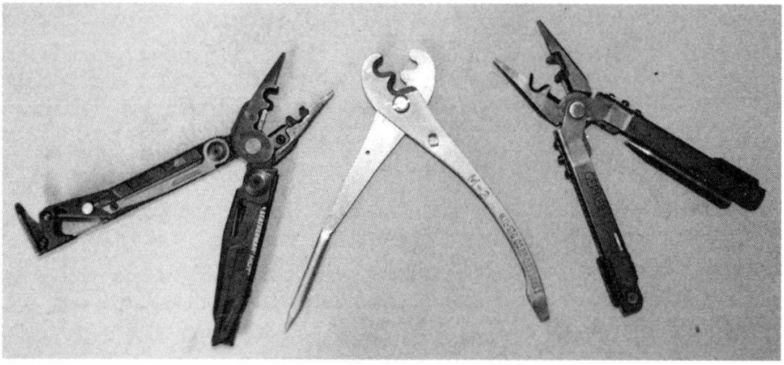

Figure 7.24 Two multitools with cap crimpers built surrounding a cap crimper.

Thus, the bomb squad must maintain demolition tools and equipment, and an appropriate supply of explosives (Figure 7.24). Tools must be maintained to support nonelectric, electric, and shock tube operations:

- Explosive crimping pliers (Figure 7.25).
- Shock tube/detonating cord cutters.

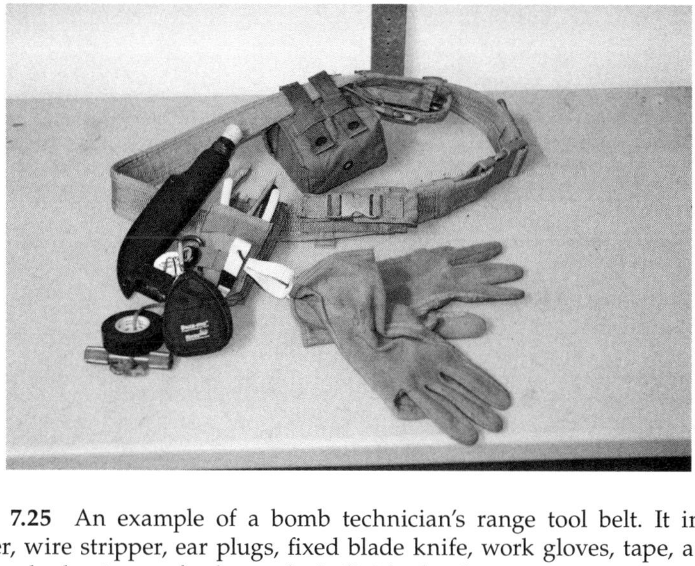

Figure 7.25 An example of a bomb technician's range tool belt. It includes crimper, wire stripper, ear plugs, fixed blade knife, work gloves, tape, a circuit tester, and other items of value to the individual tech.

- Blasting galvanometer (an electrical circuit tester specifically designed for safely testing electrical blasting caps).
- Blasting machines.
- Electrical initiation systems.
- Shock tube initiation systems.
- Firing wire (18- or 16-gauge duplex wire, minimum 300 feet, on a reel for easy layout/recovery—several reels are preferable).
- Hearing protection (plug or headset) and eye protection (polycarbonate spectacles, goggles, or prescription glasses).
- Explosives—selected for power and stability. At a minimum, cast boosters, detonating cord, and a supply of low-explosive powder.
- Detonators and low-explosive initiators (Figures 7.26 through 7.28).

The bomb squad must continuously consider changes in assignment and technology. For example, if assigned explosive breaching, small, portable, reliable firing devices are mandatory. As remote firing systems have entered the marketplace, units have adopted them for use with robotics and to aid in simplifying scene setup, relieving the layout of firing wire on a scene.

Rigging techniques are a military skill that is very applicable to civilian bomb disposal. When a robot is not available, or cannot physically function, a carefully designed rigging operation may permit the delivery of an RSP to a device, or removal of the device to either transport vessel or a location better suited for further RSP.

A number of sources provide kits specially designed for bomb/EOD rigging operations. These kits often include tools specifically designed for these operations. However, when finances do not permit acquisition of off-the-shelf rigging kits, a visit to a local hardware store, especially one that services industrial clients, will permit the tech to assemble a basic kit of supplies. These should include the following:

- 3/8 inch nylon or cotton rope of different colors
- 1/8 inch parachute line, different colors if possible
- Break-a-way pulleys
- Variety of nails, spikes, screws, screw eyes, and bolts to use as anchor points, and to attach other elements
- Duct tape and filament tape
- Variety of snap hooks and carabiners

The knowledge, experience, skills, and imagination of the technician will determine other components added to the kit.

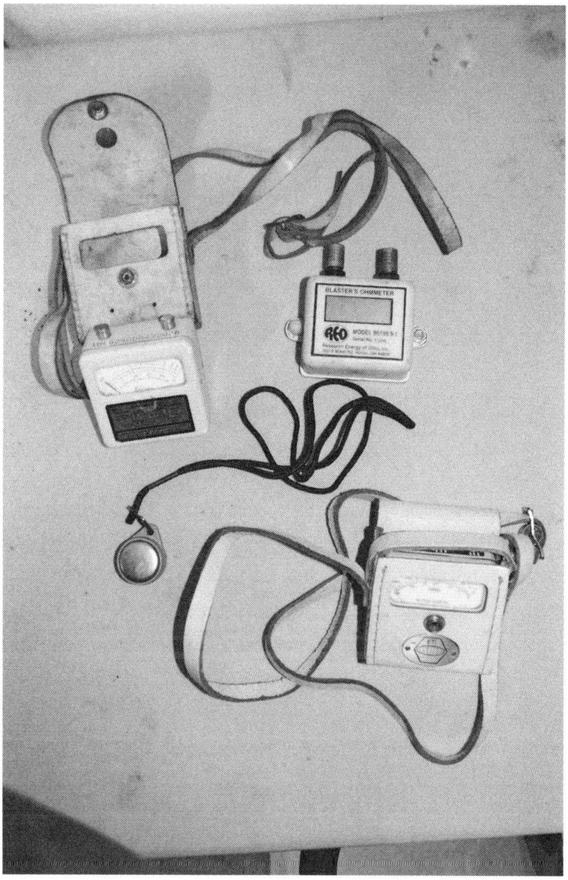

Figure 7.26 Examples of circuit testers, clockwise from top: blasting galvanometer using special silver chloride battery, blasting ohmmeter, galvanometer using 9 V battery, circuit continuity tester—vibratory.

Hand tools are important to a bomb squad. Although hopefully never needed in this role, they are mandatory for a hand entry RSP. More commonly, the technician needs to perform routine maintenance on equipment, improvise equipment, conduct inspections during VIP searches, and similar functions.

Several sources produce toolkits for the bomb squad, in both large kits designed to meet the needs of a response vehicle, and small kits able to be carried with a technician conducting VIP sweeps or going down range

Figure 7.27 Blasting machines, clockwise from upper left: two capacitor discharge machines, ten-cap twist-type mechanical generator, capacitor discharge machine, capacitor discharge/galvanometer, and US military M-34 mechanical generator.

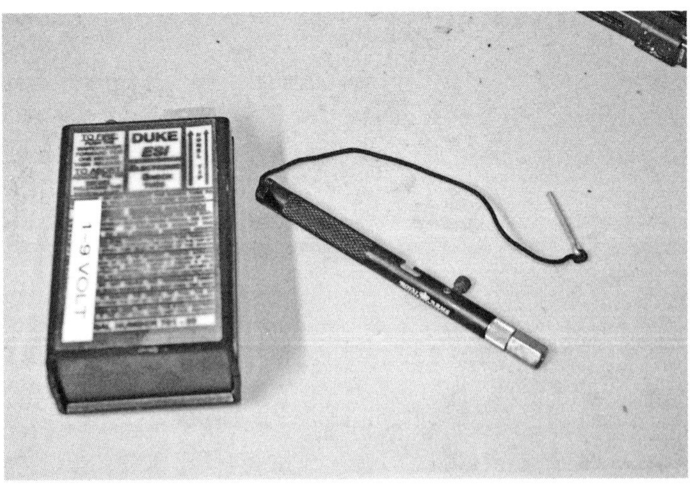

Figure 7.28 Shock tube initiators: on left, a capacitor discharge machine; on right, a modified flare gun designed to initiate using a shotshell primer.

in bomb suit to inspect and complete a remote RSP. These kits have the advantages of being selected to meet existing tool lists, and will usually be of top quality equipment.

However, a cash-strapped unit can visit local hardware stores to build a kit, and even find many items available through the evidence room, where surplus evidence such as tools are often disposed of as trash. Quality may suffer; the function of a tool being selected should be considered along with its quality when shopping for or obtaining surplus.

Every technician should have a small individual toolkit consisting of screwdrivers, slip joint pliers, wire cutter/strippers, long nosed pliers, adjustable wrench, dental mirror, scalpel handle with a variety of blades, nylon twine or para-cord, mini flashlight, electrical tape, cable ties, nonconductive probes, and a stethoscope. A main tool kit should contain all of these tools, and hacksaw, power drill with a variety of bits, brace and bit with a variety of bits, 1/4″ and 1/2″ wood chisels, assorted furniture, spring, C-clamps, a wide variety of slip joint, water pump, long nose, electrician pliers, a variety of adjustable, socket, and pipe wrenches, and indeed any other hand tools that can be acquired (Figure 7.29).

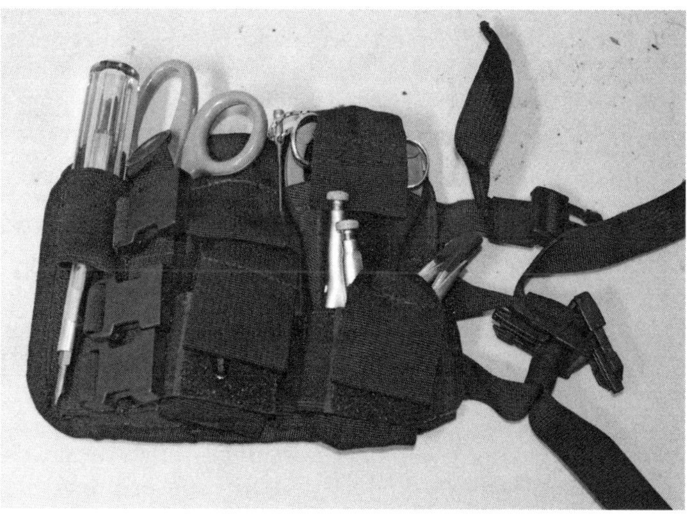

Figure 7.29 Technician's personal tool kit for approaching device while in bomb suit. Includes shears, screwdriver, clamps, mirror, flashlight; will strap on his or her arm for mobility.

Power tools should also be part of the toolkit. With the wide variety of powerful cordless tools, it is practical to collect many quality tools of this type, making field use easier. Indeed, Golden Engineering has adopted the DeWalt battery as a power source for their units.

Because the proper battery-powered tools may not be available, a power source should be maintained. Power inverters, which convert vehicle DC power to AC, are available, although they are still limited in output. More often a generator, especially one compatible with vehicle fuel or a PTO generator using the vehicle engine for power, with a 5000–10,000 watt output, should be obtained. Additionally, a supply of heavy power cords should be maintained to lead power from the source down range and wherever the tool is needed.

A wide variety of equipment is available for CBRN monitoring or field testing. It ranges from simple materials, such as pH paper, military M8 and M9 test paper for chemical agents, and chemical testing kits, through multigas monitors to give immediate feedback on chemical safety upon entering a questionable atmosphere, to a variety of electronic testing systems that can provide almost immediate analyses of questionable substances encountered.

Some of the equipment, such as pH paper and military test paper, is inexpensive. Much of the electronic equipment has moderate to high price tags, and may also be somewhat maintenance intensive. For many bomb squads that have local hazmat teams, it is more economical to develop a relationship with the hazmat unit, borrowing monitoring equipment for downrange work, and having hazmat perform analytical work with their equipment.

In consideration of potential CBRN incidents, portable weather stations are valuable tools. Most valuable are stations that can provide wind speed and direction, air temperature, relative humidity, and atmospheric pressure; these measurements can be used to determine potential plume characteristics of chemical releases. Although weather stations are available quite economically, if one is not obtained, a bomb response vehicle should at least have a wind vane/sock, with which wind direction can be determined to ensure staging in a safe, upwind location.

A variety of viewing equipment is available that can aid the functionality and safety of the bomb tech. A periscope, or preferably a pole camera, provides a tool for viewing under, over, or around obstacles. For example, in VIP searches, there are many areas that cannot be conveniently accessed. A pole camera, often with a small footprint camera and combined LED light, can be maneuvered to permit easy inspection of these hidden recesses.

Many bomb response vehicles now possess telescoping camera towers. These are especially valuable to a robot operator, who is able to observe progress of the UGV across terrain from a different vantage point than that afforded by the robots onboard cameras, providing a third dimension to his view.

At the other end of the size continuum are borescopes. Today, borescopes are available with less than a 9 mm diameter that incorporate both lighting and viewing into this diameter. Many that are optical alone are available very economically, while others which incorporate video viewing add not only cost but also provide convenient recording. An effective borescope permits the technician to exploit a small hole in a package to enter and view its contents without further molesting the package (Figure 7.30).

Photographic and video recording equipment has great value to the technician. First, a small point and shoot digital camera permits the tech downrange to quickly snap photos of a suspect device and its location,

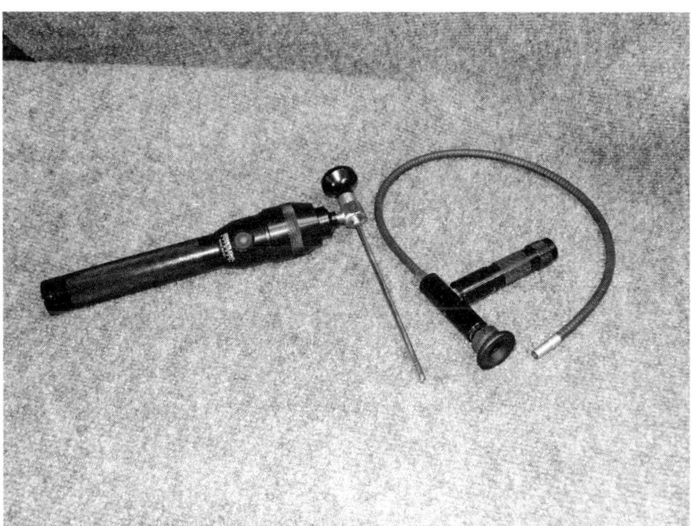

Figure 7.30 Borescopes and endoscopes are available in many styles, at many price breaks.

which can be quickly downloaded at the safe area and used in determining further tactics. Indeed, several cameras are available economically which are waterproof to 30 m, making a unit that can be decontaminated if used in a potential CBRN atmosphere.

The video is highly valuable in a number of situations. A camera, focused downrange, can be used to record operations, whether robotic, remote, or by technician, for any later date. It is also excellent for use in recording RSP operations, whether using disruption techniques or even explosive countercharge destruction; it records the actions, smoke, color, etc., for later analysis.

The recent development of sports video recorders, such as the Go Pro Hero® line, permit the attachment of a small, lightweight video recorder to the arm or helmet of a technician's bomb suit. It may be used to record all downrange actions, and upon return to bomb disposal command downloaded to permit evaluation of the device by all members of the team. It also permits safe recording of demolition operations downrange; wise placement of the armored camera permits intimate recording of energetic tool use or explosive countercharge/disposal operations, to both document the acts and permit later evaluation.

Photographic equipment is also valuable in documenting post-RSP and postblast scenes. For many teams, the primary responsibility for the investigation falls on their shoulders, thus quality photographic recording is a necessity.

Any equipment that produces a video image should also have this information recorded. Robot images may have great value at a later time, especially if the item should be destroyed by either RSP or function. Images from pole cameras and video borescope systems can often be recorded within the unit, or on a small external video recorder. Especially considering that RSP may destroy the device, these images have tremendous value for investigative and reconstructive purposes.

A variety of explosively powered disruption and breaching tools are available commercially. Remotely operated wire cutters are available for the technician to attempt to disrupt electrical or electronic functions of devices. A number of tools based upon the concept of the popular mineral water bottle RSP are available for application against targets from small packages to large vehicles. Several suppliers are producing advanced RSP devices such as the "boot banger," designed to access vehicles suspected of being used to conceal IEDs. Also, suppliers are making commercially available devices for explosive breaching, saving the technician from the chore of building improvised jigs for that purpose.

Tactical PPE is a wise investment for bomb squads. First, the inclusion of bomb techs in explosive breaching operations, active shooter searches, and similar tactical operations, alone justifies it. Technicians may outfit protective vests with pouches adequate to carry tools for search. Tactical PPE can also provide limited protection when conducting operations where the bulk of bomb suits makes them impractical or impossible to wear. A level IV tactical vest and a tactical helmet fitted with a heavy polycarbonate face shield provides some degree of protection against fragmentation at the least.

A bomb squad should maintain an evidence collection kit. In addition to a variety of paper and plastic bags (including pink, anti-static polyethylene bags), it should include a variety of sizes of clean, new paint cans—when sealed the volatile vapors of explosives will not escape. Similarly, a variety of new, clean glass bottles, ranging from small vials through approximately 1/2 pint capacity should be maintained for collection of liquid samples. Additionally, swabs and disposable droppers should be part of the kit for collection of liquid samples, and small, disposable spatulas and spoons for collection of loose powders. Finally, heat sealable nylon bags should be part of the kit; like metal cans, they do not breathe, and retain volatile vapors produced by evidence.

All bomb squads will possess explosives; for explosive disposal, for canine training, to support explosive breaching operations, and as evidence. For safety and security, magazines must meet stringent standards. Although most often just steel plate and wood, a commercially manufactured magazine is, in overall consideration, a much better choice than locally fabricated designs.

Many units have become responsible for disposal of all explosive-related materials encountered by an agency or jurisdiction. This may include evidential ammunition, surplus ammo, consumer fireworks, marine and highway distress signals, and similar materials generated by an agency or even surrendered by the public as outdated or waste.

While open burns have traditionally been used for such instruction, and continue to be the primary method for major disposal operations (such as major seizures of illegal consumer fireworks), mobile thermal destruction units that may be towed behind a small truck provide an often easier method for smaller needs (Figure 7.31). These units consist of a heavy steel housing in which the materials placed in and destroyed by exposure to high temperature incineration by a propane powered burner. Most are capable of destroying several hundred pounds of material a day.

Figure 7.31 A commercially manufactured thermal destruction unit. These may burn over 100 pounds of energetics a day.

The bomb transport trailer, while not mandated for national accreditation, is in reality a necessary piece of equipment. Whenever possible, removing a device from its location decreases the overall hazard level and permits greater variety and choice of render-safe methods. Bomb squads also encounter deteriorated explosives and shock-sensitive chemicals that, by removal to an open site, may be easily disposed of by countercharge or incineration.

Currently, two types of bomb transport vessel are available. The single-vent design was perfected by Tom Brodie in the 1960s; should its contents function during transport, they are directed upward, where they are least hazardous. Well-designed single-vent trailers have various advantages—strength, size, and financially attractive. Thus, they are often encountered with squads (Figures 7.32 and 7.33).

The total containment vessel (TCV) was devised to address the single drawback of the single vent—its open release of energy and debris. Thus, the TCV is a thick steel sphere, with a hatch that locks into the outer body when closed. The TCV also incorporates a series of bleed-off valves that will slowly release pressure after an explosion, until inner pressure is

Figure 7.32 MDPD open vent transport vessel; this is the latest incarnation of the original top vent unit designed by Tom Brodie while with the MDPD team.

equalized with ambient pressure. Figures 7.34 through 7.37 illustrate various designs of TCVs.

Upgraded TCVs, designed for potential WMD incidents, do not bleed off pressure directly into the atmosphere. Instead the combustion by-products are flushed through a scrubber/filter system, to ensure that only nonhazardous exhaust leaves the unit. These units permit the choice of direct exhaust use of the scrubber, so that the filter system does not need to be employed unless there is concern the contents may have CBR dangers (Figure 7.38).

TCVs are considerably more expensive than single-vent units. However, they have a serious advantage in urban settings, where any release may have potential for damage among tall buildings. Also, those with CBR scrubbing systems provide environmental protections not otherwise available. On the downside, TCVs take a period of time after an explosion until the pressures have equalized.

Bomb disposal is an equipment-intensive function. While it may be possible to operate out of a patrol car, it is neither efficient nor practical. Although many individual technicians operate out of SUVs, vans, or pickup trucks, units are finding they need dedicated vehicles capable of carrying a wide variety of equipment, towing bomb trailers, functioning

Figure 7.33 A charge of one-half pound of dynamite detonates in an open-top vessel; note how force and effects are directed upwards, away from the nearby environment.

as an operation center for the technicians, and providing shelter for technicians involved in a response.

A variety of manufacturers of command vehicles and fire trucks have branched out to offer custom bomb trucks (Figures 7.39 through 7.41). These manufacturers specialize in building heavy-duty, emergency response vehicles. Safety, comfort, and ease of maintenance are crucial to their stock in trade. They also routinely produce custom trucks. As squad equipment, procedures, and jurisdictional needs vary, these

Figure 7.34 TCV in tow behind response vehicle.

manufacturers can produce a truck to meet the specifications of the user, rather than a one-size-fits-all approach. For example, one agency with a part-time team designed a truck with a crew cab, to permit members to meet at squad offices and respond together. Another team, an active full-time unit, selected a standard cab with a large storage compartment behind the driver; individual members respond in their assigned vehicles, while one team member transfers his personal kit to the truck and brings it to the scene.

Figure 7.35 Interior view of TCV. (Courtesy of Palm Beach County Sherriff's Office.)

Figure 7.36 Robotic, self-propelled TCV with robotic loading arm.

Like TCV trailers, manufactured response trucks are very expensive. However, like transport trailers, they have long life expectations. These are built on heavy truck frames, often the same frames as mainline fire equipment. Diesel engines deliver low maintenance performance for hundreds of thousands of miles. It is most likely the vehicle will be replaced for obsolescence long before it will face the prospect of wearing out.

Figure 7.37 TCV at the time of detonation of one pound of explosives; note controlled release of explosive by-products by relief valves.

IMPROVISATION OF EQUIPMENT

Bomb disposal has a long and honored tradition of improvisation of equipment. Commercial equipment is expensive; manufacturers face a limited market and we cannot recoup research and development costs with bulk production. Until the mid-1990s, and even more so until after the events of 9/11, funding for the bomb disposal area was very limited, and units had to carefully budget to maintain the basic needs.

The field is also comprised of individuals who are highly technically oriented. When faced with a challenge they tend to study and develop tools to overcome it. Whether adapting an existing item, often from another field, to meet the challenge, or fabricating a new device, bomb

Figure 7.38 Control panel of TCV equipped with environmental scrubber system to permit safe disposal of chemical or biological devices. (Courtesy of Palm Beach County Sherriff's Office.)

Figure 7.39 Custom manufactured response vehicle for an urban county sheriff's bomb squad.

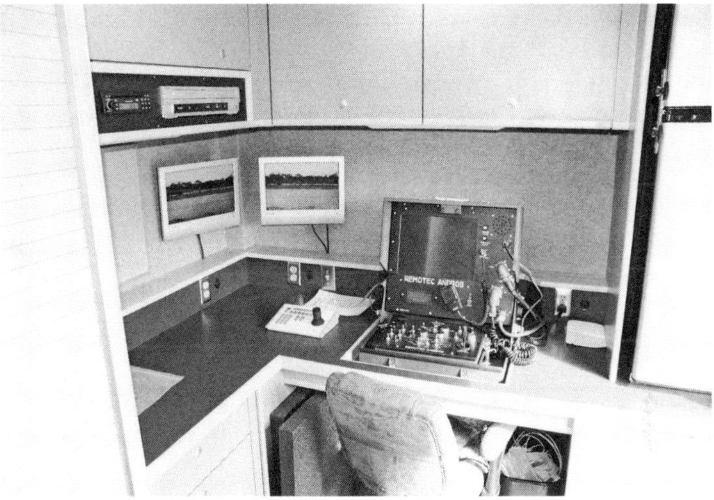

Figure 7.40 Command console of a custom bomb truck; robot(s), video, and communications may all be managed from the safety and convenience of one seat.

Figure 7.41 Storage in a custom response truck; tools, suits, explosives, etc., may be stored in closeted areas, while rear "garage" provides parking for a robot.

technicians have shown imagination and initiative beyond that is normally encountered in public safety.

As noted under commercial equipment, teams can often visit evidence rooms, government surplus centers, hardware stores, and even sources as diverse as craft stores, office supply centers, sporting goods stores, and megastores to collect a wide variety of items of value in hand toolkits, rigging kits, and even for some demolition kit supplies.

Many early disruptors were largely plumbing parts; although limited to black powder or substitute powders, they provided yeoman service to the field. Others either machined their own designs, or worked with machine shops to produce heftier units, often capable of utilizing smokeless powders (Figure 7.42). With these units came hand-loaded cartridges, sometimes fuse initiator, sometimes electrically initiated. While superseded by the accessibility of manufactured units and more dependable, factory-loaded ammunition, they remain an option for teams looking towards either lightweight designs for use in tactical support or where a disposable disruptor is a preferable option.

Many bomb squads have modified shotguns to the role of disruptors. Single- and double-barrel shotguns have been obtained from evidence

Figure 7.42 The HDS disruptor, as originally taught at the HDS. Pipe fittings, an empty 12-gauge shell reloaded with black powder and either a safety fuse or an electric match sealed with silicone sealant. While no the velocities or load variety of commercial designs, it filled the need and propelled loads of water, air, slugs, and AVON loads for many years with many devices.

and used as disruptors; initiation has been as simple as a string, or as ambitious as remote, electrically fired mechanisms. Many robots sport semiautomatic shotguns as specialized disruptors, often used with slug or Avon projectiles for door opening procedures.

Many single-vent bomb transport trailers have been locally designed and constructed. Indeed an early publication from the IACP National BDC provided guidance in the fabrication of such trailers, in recognition of the cash poor status of most early bomb teams.

Many bomb squads continue to use converted vehicles for bomb response. Often a retired cargo or delivery truck will be donated to a team, or a retired ambulance transferred from an EMS agency to serve the bomb squad (Figure 7.43). Often members of the squad, trained as carpenters, electricians, etc., are able to cheaply fabricate highly functional storage and command modules in these converted vehicles. Usually, these vehicles have been retired from their original purpose, not because of actual wear, but because of replacement policies to avoid costly repair. Customized to the needs of the bomb squad, and facing a lighter usage than their original purpose, they can provide a team years of service.

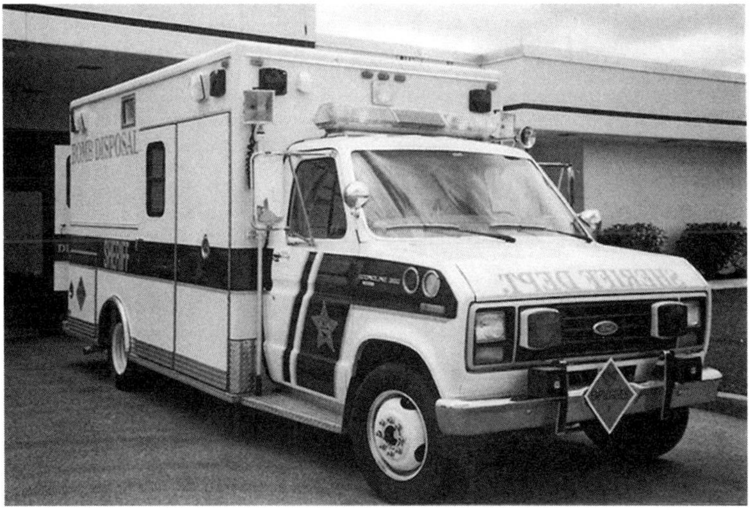

Figure 7.43 Retired ambulance transferred to the sheriff's office, where it filled the role of response vehicle for more than 10 years.

However, much of the greatest improvisation has been in the areas where no tool or jig exists to be acquired. Some of the items designed over the years are the following:

- Remote car opening tools
- Remote pipe bomb openers
- Stands and holders for x-ray cassettes/film
- Explosive breaching materials
- Special charges for attacking devices inside vehicles or other difficult containers
- Adaptations to rigging equipment to permit complex remote movement

Figure 7.44 The bomb sled—locally fabricated device, based upon a wheeled chassis, 1/2″ plate steel armor, and manipulators to permit standoff handling of devices or placement of tools. Dade County went so far as to mount one on a riding lawn mower for propulsion.

Figure 7.45 While commercial "cap protectors" are available to place an unshunted detonator into pending completion of an RSP, as illustrated here, a large phone book can act as an improvised protector, absorbing energy and fragmentation should the cap energize.

- Mechanical and electronic inspection aids
- Remotely functioned tools for robots
- Trailed delivery systems for robots
- Methods of remotely observing surveying CBR monitors carried by a robot

The ability of a bomb technician to improvise, adapt, and overcome should never be underestimated. Dealing in a small field in which it is difficult for manufacturers to economically design and market tools to answer many needs, it is the imagination and technical insight of the technician that rises to develop and build answers to impediments encountered on the job.

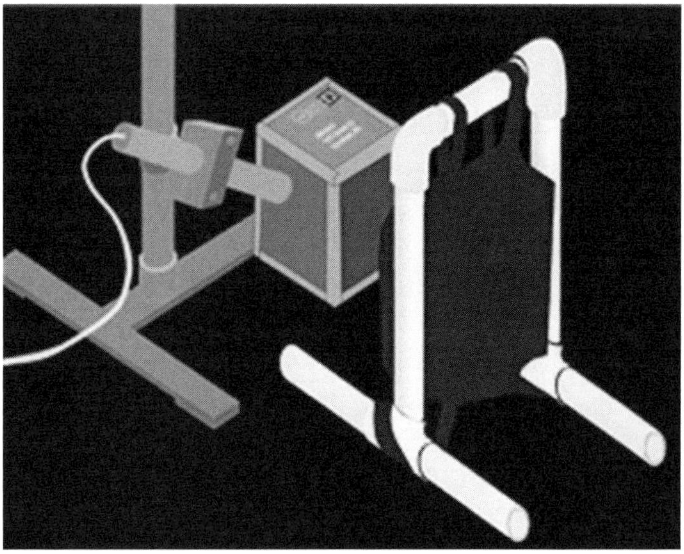

Figure 7.46 Sketch of plan for PVC pipe frame to suspend obsolete soft body armor, to prevent fragmentation from traveling to the side at a disruptor shot.

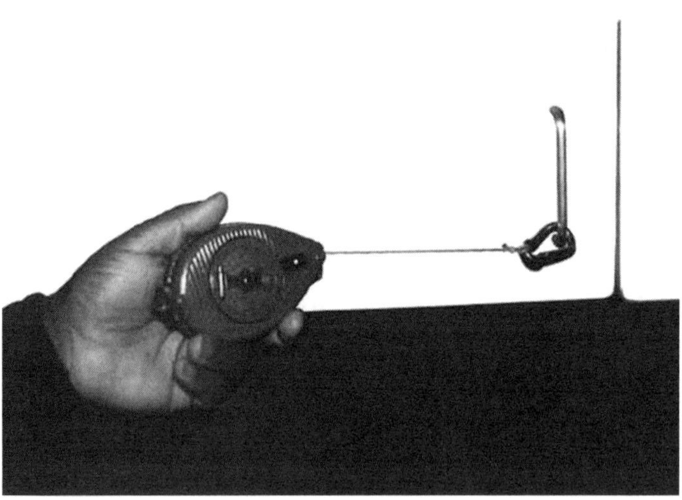

Figure 7.47 Chalk line adapted as rigging tool. (Photo courtesy of Bill Borbidge.)

A valuable resource for any bomb squad is the FBI CD published in the 1990s, based upon Philadelphia PD Bomb Squad's William Bobidge's research; he collected information on a wide variety of improvised tools and through the FBI was able to disseminate that information. Also, squads should be familiar with the US Department of Defense's Defense Logistics Agency. This agency is responsible for disposal of surplus military materials, ranging from uniforms through vehicles. Agencies have acquired demolition kits, robots, and a wide range of other equipment either for direct use or for use in improvised tools (Figures 7.44 through 7.47).

8

Response Concepts and Considerations

THE GUNPOWDER PLOT

It is early morning, November 5, 1605. Alerted by a loyal Catholic member of Parliament, Sir Thomas Knyvett, the Justice for Westminster, oversaw a search of the many cellars that undermined the buildings of Parliament. For the second time that evening, a man identifying himself as John Johnson was found in a cellar built off of a nearby residence. Earlier, when confronted, he told the officers he was a servant of Thomas Percy; that name raised eyebrows, as Percy was suspected of being part of a plot against the king. Searching "Johnson," he was found to be in possession of a pocket watch and slow matches. An extended search of the cellar resulted in the discovery of 36 barrels of black powder. "Johnson," determined to be Guy Fawkes, a mercenary whose knowledge of explosives and tactics had recruited him into a plot to assassinate the king and Parliament, had been preparing to initiate the fuse (Figure 8.1). The location of the cellar—under a portion of the Parliament where the king and many high other ranking officials would attend the State Opening of Parliament in a scant few hours—would very likely have seen the king and many others killed. Sir Thomas Knyvett and his deputies may well have, unknowingly, been the first bomb squad in history, their successful actions resulting in the celebration by the subjects of the United Kingdom, to this day, of The Gunpowder Plot.

There are a variety of considerations that affect any response. These will include national guidelines, local capabilities, situational analysis,

Figure 8.1 An engraving of Guy Fawkes (third from the right) and eight of his 13 coconspirators depicted here. (Engraving by Crispijn van de Passe the Elder, public domain.)

and the abilities of individual technicians. Although circumstances dictate procedures to be used on an incident, every team should have in-house procedures, really guidelines, promulgated with respect to national guidelines, team capabilities, and local community aspects (size and type of population, physical size, architectural layout, etc.) to make unseen decision-making simpler.

SUSPICIOUS ITEMS/DEVICE RESPONSE

Whether a suspicious item at a bomb threat search, an item found/deposited as a result of another criminal act (robbery, active shooter, etc.), or any item encountered by another member of service or civilian, it must be treated as an explosive device. No further attempts to identify it, prior to it arrival of a bomb team, should be taken. Any agency policy should state such, and that all possible steps to evacuate or safely shelter in place shall be put into effect. No attempts should be made to further evaluate the item with either canine or electronics; it is an unnecessary endangerment of personnel and resources, and can not be relied upon to eliminate a threat.

Whereas few jurisdictions have authority to order evacuations for a threat, the presence of a suspected bomb changes that. It is a public safety hazard that must be addressed; it is a crime scene that could expand in area in a millisecond. If at all practical, all personnel should be removed, minimally, pursuant to the tables published by ATF/TSWG. Thomas G. Brodie stated, succinctly, always move the people from the bomb, never the bomb from the people. In some rare instances a complete evacuation is not possible; then shelter in place actions must be implemented for those who cannot be removed. Personnel conducting the evacuation must maintain vigilance for secondary devices, other hazards, and environmental threats.

Bomb squad support should be immediately requested. Personnel must understand that bomb technicians require time to marshal their equipment and response; these are potentially life-and-death variations of beat the clock.

Fire and EMS support should be requested and staged at a safe location. They need immediate access to the scene, but do not need to have a front seat where they and their equipment may be imperiled in event of an explosion.

Any device event may be looked at in terms similar to a hazardous materials incident. The total evacuation zone is the hot zone. What would constitute the warm zone for a hazmat should be maintained as a secure area for staging of the bomb squad and its immediate support forces. The cold zone should be used for staging of all other public safety personnel—command, fire and EMS support, all officers providing security support, etc. Outside of this ring is uncontrolled, open to the public.

Agency policy must provide for bomb related decision-making to be solely the realm of the bomb squad. Further, policy should provide that the bomb squads staging and operational area should only be occupied by bomb squad and necessary support—possibly fire rescue if a close relationship exists, immediate investigative support, possibly an interface to the command post. If possible, one bomb tech should be assigned to the command post to brief them, rather than crowding the bomb operational area.

Security is a prime consideration of bomb responses. Not just maintaining a secure perimeter from intrusion, but also being wary of other dangers. The need for secondary device awareness requires all responders look for indicators of potential secondaries. An often overlooked aspect is protecting the scene from hostile entry. At a minimum, officers on the perimeter must maintain vigilance against any attempt to assault technicians. Although most technicians are police officers, when on a response their attention must focus on their mission; they are not in a position to also maintain security. Indeed, in Arapahoe County, Colorado, the sheriff, a former bomb technician, assigned SWAT snipers to respond to bomb calls, take high overwatch positions, and provide intelligence to ground units.

Prior to arrival, responding bomb technicians should be provided as much information as is possible, to permit efficient use of response time. Upon arrival, all available information must be shared with them. This should include civilian witnesses to the device, officers with intelligence information, persons with knowledge of the scene layout and possible hazards, and any others who may have input of value to the technicians. Ultimately, safe decisions can only be made when technicians are fully informed as to all aspects of a situation.

Render-safe decisions will be made by bomb technicians on the scene based upon a variety of considerations. The technicians' training, available equipment resources, intelligence, nature of location, weather, policy, and national guidelines will almost always be factors. Others, dictated by circumstances, may influence the tactical approach.

Many incidents are resolved on site; however, if it is safe to do so, bomb technicians may opt to relocate a device to an open location where potential damage is minimal. If a bomb squad lacks a bomb transport vessel, it may improvise with a dump truck load of sand. The vessel transporting the item must be part of an escorted convoy, the convoy including police escort vehicles at front and rear, and fire/EMS vehicles. For safety, the vehicle following the transport vessel must maintain a long lag. Also, where escorted convoys have units leapfrogging intersections, this should not be considered a safe technique; it would be a very unfortunate, perhaps tragic, occurrence for a speeding car or motorcycle to pass a device as it cooked off.

An improvised disposal site should be chosen with regard to traffic, public, potential hazard (e.g., hazmat, power transmission lines, etc.) as well as being as close as possible while being large enough to safely handle a high order detonation of the device. This may be as close as a neighborhood ball field when dealing with a pipe bomb, to a distant area of pasture when dealing with a large device or explosive recovery.

Any bomb incident draws media and public attention. Policy should establish who conducts public information dissemination. If it is required of the bomb squad, it must be understood that there is no briefing until their primary role is complete—public safety and their safety takes precedence over public information. If a public information officer handles this role, that individual must understand that a bomb squad will not release intimate details of a device, nor specific information on render-safe procedures. A knowledgeable PIO understands these needs, as well as how to satisfy media needs without endangering either future public safety or bomb tech safety.

VEHICLE RESPONSES

The involvement of vehicles and bombs is a multifaceted area. With a large vehicle bomb, they provide concealment, transportation, and fragmentation. Often, bombs are encountered when being transported to a target site by vehicle. Many a vehicle has been the target of a bomb, either itself or to victimize the vehicle occupants.

A vehicle bomb is also not limited to a car or truck. Motorcycles and bicycles are commonly encountered as vehicle borne devices. The tragic assault on the USS Cole used a boat as a vehicle borne suicide device. The Philippines have encountered several incidents where oceangoing ferries have been targeted by terrorists. Beginning in the 1950s, bombs have been directed at aircraft for personal gain, political intrigue and assassination, and in terrorist actions.

Vehicles present a number of challenges to responders and technicians in particular. Any vehicle can easily conceal a suitable amount of explosive, radically expanding the hot zone evacuation area. A bicycle frame may hide 10–25 pounds of explosives ... a semi trailer cargo van up to 60,000 pounds. Those 10 pounds will require a minimum evacuation of about 1000 feet; 60,000 pounds requires a minimum evacuation of 7000 feet. Consider first the manpower needed to safely and efficiently evacuate those radiuses. Then factor in maintaining security over that area. Finally, what logistical support as needed—hydration for security and fire personnel, medical support for the evacuated population, etc.

For the bombs tech, those radiuses also pose major challenges. Most bomb response robots are designed for 300 foot control, not 1000 feet, not 7000 feet. British military and police bomb techs found themselves using armored vehicles to permit safe approach at the extreme of a robots range, with the technician and his driver both dressed in bomb suits, and using buildings to provide them further barricading. How many bomb squads have access to armored vehicles for this purpose?

The construction of vehicles greatly limits access. A robot may not be able to flex its arm to look under and in. It may be able to look in, and use some tools through, vehicle windows. Then again, it may not. It cannot function under seats or dashboards, common concealment places of anti-occupant devices. It may not be able to climb up into cargo areas. It may be too big to drive down the aisle on aircraft, bus, or train, or to operate on or even gain access to a small boat.

A bomb tech may be the only logical method of operation in such confined spaces. However, this requires further decision-making, especially as to PPE. Bomb suits may become a dangerous hindrance in the close confines of cars, trucks, small boats, and smaller aircraft. Thus the technician must decide if armor is practical, and if so, what level permits safe and efficient function.

There are thousands of different models of motor vehicles, aircraft, boats, and other types of vehicles in operation. The wide variety makes it unfeasible to commercially prepare tools for remote opening manipulation of them. Thus improvisation has become the key to such tools. It has run the gamut from simple tools using tongue depressors, fishhooks, tape, and locking pliers, to custom machined tools giving a team readily usable equipment.

In the aftermath of a major vehicle bomb in downtown Los Angeles, LAPD developed a remote-controlled, robotic forklift designed to permit long standoff manipulation of a vehicle. Since then manufactures have introduced similar units. Usually designed with quick change tools, these giant UGV's provide the ability to attack a vehicle with a disruptor, emplace explosive countermeasures, or remotely move a vehicle from command distances of up to 2 miles.

A wide variety of explosive countermeasures have been developed for accessing vehicle interiors or general disruption of a vehicle borne device. Many of these items are readily improvised by a knowledgeable bomb techs; additionally, several providers produce devices to which the bomb squad merely adds water tamp and explosives.

Some jurisdictions have forbidden their bomb squads from using such tools. They overlook a significant fact—that if not rendered safe, the device most likely will function and extensively damage a large area. While it must be understood that any use of any render-safe technique may result in a function of the device as designed, the probabilities are much greater of success. These techniques may cause some collateral damage, but infinitesimal compared to that of a high order by the device. Further, due to the use of water in the design of these techniques, almost all of the explosive energy of the technique is used within a few feet or yards of the tools; most collateral damage will be limited to broken windows or other weak and fragile items, rather than serious structural damage.

When confronting a vehicle incident, if reasonable within the time frame, an identical vehicle should be brought to the bomb squad's command post. This provides the technicians ready reference to the construction of the vehicle, permitting them to understand the design of the vehicle, door, hood, and trunk opening, and to test manipulation methods safely. Indeed, it is valuable for bomb squads to visit a variety of car, truck, boat, equipment, and aircraft dealers to study their design as part of their in-service training.

In 1993, during preparation for a parade to honor President George H. W. Bush for his liberation of their nation, Kuwaiti security forces recovered a pickup truck that had been planted as a bomb along the route. Major internal voids in the body, hood, doors, floor, etc., had been packed with hundreds of pounds of explosives; they could not be detected by casual or even routine security inspection. This is a situation bomb techs need to prepare to face and safely respond to.

FIRE AND MEDICAL SUPPORT

Almost all bomb responses should have fire and EMS standby. Whether conducting RSP of suspicious item, handling recovered military ordnance, disposing of deteriorated explosives, or providing support to tactical law-enforcement operations, there are serious elements of danger to the technicians.

In the United States, there is a dichotomy in the makeup of local fire and medical services. About one half of jurisdictions use separate fire and EMS agencies; the others have combined services, often referred to as fire rescue. When the services are independent, this requires at least double the groundwork by a bomb squad in establishing protocols and training up the supporting personnel. The following remarks are applicable to working with a fire department, fire rescue, or EMS service.

The American public safety triad of police, fire, and EMS have always had a certain amount of interservice rivalry. For the bomb disposal field, it is crucial that this rivalry be minimized, and the cooperation and a sense of camaraderie be established. A strong bond among emergency responders on the bomb scene not only is necessary for technician safety, but also gives the bomb squad a force multiplier and dependable, professional support.

At the least, fire rescue should be on the scene during most of these bomb squad operations. It is important that the personal understand their services are needed in a standby mode until released by the bomb commander. It is very disheartening for bomb tech to see EMS support driving off as the bomb squad is preparing to conduct a disposal procedure because the medics assumed the scene was safe.

Training helps remedy this. Firefighters and medics are constantly training, or looking for programs to aid in maintaining their competency. A bomb squad can offer an agency a wide variety of useful training—working with bomb techs, understanding bomb suits, conducting rescue at the postblast scene, securing staging areas, etc. Couple this with joint training, drills, and exercises, and a strong bond is built between the services.

Once these bonds have been established, the bomb techs will find members of the rescue services imbued with a greater interest. Since few in the bomb field have strong medical backgrounds, identifying medics with a greater interest provides allies who can research the medical aspects of the work. What are the most life-threatening injuries (usually concussive blast effects, as opposed to physical injury such as burns, fragmentation, or laceration)? How to best handle potential spinal, cervical, and cerebral/cranial damage? Establishing flight protocols for medevac of blast victims (although most medical helicopters only fly 500 feet above the ground, a nap of the earth flight in mountainous regions may range over several thousand feet of altitude). Having an interested, knowledgeable professional involved will help ensure that proper protocols are adopted by the rescue agency.

If the bomb squad serves a jurisdiction with a hazardous materials team, a highly beneficial symbiotic relationship can be forged. Consider first two important similarities. First, by definition, bomb disposal and hazardous materials technicians are hazardous materials mitigation specialists, as explosives are a specialized niche of hazardous materials response. Second, both approach their responses in the same manner—a methodical, cautious, highly cerebral process.

Establishing a close working relationship with hazmat eases the burden on the process and the bomb squad. First, while the fire response agency may adopt a general response protocol, it is easier to work with the hazardous materials response team to develop a specific bomb squad support plan. Second, training is eased; instead of in the entire agency, only one specialized unit needs to be trained up. Because hazmat medics are already trained in specialized treatment protocols, their interest may often be piqued to conduct research to upgrade their skills to include blast effect injuries.

An alliance with hazmat is also a true force multiplier. Training the relatively limited manpower of a hazmat team permits much more in-depth training. The hazmat techs may be trained in many support skills—loading and setup of disruptors, electric and shock tube initiation system setups, donning and doffing of PPE (especially important skill for understanding rescue of a downed bomb technician in a bomb suit), to permit assistance in setup at a scene and accessing tools. Consider that most bomb squads will respond with two to four bomb techs; a hazmat team will usually respond with up to twelve technicians. This is a major manpower boost, relieving the bomb squad from fatigue inducing activity by delegating many support activities to these professionals.

Close relations also permit other benefits. Hazmat teams practice a system of rapid intervention team's (RIT). An outgrowth of two in/two out rules of respiratory protection, the RIT team is a rescue force, dressed out in appropriate PPE, standing by to make a rescue of the entry team should the need arise. A number of agencies with a close working relationship with their hazmat teams have extended their training to include use of SR5 search suits, provided by the FBI, by RIT personnel. Dressed out in this PPE, the RIT team can enter the hot zone with a bomb tech, take cover behind adequate barricading, providing much faster rescue should the technician go down for medical reasons or due to an explosion.

Another benefit is that, with a close working relationship, the hazmat techs understand basic bomb technician operation protocols, and know their bomb technicians—both personality and medical concerns. On an incident a ranking hazmat technician may be employed as the safety officer, with one assignment—to observe the overall scene and bomb techs, with the authority to stop operation if it appears either a previously unrecognized hazard is present or that the technician, for medical or fatigue reasons, is not following safe practices.

When a local squad and fire agency establish a strong relationship, it may also solve out of jurisdictional support issues. Except for a few major metropolitan areas that are populated by many bomb teams, most bomb squads provide regional support. Logistically it is difficult if not impossible to establish relations with the wide variety of jurisdictional agencies encountered. However a strong relationship may see a supporting fire rescue establish protocols providing for out of jurisdiction support to their bomb squad. Thus upon arrival at a remote location, the bomb techs have knowledgeable assistance, rather than fire or EMS providers who do not understand the needs or hazards being faced.

Fire rescue support for bomb squads can be a two-way street. Especially in the western United States, explosives are used in fighting brush and forest fires, being used to establish firebreaks. In some collapsed structure response, explosive entry may provide rescue personnel access quickly that may otherwise waste valuable time. Explosives have long been used in hazardous materials mitigation, to destroy stocks of hazardous materials, released uncontrolled pressure building in vessels such as drums, or even to provide controlled explosion of materials, such as was pioneered by Lt. Billy Poe of the Louisiana State Police Bomb Squad in handling railway emergencies. Also, larger platform robots can provide important services, dragging fire hoses into otherwise inaccessible locations or providing unmanned monitoring platforms. Small foot print robots proved their value in search operations in 2001 at the World Trade Center, when US Army EOD provided a variety of small units that searched areas both inaccessible and inhospitable to human searchers.

For some units it is not possible to either have a singular agency to provide support or to establish the training and procedurals. This is especially true of state police agencies that are the singular provider of bomb disposal services, particularly in physically larger, rural states. The best that may be hope for here is to offer as much training as is practical across the region, plus to promulgate and distribute educational material to the fire and EMS services of the area they support. It is far from ideal, but in a real world, such a limitation must be dealt with. If nothing else is possible, having fire and EMS support on-site, briefed as to the specific needs of the bomb squad, is far better than responding with no support at all.

TACTICAL SUPPORT RESPONSES

Earlier, the increasing role of bomb disposal and tactical response was examined. As noted there, the philosophies of bomb and squads are very different, bomb disposal in a deliberate, highly methodical process, SWAT, when in action, a highly dynamic, fast-moving concept. When incorporating the two, there must be well understood procedures in place to ensure that, for the situation at hand, the appropriate philosophy applies. Obviously, when bomb techs are only providing support to dispose of malfunctioned distraction devices, chemical agents, or explosive breaching materials, there is no functional interaction; tactical personnel will complete their mission, then bomb disposal will handle any failed munitions. Similarly, SWAT support on a bomb call is primarily observation, intelligence gathering, and preservation of a perimeter outside of where the bomb techs are working.

Integrated operations are a very different case. A bomb tech integrated into an entry team as a breacher must function as part of that team, even if not advancing after firing the charge. A tech aiding in device and booby-trap sweeps during a teams entry/search or as part of an active shooter response will have to use different procedures than during a typical bomb response. These may include partial render-safe, marking items to be avoided by immediate responders, or other steps designed to smooth the tactical operation. Procedures must acknowledge that these incidents require serious deviation from routine bomb disposal operation, with the bomb techs immediate concern to identify hazards to the entry personnel, only completely rendering them safe if it can be accomplished without serious impediment to the tactical operation. At the same time, procedures must ensure tactical operators understand that any item marked by EOD must be considered a hazard to be avoided, that techs will identify a clear path, and that once the objective is secured, the scene will revert to a bomb scene to permit complete RSP of all potential hazards.

SUICIDE/SURROGATE BOMBERS

The rise of the suicide bomber as a terrorist tactic, and the use of surrogates as suicide bombers, has opened an entirely new aspect to bomber response, one that is fraught with considerations. Long before an agency confronts such an incident, it needs to have carefully considered the subject and develop guidelines for its patrol, tactical, and bomb response elements.

For this book, only the response to a suicide type incident will be examined. Prevention, whether by intelligence gathering, physical design, or security measures, is a wide field, and beyond this book's scope.

Security must be a primary consideration in any suicide bomb response. The gathering of public safety responders to control an in progress suicide bomber is a highly attractive target for a second wave, whether a secondary device, secondary bomber, or armed assault.

A postblast also makes for a similarly attractive target. Also, in one suicide bombing in Jordan by a husband and wife team, her device failed to function, and she was found still at the scene, desperately trying to activate it.

Responding to a suicide bomber is much more complex than killing the bomber proactively. The decision to shoot requires legal and tactical consideration. Tactically, how large is the explosive? Can the location withstand such a blast? Is there a skilled sniper capable of a precision headshot at upwards of 300 yards available? Can the sniper be safely deployed, considering the potential of the device functioning? Is the individual a suicide bomber, or a surrogate victim? Is the suicide bomber, if not a surrogate, an individual recruited based upon diminished mental capacity? To assist agencies in establishing local policies and procedures, DHS offers its program, Prevention and Response to Suicide Bomb Incidents, through its partners at New Mexico Tech. This program does not dictate a set method to respond; instead it feeds its attendees information of prior incidents, technological considerations, intelligence renderings, etc., to aid them in returning home then developing programs appropriate to their locale.

Local policies should incorporate input from a number of fields. The local bomb squad should know its agency capabilities and tools—negotiation skills, sniper skills and equipment, armored vehicle support (an armored vehicle may be a tool, but only if its design permits safe employment of a marksman). Legal advice, both civil and prosecutorial, whose input should reflect local sentiments and help ensure a policy that protects responders from later repercussions.

Suicide postblast investigations also differ from other scenes. First, carnage. A suicide bomber is a delivery system designed to target a maximum number of individuals as close as possible. Thus the scene is much more sanguine than most other bombings, as the bomber will have attempted to be located among a large group of victims. Bloodborne pathogen PPE is a mandate, as the health of the victims is unknown. There have also been reports of groups recruiting individuals with serious bloodborne illnesses, such as hepatitis and HIV, with the intent of adding a biological component to the devices effect.

Reports from Israel describe bombers coating shrapnel in suicide bombs with rat poison, an anticoagulant. The intention was to increase blood loss and interfere with emergency life-saving efforts. However, this also presents a hazard to responders, who may ingest the chemical while breathing, or if injured from handling debris. Again, all responders must use appropriate PPE to protect them from this potential.

While much of the postblast investigation will proceed like any other case, in some cases one aspect of evidence is unusual, but valuable. In most cases where a suicide bomber wears a vest, orthopedic belt, or prosthetic chest/belly, the bomber's head is torn from the torso with minimal facial damage. Depending upon the bomber stance, hands may also be explosively amputated. This provides valuable evidence towards identifying the perpetrator.

North America has, thus far, been spared successful suicide bombings. There has been one successful surrogate bombing, and several hoax suicide bombers, but nothing like many other parts of the world have experienced. We must prepare for this sort of violence before it becomes common.

WEAPONS OF MASS DESTRUCTION RESPONSE

Following the issuance of PDD 39 by President William Jefferson Clinton, the FBI identified the bomb squads of the United States as its local response force for WMD incidents. This was in recognition of several factors.

- Explosives are often used in chemical and radiological dispersion devices
- Mechanical dispersion devices lend themselves to similar RSP as explosive devices
- The existing relationship between the bomb disposal community and the FBI
- The ability of the FBI to provide specialized training to bomb technicians via HDS

Since that time, most bomb squads have significantly incorporated their operations into a complete CBRNe model.

In actuality, most of the bomb squad function remains the same as it was prior to the addition of WMD responsibilities. Its greatest changes are

- Additional PPE requirements
- Interfacing with hazardous materials personnel
- Incorporation of CBR monitoring equipment
- Greater reliance on diagnostics
- Movement from general disruption and countercharge techniques to precision disruption techniques
- Maintaining hazmat skills

Since the late 1990s, every new HDS student has had a mandate to be certified under OSHA 29 CFR 1910.120 as a hazardous materials technician; indeed, now new HDS students attend the certification training at the DHS Center for Domestic Preparedness as their initial week of HDS training. This achieves two important effects. First, the new tech understands the selection and use of PPE for chemical, biological, and radiological protection. Second, the technician understands the basics of selection and use of monitoring equipment for chemical and radiological situations.

For those teams that enjoy a close association with the fire service, or better yet, a hazmat team, selection, acquisition, and maintenance of the PPE is greatly simplified. By investing in the same models of equipment, the bomb squad can, first, tailboard onto fire service purchases of equipment; the bulk in which a fire agency purchases an item such as SCBA permits a much lower price break than a bomb squad, with its limited number of units, would receive. The fire service will usually have on staff personnel capable of maintaining and testing the equipment, where a stand-alone bomb squad would have to contract the services.

Every bomb squad should maintain a set minimum number of various items of PPE. Sizing—of equipment and of members—needs to be taken into consideration. The equipment itself should include

- SCBA, with each technician having an assigned, correctly sized mask.
- APR or PAPR, with adequate supplies of filters, assigned to each member (note that some manufacturers are able to use the same mask among their SCBA, APR, and PAPR lines).
- Coverall ensembles.
- Fully encapsulating (level A) suits.
- Level B/C suits. There are a variety of materials available.

Numerous items of protective gear have been developed specifically for tactical operations. Suits should be obtained in different materials: Tyvek® or equivalent for low hazard (e.g., biological or radiological) and training, Tychem® or equivalent for greater chemical protection.

- A wide variety of gloves should be maintained in stock: Nitrile (surgical), butyl, Silver Shield®, plus cotton under gloves, Kevlar® cut resistant gloves, and leather work gloves.

There is a wide variety of monitoring materials available. Some, such as pH paper, military M-8 and M-9 papers and M-256 kits, are relatively inexpensive and have long shelf lives. Some items such as radiological survey meters may be discovered in agency or jurisdictional supply points, where old civil defense materials have been stored away. With inspection and minor maintenance, many of these can be put into service.

Many electronic meters, such as multigas meters and a variety of electronic analyzers, are somewhat expensive, require routine maintenance, and employ parts or sampling supplies that may have shelf lives. Here, a close relationship with a hazardous materials team is beneficial, with the hazmat team providing access to this equipment when needed.

The ability to interface with hazardous materials personnel is a valuable benefit to bomb techs responding to potential WMD incidents. Although a bomb squad has PPE and monitoring equipment, it is unusual for a bomb tech to maintain a keen level of knowledge in their use and interpretation. The qualified hazardous materials response technician is proficient at PPE selection, use of monitoring equipment, and interpretation of their results. By interfacing the two, a synergistic team is produced, capable of addressing situational conditions and analyzing the combined hazard encountered.

One major difference in a WMD approach over an IED approach—activity must use a two-man team, as opposed to the single bomb tech. This is a necessity under OSHA, where any ingress while using a respirator requires a two member team. However, this is where the two are used to their best abilities, combining the bomb tech and hazmat tech skills and knowledge. Also, the hazmat tech, except when closely monitoring the device, can remain at a greater, safer distance while the bomb tech works.

In addition to chemical and radiological monitoring, the tech has other tools available. X-rays serve an especially valuable role in both evaluating the device and in precision aiming of disruptors. At least one commercial provider of training has developed a system to permit analyzing an image and accurately targeting specific device components.

If x-ray interpretation determines it to be safe, fiber optic borescopes can be introduced into the device through a small hole in a device. Especially if capable of video recording, the borescope may provide significant detail on the interior layout and components that can be applied towards the render-safe.

Originally, disruptors were designed for general disruption or delivery of relatively large projectiles. In consideration of the need for pinpoint accuracy, several disruptor manufactures have introduced small caliber disruptors, designed around 9 mm, 10 mm, or 11 mm bores which use high velocity solid projectiles. These tools are capable of destroying a specific component while not causing collateral damage to the remainder of the device.

One of the largest manufacturers of bomb disposal equipment produces an item that looks like a geodesic dome tent. This tool is designed to be placed over a device, a countercharge or disruptor employed within it, and then filled with proprietary foam. The foam incorporates a universal decontaminant, and is designed to absorb considerable explosive energy and remain intact. Upon application of the RSP, the explosive energy will be contained or significantly reduced, while a chemical or biological hazard will be neutralized by the decontaminate chemical.

In many circumstances, the situation may be contained and sufficient evacuation established that robotics may be employed in lieu of a technician going down range. Several robot manufacturers have introduced systems to mount CBR monitoring on their robots and either provide video or electronic feedback. QinetiQ's Talon robot is designed to permit decontamination of the unit after exposure to CBR or other contaminants.

TCVs are available that are fully airtight, and which exhaust explosion by-products through a scrubber system which only releases water vapor into the atmosphere. One step further, NABCO produces a TCV unit mounted on tracks, and which has a large robotic arm. This unit may be controlled remotely, pick up a package, place it inside the TCV, secure it, and remotely remove itself from the scene.

Explosives have been the primary weapon of terrorists by a wide margin for many years. However, attempts have been made, luckily not very successfully, to employ CBRN devices. Especially in the United States, public safety bomb disposal will be the primary operational response force. Every bomb squad must maintain its training and ensure on an appropriate equipment for safely dealing with a potential WMD incidents.

EXPLOSIVES DISPOSAL

Hell in a Small Texas Town

The SS Grandcamp was docked in Texas City, Texas, taking on cargo of tobacco, 2400 pounds of ammunition, and 2400 tons of ammonium nitrate fertilizer on April 16, 1947. Possibly due to careless smoking, at about 8:00 AM a fire ignited in the stored ammonium nitrate. While AN was used among the military munitions of the Second World War, its explosive properties were not well recognized in the civilian and agricultural world of the 1940s. Thus the local fire department was called upon to fight the fire. In an attempt to minimize damage to the cargo, it was determined to flood the fire with water, converting it to steam, to asphyxiate the fire. Without good understanding of the hazardous properties of AN, no one realized that it would continue to burn even as oxygen was deprived, and that the steam would increase atmospheric pressure, making the hazardous cargo more sensitive.

At about 9:15 AM the AN detonated. Of the 27 member Texas City Fire Department, all but one, who had not arrived on scene, died, plus three members of the neighboring Texas City Heights Volunteer Fire Department died in the blast; in total, 468 died, between the initial detonation of the Grandcamp and the subsequent, sympathetic detonation of a second freighter, SS High Flyer, docked some 600 feet away, and carrying a cargo of 961 tons of AN. One anchor from the Grandcamp, weighing 2 tons, was projected over a mile and a half, causing a 10 foot crater on impact. The resulting fire destroyed most of the docks, industrial, and residential sections of Texas City.

Contrary to popular opinion, the most hazardous aspect of bomb disposal is the disposal of explosives, shock sensitive chemicals, and unstable flammable materials. Ill stored explosives may deteriorate, decomposing into different, more sensitive and unstable chemicals. If improvised explosives, they may be sensitive, unstable, and contain contaminants that may further increase their reactivity.

Prior to conducting any disposal of explosive materials, the bomb technician must have training. During training at HDS, the new technician receives introductory training in disposal operations. Since about 2000, ATF has offered the Advanced Explosive Destruction Training Course, an in-depth program dealing with safe disposal with a variety of materials. While not a disposal program per se, the homemade explosives course offered by the FBI through its field offices provides valuable information on handling of various improvised explosive materials.

A growing number of bomb disposal units possess thermal destruction units, trailers which are designed to use high temperatures to destroy ammunition, marine distress signals, fusees, and consumer fireworks (DOT class 1.4, formerly class C). Often these agencies will partner with local sanitation or environmental authorities to provide disposal services through which surplus ammunition and marine distress flares, generated by the public, may be safely disposed of in an environmentally friendly manner. In at least the state of Florida, the state environmental authority has developed a permanent permit for squads using these devices, alleviating the need to file for a permit every time the unit is used.

Planning for a disposal operation must be carefully conducted. Obviously, logistics must be considered. If fireworks or illegal pyrotechnic devices are being destroyed thermally, in open burns, material such as fencing or screening may be used to prevent fly out. For open burning some type of dunnage may be needed—paper products, straw, wood waste, even surplus uniforms. A flammable fluid such as diesel is often used as an accelerant, due to its low volatility and safer use than a material such as gasoline. A low explosive initiation charge is used, being initiated electrically from a safe distance by an electric match.

Safety precautions must be taken. Personnel should stage in a safe location, taking note of wind conditions. Fire support should be present, at least an engine, although the terrain may be better served by having brush fire trucks on the site. Not only is the fire support available to suppress any attempts by the fire to spread, but they may also wet down the surrounding area prior to initiation, and can inspect debris upon completion of the operation to ensure all hotspots have cooled off.

Personal protection is also important. Each technician should be clothed in a coverall garment of a flash fire resistant material such as Nomex®, plus a full head hood of such material, and gloves of such material or leather. Either leather or fire boots should be worn when working a destruction. Helmets and either goggles or face shields should complete the ensemble.

In addition to the clothing, hydration considerations are important. Water or a suitable sports drink should be available in sufficient quantity to ensure all personnel remain hydrated for the anticipated work period. Since these operations often take a full day, all personnel should either bring a box lunch or a runner should be prepared to cater a midday meal; additionally, some type of snack should be available for use as needed.

Paperwork is an important, unavoidable aspect of the operation. Especially as it is a hazardous materials operation, an incident action plan (IAP) should be prepared by the incident commander and shared with all participants. This IAP should include the incident command structure, so that all participants understand their role and chain of command.

Long before even entertaining the idea of a disposal, liaison should be established with all applicable environmental regulatory agencies—local, state, and possibly federal. A good relationship goes a long way towards easing the burden on a squad commander; indeed regulators who know and respect a team's work will be likely to work with them, and to consider them a resource in their emergency responses.

In preparing to conduct a disposal, recognize that a permit will be needed. Failure to obtain a permit exposes the agency, if not the individual, to regulatory action (often hefty fines) and potentially criminal sanctions.

Every jurisdiction will face a different regulatory matrix; possibly only state or federal, possibly local and state, and possibly all three levels. Make introductions, and include them in the planning process.

As an example, the rules of the Florida Department of Environmental Protection provide for issuance of emergency hazardous waste disposal permits to bomb squads. Traditionally, DEP recognized the following three different circumstances:

- A true emergency (e.g., a bomb disposal) where action must be taken immediately in the interest of public safety—in this event, a squad will take necessary action, and immediately afterward apply for a permit.
- A pressing response, for example, an operation where a disposal must be made, but not unduly urgent. In this event, DEP requested a telephonic communication; they would verbally issue a permit, and follow-up with paperwork after.
- A scheduled disposal, for example, a planned disposal of materials (not involving a permitted thermal destruction unit), in which case a permit should be obtained prior to the operation.

In any case, upon completion of the operation, finalizing of the permit would include submitting a report detailing location and description of the methods of disposal (open, covered charge, etc.), plus publication of a legal notice of the operation. A final permit would then be sent to the agency for filing with their records.

Explosives disposal is both physically dangerous and administratively complex. Preparation, not only for specific operation, but to lay a predicate long before needing to conduct a disposal, it is mandatory to ensure a safe and legal outcome.

EVENT AND VIP SUPPORT

Death of a Monarch

On March 13, 1881, Alexander II, czar of the Russian Empire, followed his usual Sunday routine, traveling to a major public square to review the troops. Nikolai Rysakov, a member of the People's Will terrorist organization, threw a small bomb, which landed beneath the emperor's armored carriage. The ensuing explosion damaged the carriage, killed a Cossack escort, and wounded the driver and spectators. The czar, ignoring the concerns of the local chief of police, Cossacks, and guards to stay in the safety of the armored carriage, instead alighted to inspect the scene and lend aid to the wounded. A second assailant, Ignacy Hryniewiecki, approached and, standing by the emperor, dropped another lit bomb at his feet. This blast killed the assailant and mortally wounded the czar, who bled to death from traumatically amputated legs.

The world has changed significantly for major event and VIP security. Not long ago, a major event included the Super Bowl, World Series, national political conventions, or Olympics, but with the new tactics of terrorists, a growing number of Columbine-like incidents, and more lone wolves, a venue as small as a high school graduation or local ballgame may be considered a target. VIPs are no longer limited to national politicians, leading actors, and major-league sports figures. Threats arise at town council meetings, against musicians and rising actors, and a wide variety of athletes.

In planning, officials are told to consider any event attracting about 12,000 people, or sporting event attracting over 7000, as being a potential for a terrorist incident. How many community events (fairs, Main Street festivals, etc.) attract 12,000 attendees? Many sporting events attract over 7000—almost every college football game, and many high school games.

It is difficult to secure entry to many of these events. Most are considered community events, and the community will not be pleased to have to run a security gantlet to attend a street festival or high school athletic event. Thus the bomb squad must look at its role as primarily reactive, available to respond to a threat or incident. Proactively, it may be able to conduct preevents sweeps of the venue and secure it, but in between, is just a standby.

In the shadow of Columbine and gang activity, many public events generate a higher level of security than previously. Many high school graduations now are controlled access, with locations searched and secured prior to the event. Often a combination of bomb technicians and canine support conduct the sweeps, pairing their knowledge and talents to conduct as effective a search as is possible.

Events of national stature generate security under the auspices of the the Super Service. National political conventions, Olympics, World Series, the Super Bowl, and select other events demand increased security. These are mammoth undertakings, coordinating dozens of agencies. At a recent Super Bowl, seven local bomb squads, local explosives canine support,

ATF and FBI explosives personnel, military EOD, and CBRN support from local hazmat teams and a National Guard Civil Support Team coordinated the bomb/WMD support alone. Currently, the US Secret Service, housed under the Department of Homeland Security (DHS), is tasked with overall command and coordination of these national event security responses.

VIP support will also vary. Security for national leaders is the responsibility of the Secret Service, which coordinates bomb support with local bomb squads and military EOD. Often, EOD conducts the lion's share of these sweeps, with bomb squad personnel staged for response and conducting route sweeps ahead of a convoy. Other "lesser" political figures may also have their own security contingents, but depend on local bomb squad support to a greater extent for sweeps.

Nongovernmental VIPs may have accompanying security personnel, but may request bomb squad support for all sweeps. Much of this will be based upon the assessment of the threat—many entertainers or athletes may only fear a physical, personal attack by a deranged "fan," where others with involvement in controversial fields, whether political or otherwise, may have greater fear of an explosives attack. What tools should bomb squad bring to these operations? For most, eyes, ears, and sharp minds. Personal toolkits incorporating a selection of hand tools, mirrors, lights, probes, tape, and line should be carried by each technician on the assignment. A variety of other tools are also advantageous. Inspection mirrors, pole cameras, fiber optics, and borescopes aid in a variety of searches. Small discrete radiological monitors, chemical monitors, and a variety of chemical and explosives test strips/kits are very valuable. X-ray equipment aids in positively clearing items. If access control comes within the purview, baggage screening x-ray and magnetometer portals may be necessary. Explosive detection canine is always a prime tool in any such security operation.

Special events and VIP missions involve bomb squads to a much greater degree than ever before. These are time consumptive operations, fatiguing to the participants, and make cause conflicts for small teams with inadequate backup should another issue arise. Because of changes in society, in the targeting by terrorists, and mobility of the society, these events are no longer limited to major metropolitan areas. Small units that support significant regions find themselves involved routinely, and under a greater stress than their larger compatriots. Every bomb squad needs to understand its area of operations, assess its potential draws and targets, and prepare accordingly.

MILITARY ORDNANCE

Deaths in Paradise

Sunday, April 5, 1987, saw two teens in Miami, FL, experimenting with a device they had stolen from a car parked at a mall in downtown Miami. The green plastic box, roughly 10 inches by six inches by one and a half inches thick, was convex curved; one side was marked "Front Towards Enemy" (Figure 8.2). At some point, possibly by deciding to plug its loose wires into power, it detonated. The M-18 Claymore Mine, about 1.25 pounds of C-4 behind some seven hundred 1/8" steel balls, is designed to spray an area downrange with shrapnel, to protect a position, with an effective downrange of 100 m. More so, it has a significant back blast of explosive power as well.

The two young men died; one immediately, the second later in a hospital. The explosion tore two walls off and the roof of half the structure was destroyed.

The source? Unknown. Military ordnance finds its way to the streets, walking off bases to be secured for private caches, traded for drugs, or just kept as souvenirs. In 1980s Miami, Cuban freedom fighters were still an active element, with many well equipped from contacts in earlier days with various intelligence agencies.

Figure 8.2 M-18 Claymore mine: designed as a shotgun, capable of killing or wounding over a 100 yard area.

For over 200 years, militaries have used explosives in warheads, numerous types of mines, and many other forms of ordnance. It is encountered in a wide variety of manners.

- By divers exploring wrecks or former training waters
- During excavations of military dumps or caches of stolen military materials
- In museums and displays
- On the street, where often stolen munitions surface for illegal use
- Among the effects of veterans who kept souvenirs of their service
- Items found by hikers, campers, etc., using military training grounds or former sites for sport and which are collected as souvenirs

Various examples of military ordnance recovered are depicted in Figures 8.3 through 8.13. For extensive coverage of this, a must-have book on ordnance identification is Tom Gersbeck's Practical Military Ordnance Identification, also available from CRC Press (2014, ISBN: 978-1-4398-65058-9).

Figure 8.3 Reloaded Mk-II hull, showing the amount of smokeless powder recovered from it.

Figure 8.4 M-25 hand grenade. Uses an explosive burster to spread CS irritant agent over a wide area.

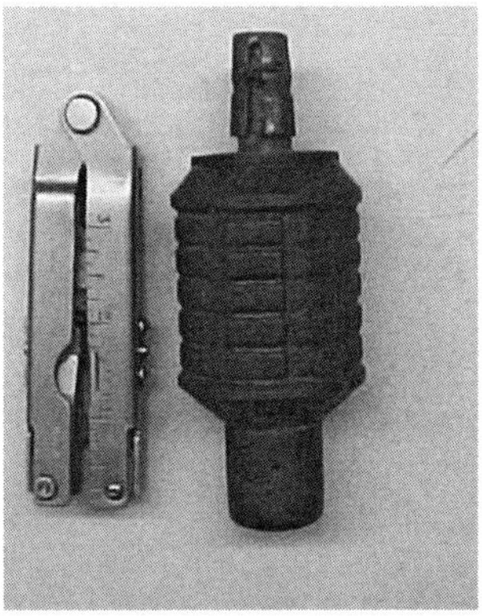

Figure 8.5 World War II Japanese hand grenade. Due to lack of resources, Japanese military often substituted picric acid, a shock sensitive chemical, for high explosives. It forms highly sensitive compounds with metals. Often found in museums or among veterans' souvenirs.

Until recently, most bomb squads would merely collect ordnance when familiar with it, or safeguard it and contact military EOD to handle it further. The nature of the global war on terrorism has significantly affected the availability of EOD assets. Previously, Army EOD was responsible for response to all ordnance support above the mean high water mark, and Navy EOD for all responses below that line. Marine and Air Force EOD

Figure 8.6 Dutch V-40 "mini" hand grenade. This one was recovered by Miami-Dade PD bomb squad from a trash can at an airport.

only ventured off-base when their base commanders deemed it acceptable to support local authority.

In the early 1990s, Army, facing budget constraints, began to reorganize EOD by merging units, formerly referred to as detachments, into larger posts referred to as companies. This did not significantly degrade response, as many of the units had previously shared some response areas. However, with the demands of asymmetrical warfare on EOD in combat theaters, the Army has merged various companies to create battalions. These battalions now provide regional EOD support within the continental United States.

At the same time, the Department of Defense decreed that all military EOD would share in stateside civilians support, dependent upon the needs of their home base. However, all military EOD units are affected by the requirements of this war; most units have personnel deployed to combat assignments, decreasing their base manpower.

Couple this with the primary responsibility of EOD—to provide emergency explosives support to the military. Keeping the military safely functional is the priority of EOD—any incident involving explosives must be

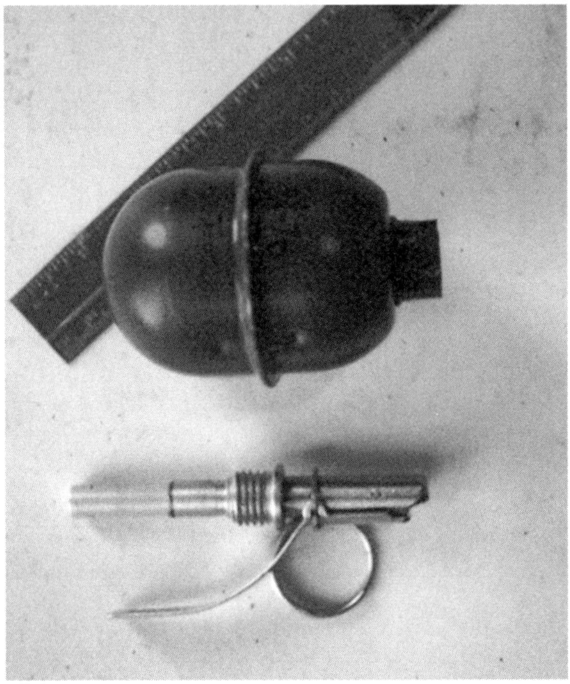

Figure 8.7 Soviet RGD-5 hand grenade, recovered in the wake of the Mariel boatlift of 1981.

responded too quickly, to ensure military operations are not shut down. This combination of circumstances means off base responses to support the civilian community may not be as timely as they once were.

HDS teaching has always been that public safety bomb disposal handles explosives and improvised explosive devices, and when confronted with military ordnance either collect it if safe for EOD to later collect, or secure it for the arrival of EOD if safety was of any question. Some items, such as naval marker flares in coastal areas, might be so commonly encountered that public safety bomb disposal came to handle them without support. Other items, especially hand grenades, were often improvised, being practice hulls repacked with explosives and using either nonmilitary bouchon fuzes, or repacked fuzes, and actually now an IED (Figures 8.14 and 8.15). But overall, most ordnance would be referred to military for disposal.

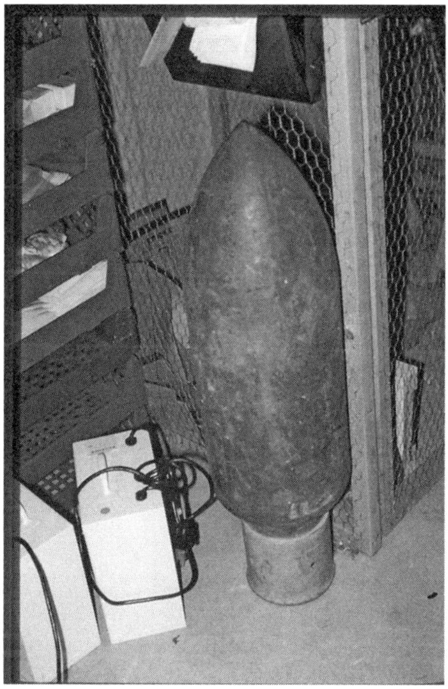

Figure 8.8 AGM-12 Practice warhead.

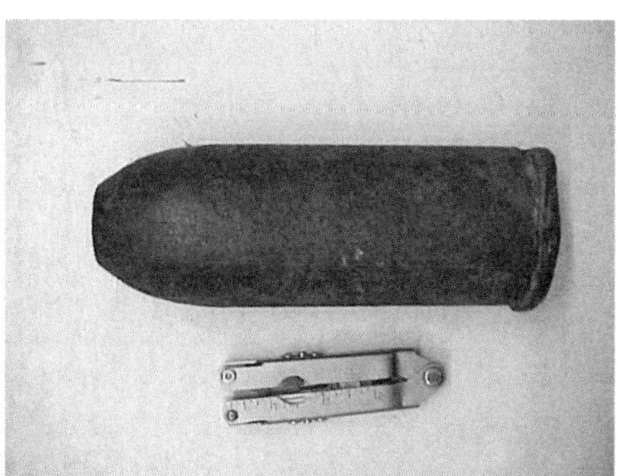

Figure 8.9 Early 1900s artillery projectile; these may be found in collections, museums, or recovered from former training sites.

Figure 8.10 World War II 100-pound white phosphorous bursting aerial bomb, recovered by sport divers off Florida beach.

The limited access to EOD is presenting a variety of problems to public safety bomb disposal. At the same time as the military has been taxed with a war response, public safety has seen significantly growing economic constraints. Assigning bomb techs or even officers to safeguard an item for many hours or even days is rarely justifiable. Knowledge is a crucial shortcoming. Most current and recent ordnance is classified, especially RSP

Figure 8.11 Explosion when WP bomb countercharged on bomb disposal range.

Figure 8.12 Smoke from destruction of 100-pound WP bomb.

Figure 8.13 Cannon balls are often located in areas from Revolutionary, 1812, Civil War, and Indian Wars. Some may be iron spheres, but many are fuzed with explosive (black powder) charges. With age of the powder, they should be treated as extremely sensitive.

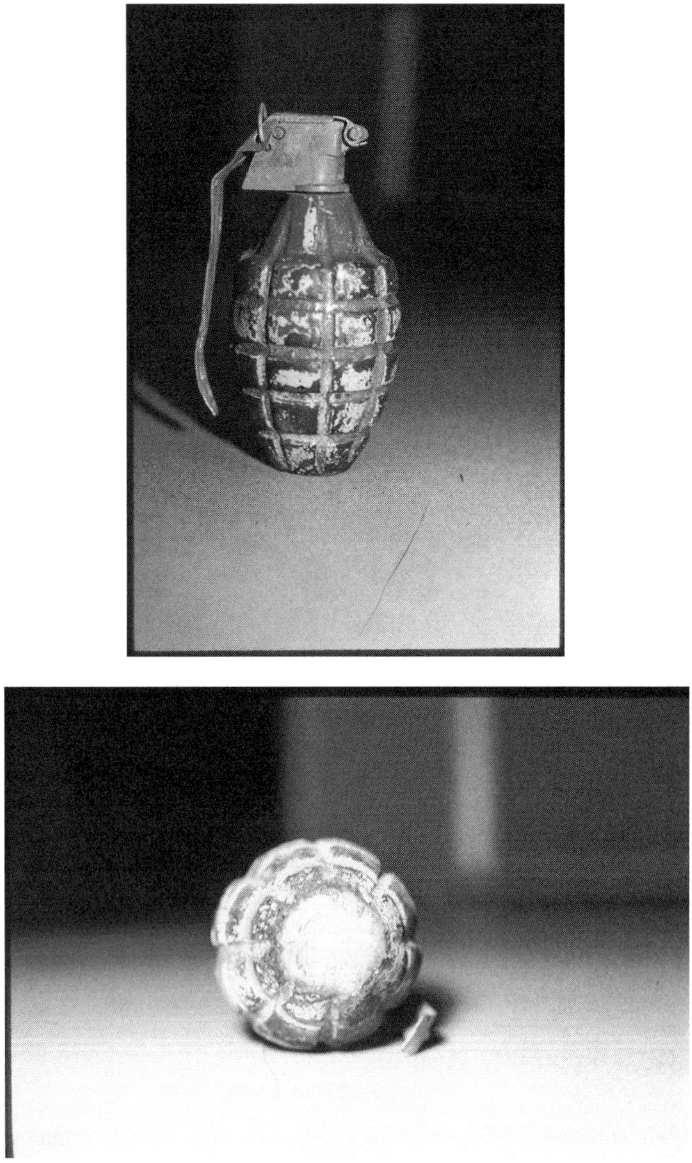

Figure 8.14 A practice Mk-II hand grenade hull, modified by filling the exhaust port, adding a live fuse, and filling with low explosive.

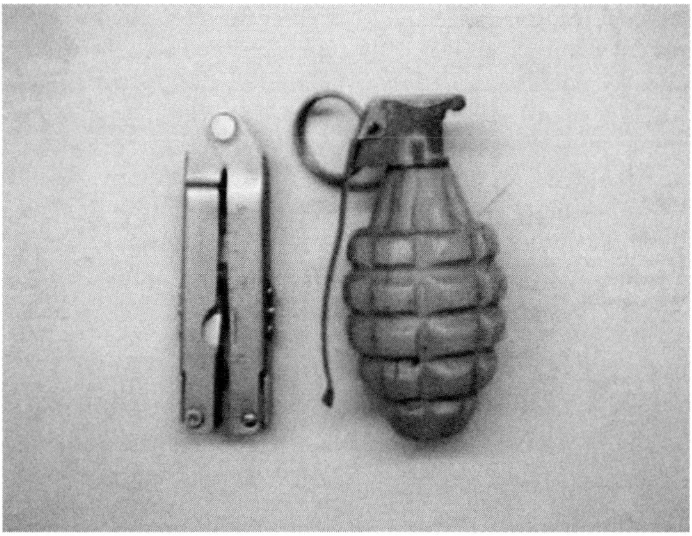

Figure 8.15 Early World War II Mk-II hand grenade; at that time, they were painted yellow, as opposed to later olive drab green, which can mislead some to think it is not dangerous.

techniques. Much of this is also highly sensitively fuzed, and extremely hazardous to handle without training, knowledge, or equipment.

Identification of ordnance is not always straightforward. Some is not well documented. Commonly, people may repaint an item, either to make it presentable or to camouflage its true nature. Blue is considered, under current American doctrine, training. How difficult is it to paint an item blue, when it is actually a high explosively loaded item?

Overtime, color codes have also changed. Prior to 1941, American hand grenades were painted yellow; it was only the onset of World War II that saw them colored olive drab. Also, paint wears off due to time, corrosion, etc. On at least one occasion, an artillery projectile was recovered during and excavation. Military EOD responded, and mistook it, in its bare steel configuration, as a high explosive projectile. It was then countercharged, and the EOD team was exposed to mustard, a blister chemical agent. Color, basic appearance, and third hand knowledge does not replace diagnostics and reference materials.

All US military EOD personnel are graduates of the Naval School EOD at Eglin Air Force Base in Florida. The school entails six months of intensive training. Navy EOD personnel undergo further training, to encompass dive and parachute training. Additionally, EOD personnel will attend a variety of chemical, biological, and nuclear/radiological classes, as well as specialized, advanced training to reflect service demands.

Current Department of Defense regulations provide that EOD may, upon request of federal or civil authority, provide support to them regarding IED's, nonmilitary commercial explosives, or similar dangerous articles, when in the interest of public safety. Explosive ordnance of American or foreign militaries is a primary responsibility of military EOD. Further, through Army EOD, military EOD is tasked with support to the US Secret Service and Department of State for VIP protection, and to the FBI and Department of Energy for improvised nuclear device response.

Under DOD regulation, Army EOD has primary responsibility for all land mass areas. US Navy EOD has primary responsibility for all rivers, canals, and closed bodies of water, and coastal areas below the high water mark (Figure 8.16). Air Force and Marine Corps EOD are primarily responsible for support on their respective facilities; however, Navy, Air Force, and Marine EOD may provide support to land mass civil authority

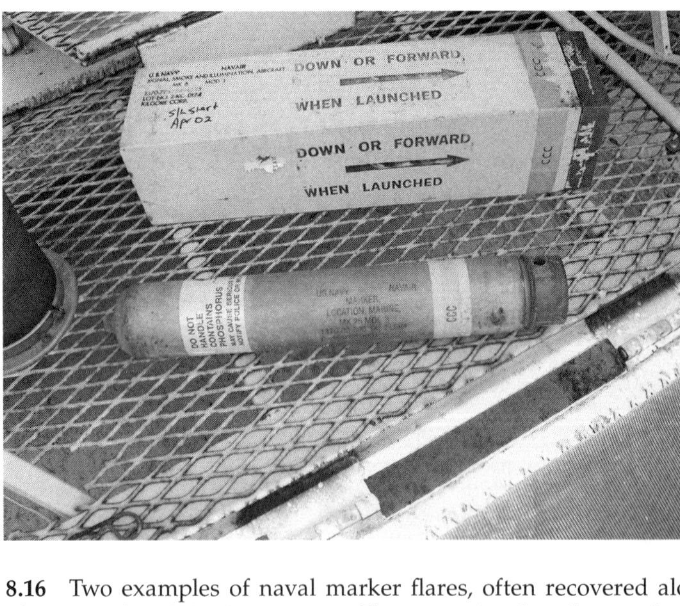

Figure 8.16 Two examples of naval marker flares, often recovered along seashores where naval activity is common. They contain phosphorous incendiary loads and may have scuttling charges.

at the discretion of their base commanders. This latter will be subject to careful consideration; it may not be safe, from a military aspect, to respond an EOD asset, especially one stretched thin by combat deployment, from an active base at which military ordnance are commonly in use.

The Posse Comitatus Act limits the role of military forces in enforcement of civil laws. As it is applied to EOD operations, it limits military EOD to taking appropriate RSP actions to preserve the public safety. EOD is not permitted to aid in the collection of evidence. Further, while they are permitted to testify in civilian courts, they are limited to testimony as to device description, componentry, and function, will treat IED RSP as "for official use only," and are expected to confer with military JAG/legal affairs prior to providing testimony. Also, many ordnance RSP's are classified, and if employed may not be revealed.

Under NBSCAB certification/accreditation standards, public safety technicians must be graduates of HDS. This is not to disparage the capabilities of an EOD tech; especially with the current level of terrorism related deployments, EOD personnel are facing greater numbers of IED's than were ever anticipated by any American bomb disposal function. However, requirement for HDS attendance achieves two purposes; first, that all hazardous device technicians share a common standard of training, much as all military EOD attend the Naval EOD school. Second, being a component of the criminal justice system, civilian bomb disposal must recognize evidential concerns and handling of explosives and devices; while military procedures often incorporate evidence handling as a method of intelligence gathering, the steps and considerations for a public safety technician are much more inclusive. However, civilian administrators should recognize that former military EOD techs are a valuable resource for recruitment; their attendance of HDS only serves to add to or refocus skills they already have considerable training with.

BOMB DISPOSAL AND EXPLOSIVE DETECTION CANINES

There is no doubt that a canine is the most efficient tool for explosive screening. The olfactory senses of a dog are superior to any electronic system currently available. The canine is capable of faster search and monitoring devices. When a dog's "batteries" wear down, a short rest and a bowl of water will replenish them. The introduction of a new family of explosives merely acquires training to imprint the news sent onto the dog's memory. However, several issues need to be appreciated in relation to bomb detection canines and the bomb squad. The first is whether explosives detection dogs should be part of the bomb squad, or located elsewhere in agency's make up.

It must be understood that a K-9 handler has an intense job. Whether patrol, scent discrimination, or dual-purpose, most of the handler's time is spent in maintenance of the dog and continuing training. Although it has been done, it is stretching an individual's capability to be trained and functioning as both a handler and a bomb technician. One issue regarding using a technician as a handler is, what is done with the dog when the master's hat is turned to the technician's side? Safe facilities must be provided for the dog to stand down while the handler works as a technician (Figure 8.17).

For some large bomb teams, assigned to major agencies, having explosive canines on board has worked. For these units, there is sufficient call for canine services to keep the handler teams active. However, most agencies find it more efficient to incorporate dual-purpose dogs into their patrol log function, with possibly explosive detection only dogs used for assignments such as airport, courthouse, port, and similar locations with high interface with the public.

Many dogs are cross trained for patrol and explosives detection, and handle two roles well. The dog should never be cross trained for explosives detection and another specific scent discrimination, such as drugs. Quite simply, how do we determine whether the dog is alerting for contraband, or a bomb? Officer and public safety would be endangered, and potentially the dog's reliability for probable cause may come into question.

Nonhandlers need to understand that the dog is, primarily, designed to search an area. It is not specifically pinpointing the material it is alerting to, although a well-trained canine team canine may be able to.

It is also important to understand that an explosives canine is a screening tool. It is used in events, to efficiently and quickly clear a large area. It is used on bomb threats to assist physical searches. It may be used to screen unattended packages to which no threat has been attached. However, they should never be used in conjunction with a suspicious package, that is, an item which may not belong where it is located, to which a threat has been attached, which has no logical explanation for its presence. Even if the canine reacts negatively to the suspicious item, the item's demeanor requires final clearance by a bomb squad. Simply put, there is never a valid reason to expose a valuable canine team to what must be considered a deadly weapon.

Especially when using a cross trained (patrol/explosive) canine to conduct an area search or even an unattended package, the scene or

Figure 8.17 A happy explosives detection canine during a training operation.

immediate area of the item should be evacuated. The dog and handler are concentrating on their screening search. An unexpected appearance of a person could startle the canine, which could revert to protective status, biting the innocent but foolish person interfering with the dog's work.

Training aids are an important aspect of the canine continuing training (Figure 8.18). While pseudo-explosives are available, questions arise as to their efficacy. A bomb squad can maintain contaminant free standards of the main families for in-service training. While a variety of methods are used, it is best to provide portable magazines for each handler to store their training aids, with each item then stored in its own, airtight packaging to prevent cross contamination. Scheduled rotation of these supplies ensures that the material in used for training remains contaminant free.

Currently, the major police canine associations are working with the federal Scientific Working Group on Dogs and Orthogonal Detection Guidelines (SWGDOG) at Florida International University to develop better guidelines for working dogs. As a result, standards have already been developed for training of canines and handlers, and specific certification testing standards for explosive detection canines. Working in conjunction is the National Explosive Detection Dog Advisory Board (NEDDAB), which has coordinated with the various canine certification groups and which have adopted the same standards.

Federally, ATF, the FBI, and DHS are active in canine training. Through its canine training facility in Front Royal, Virginia, ATF has trained and placed many explosive detection canines with local agencies, as well as

Figure 8.18 A portable magazine, secured in the trunk of an explosive canine handler's car; small amounts of live explosives are maintained here to permit constant training.

dogs used to support its own mission. DHS, through TSA, trains detection canines which are placed with local agencies that provide security at commercial airports nationally. The FBI maintains explosive detection canines at most of its field offices to support both the FBI's investigations and those other events it is assigned to support.

The explosives detection canine is a valuable resource to agencies facing bomb threats were security screening responsibilities all—techs, commanders, handlers, administrators—must remember that handler and technician roles require they think differently. Technicians look at the scenes for signs of threat. Each brings a valuable and important set of capabilities to a scene, which provide life-saving services to the community.

9

Explosive Evidence Handling

Explosives recovered in criminal investigations are evidence, same as burglar tools, firearms, narcotics, or any other items collected in criminal cases. The same rules apply as with any other evidence—properly marked and sealed containers, receipts, and other documentation, a strong chain of evidence. However, there are several significant differences the technician must be aware of, to ensure proper handling.

The first difference—these are explosive materials. They must not be stored in agency evidence and property facilities. The agency should have magazine facilities, or arrangements with another public safety agency bomb squad to share their magazines. Since a bomb squad also maintains stores explosives for their own use, magazines are not difficult to justify.

Many agencies operate multiple magazines, one solely for high explosives storage, one for low explosives and initiators, and often a third for material pending disposal, especially waste ammunition, marine distress flares, consumer fireworks, and similar materials (Figure 9.1). Separation meets regulatory needs, eases housekeeping, and helps ensure items destined for disposal stay segregated from either active case materials or on-hand supplies.

It is a wise investment for a bomb squad to study its agency's primary evidence system and attempt to emulate it in operating its explosive evidence function. As long as space and facilities are provided, segregate evidence from stock explosives. For major seizures, which are often recovered in their original packaging, it is best to document and catalog the contents of the container, return them to the container, label, and seal it. Smaller seizures, after being documented, should also be packaged. Previously, packaging meant bags, whether plastic or paper, which are

Figure 9.1 Two commercially available magazines in use to store an agency's explosives and explosive evidence.

still viable alternatives. However, as has been learned in the evidence room, sealed boxes provide far easier, neater storage on shelves. A variety of sizes of new boxes can be obtained and maintained, and an applicable box is selected when needed. Box the evidence, seal, and label it for easy storage in the magazine on a shelf.

Obviously an intricate, computerized, bar-coded evidence tracking system is not justified for most bomb squad evidence systems. However, a logbook or a computer spreadsheet will provide an adequate tracking system for the relatively limited quantity of evidence. In addition, every evidence item stored in the magazine should also be logged into the explosives storage inventory, which is a mandate for every magazine, providing a backup should the evidence manifests be neglected.

Gross amounts of explosive material are easily stored. Not so with minute amounts, either samples are drawn for submission to a lab or post-blast samples. Here, due to the inherent volatility of many explosives and even more so, specialized packaging of their residues is needed.

First, recognize the container must be vapor-resistant. Volatile explosive materials may off gas and dissipate, leaving nonreactive materials for lab analysis. Thus paper bags, pasteboard boxes (druggist boxes), and polyethylene plastic bags are unsuitable for such evidence storage.

Glass jars, metal cans, and nylon bags are suitable for these materials. These are generally small samples, and the containers are small. New, unused paint cans, which form airtight packages when their lids are sealed, are excellent. One pint and one quart cans are generally adequate for these samples.

Chemical specimen vials and jars are also very suitable. These may be found in small sizes such as one ounce and eight ounce. One ounce vials are an excellent size for lab samples of explosive materials; the eight ounce is for obtaining liquid samples at a scene. Screw on, phenolic tops with Teflon® liners provide airtight packaging.

Heat sealable nylon bags are common in the area of fire investigation. While care must be taken at the sealing of them, once sealed, they are impervious to off gassing, a fault of polyethylene bags. These are especially valuable for storing swabs used on surfaces, small samples of debris and dirt from the site, scrapings of suspected residue, etc.

One item has come into use as a safety measure. This is the pink, antistatic plastic bag, commonly used for electronic components. While the volume of materials collected as lab samples is very small, and poses little explosive danger, it is still static sensitive, especially low explosives or a variety of precursors. Using a zip top style antistatic bag to overpack a class vial, glass jar, or nylon bag containing such a sample minimizes the potential of a static discharge initiating the contents.

A wise investment in handling lab samples is to collect three samples of each item selected for lab analysis. One item will be submitted to the lab chosen for the case. A second sample is maintained for defense analysis, if the defense should choose to conduct independent examination. The third provides a fallback, should either other sample be lost.

Lab submission is also different from routine lab submissions. If the bomb squad has the convenience of hand carriage, it will proceed as any other submission. However, it is long-distance submissions where rather extraordinary procedures applied.

If the ATF lab system is selected to conduct analysis, it is somewhat simplified. ATF labs do not directly accept submissions from outside their agency. Instead, transfer the evidence to a local ATF agent, who will assign the evidence an ATF case number in order to assist and arrange delivery to the appropriately located lab.

The FBI do accept submissions from outside agencies, as it functions as the nation's open access crime lab. However, explosive material cannot be routinely shipped by either postal service or courier services. To overcome this impediment, the FBI lab retains a supply of special containers designed and approved for common carrier delivery of minute amounts of explosive materials or other highly reactive items. To arrange shipment, first contact the Materials and Devices Section at the FBI lab in Quantico, Virginia. After explaining your case to them, they will arrange to send a shipping unit to you. Package the sample, place it in the container, and enclose the appropriate cover letter for the FBI, then return it to the FBI laboratory using a courier service.

The bomb disposal field does not deal with explosive evidence in near the quantities or frequency that, for example, street patrol or narcotics investigators deal with drugs. However, when confronted with explosive evidence, the bomb technician will be more intimately involved in its collection, storage, transportation, and eventual disposal than any other single component of the law enforcement community with such evidence.

10

Documentation and Record Keeping

THE MAD BOMBER

On November 18, 1940, the NYPD bomb squad responded to a pipe bomb at the Con Ed headquarters facilities. Interrupted by the Second World War, this would mark the first of some 33 responses attributed by the press to the Mad Bomber of New York. Over a 16-year period that spanned two generations of bomb technicians, the NYPD bomb squad rendered safe or conducted follow-up investigations on each of these incidents. Through careful render-safe, evidence collection, cutting edge psychological assistance, dogged shoe-leather detective work, and maintenance of quality records, in 1957 they identified a paranoid former Con Ed employee, George Metesky, as the perpetrator. Metesky was determined to be insane, and spent 16 years in a state insane asylum.

Like any other investigatory field, bomb disposal generates reports. However, it generates more than a typical investigative position. Along with case reports, there are Bomb Arson Tracking System (BATS) reports, evidence and magazine logs, an array of records maintained for regulatory purposes, often budget and purchasing records, and even internal logs and reports.

Before continuing, consider some general aspects of records management. Every state has different laws on regulating public records, such as criminal records, photos, videos, personnel records, and many or most other forms of governmentally generated records. Some states like Florida, have very open public access to records; in Florida, almost all records not defined as active criminal investigation or active criminal intelligence are open to public inspection. Other states have much more limited access to records. It is important to understand your jurisdiction's laws, especially as a unit often maintains records such as x-ray images.

Record retention is another area to be aware of. Again, every state has its own retention schedules. For example, Florida requires criminal records be maintained until the statute of limitations has expired, while personnel records such as training records must be maintained for 50 years after the employee's separation.

Record security must also be considered. Law enforcement accreditation standards mandate that certain records be maintained in secure storage. These include original criminal investigative records and personnel records. For most units, a locking file cabinet will be suffice to provide secure storage for such records that they deem to maintain.

For many units, it may be most beneficial to maintain only copies of records and store all originals as part of the appropriate agency recordkeeping. For example, especially with digital photography, all photos and x-rays are stored as part of the agency's case photo records, while individual training records are shipped to the personnel unit for storage. This removes the unit from being considered as a record-keeping site, and thus not responsible for dissemination or purging of records.

Film-based x-rays pose a more complex storage dilemma. If positive print x-rays are used, then these comprise the original document, and hence should be treated as such. Whether 3½ × 4½ or 8 × 10 prints, they are an odd size for normal storage. One option is to first digitally scan the originals, providing a backup image, for either maintaining the original print in a dedicated file or by filing with the agencies other original records. Maintenance of 8 × 10 negative film is more complex. First, it must be ensured that the film has been properly treated to guarantee it will not degrade in storage. Envelopes or clear acetate sleeves should be used to individually store the transparencies that are delicate. They should then be stored in a dedicated file, observing agency film storage protocols.

The movement into digital photography, while initially causing some problems to the criminal justice system, has ultimately eased storage and retrieval of photos, while significantly lowering expenses. Most agencies have established procedures for the storage of digital images. These procedures may be applied to all images, photographs, and radiographic images.

Perhaps, the most important aspect of storage of digital images is to ensure all original images are maintained as such. For printing or viewing where manipulation is needed, a copy should be made of the original image, and the copy be used for all such manipulations. Thus the credibility of the original image is preserved.

Although not an operational record like an incident report, the ATF BATS is a valuable record system. Being the latest incarnation of information submission for the BDC, it provides a multifaceted data management program. BATS provides major improvements over previous BDC reporting systems. As an online system, it eases the actual submission, storage, and dissemination of information. By providing direct access to all qualified bomb commanders, technicians, and investigators, it simplifies reporting and makes research of the database for investigative purposes accessible to all potential users.

It has also improved on the nature of information stored. Details of devices encountered have been expanded, which are especially valuable for an investigator attempting to link to other incidents. It also permits even more in-depth logging of administrative information on activity, whether actual device responses, special events support, outreach training, squad training, etc. The bomb squad commander thus enjoys better documentation of unit activity; moreover, BDC, HDS, NBSCAB, and others with access have a more complete view of each agency's activities as well as the overall picture.

In order to maintain accreditation through NBSCAB, the bomb squad must maintain training records. These include individual technician training, such as certificates of formal training related to the field, and a record of all in-service training conducted, including description of each training session and annotation of which team members attended the session. The commander needs to organize these records such that they are easily referenced by the FBI SABT conducting accreditation inspection for NBSCAB.

Many states require registration of x-ray equipment and individual dosimeter records for each user of radiographic equipment. Dosimeter analysis reports may be issued on monthly, quarterly, annual, or other periods. These should be maintained accessible for regulatory inspection, along with the permit or registration, a copy of specifications for each model of x-ray machine in use, and copies of any service documents or reports.

Some jurisdictions exempt public safety from explosives licensing; others require it. Many teams also possess federal explosives licenses, to ease purchase of explosives. Copies of all licenses should be maintained, to provide ready reference for revelatory inspections and to show compliance to inspectors.

Previously the role of explosives magazines was discussed. The log for the magazine is a crucial document, open to regulators for inspection, supremely valuable in the event of theft or other loss of product, and important to permit the agency to both know its current inventory and prepare future budgeting. The log should be routinely updated; no product, including evidence, should be entered without full description and inventory. Likewise, every item removed, whether for agency use, lab evidence, or for destruction/disposal, must be logged out with a notation explaining its destination. Regulators state that one of the leading deficiencies noted in inspections are incomplete or inaccurate explosive inventories. Not only such recordkeeping may fall into regulatory fines, but may expose the agency to public criticism in the event of unreconciled records becoming public information.

Although not a form of recordkeeping, one final compendium of paper is valuable to the bomb squad. This is the maintenance of a reference library. This library should include a wide variety of materials as possible, including the following:

- Commercial/academic explosive books
- Catalogs
- Military manuals
- Equipment manuals
- So-called "underground" explosives and bomb books
- Hazardous materials references
- Video and other training materials

The library has significant value to the team. For general reference, training, and similar purposes, a library has great utility. For identification of materials, such as commercial explosives and military ordnance, the books are invaluable. Investigatively, books and catalogs have great value in identifying componentry. Indeed, many technicians have located identical designs to a device by reviewing "underground" books, providing important clues to follow-up on and search for during subsequent searches.

11

Looking Ahead

It was not very long ago the bomb disposal was considered by public safety administrators and the greater governmental sphere as a minor component. The assignment of CBR response to the bomb community increased its value somewhat; the events of 9/11/01 were very significant. Where may the future lead?

On the one hand, we have entered the age of terrorism. Extremist Muslim groups have demonstrated a high degree of patience; one book, *1000 Years for Revenge,* aptly chose this title from their concept of conquest. At the same time, terrorism has emerged as the tool of disillusioned peoples or causes, who either lack the patience to work within the political system, or who wish to impose their will on an overwhelmingly opposed majority. These groups include extremists from environmental and animal rights organizations, radical abortion opponents, a variety of extremist religious sects, neo-Nazis, racial supremacy organizations, nationalistic ethnic groups, and a variety of minor, extremist political fronts.

Criminal bombings will continue and increase as well. Until society determines a satisfactory solution to drug abuse, the profits to be made ensure a continuing criminal presence. Narco terrorists, many of which evolved from terrorist groups and some of which continue to receive economic support from terrorist organizations, find explosives as convenient tools for imposing discipline, warring with rivals, and confronting the justice system. Lesser drug syndicates find similar value in explosives as well as for use as booby-traps to protect their production facilities.

The fluid evolution of drug manufacturer also continues to involve the bomb disposal field. Whether 1980s manufacture of cocaine, the shift to production of TCP and designer drugs, or current manufacture of methamphetamines, the explosively volatile nature of these chemical processes continue to involve bomb technicians in the safety aspects of investigations.

Traditional organized crime will also continue to use the bomb as a tool and weapon. It's now truly international appearance, with Russian and Eastern European groups, Sicilian Mafia, American Mafia, Latin American organizations, and a variety of Asian groups have increased the presence of sophisticated criminal activity and brought more into conflict.

Outlaw motorcycle gangs have grown and spread internationally. Involved in a variety of drug enterprises, theft, white slavery, and numerous semi-legitimate fields, they often turn to the bomb in matters of discipline or conflict.

Juveniles have long been drawn to explosives for experimentation and minor vandalism. Today, this has expanded to encompass almost terroristic activities. Information access such as the internet, mixed with misguided interpretation of television and motion pictures, has often fueled both the knowledge and the impetus to use bombs.

The information revolution has also aided in the growth of bombs. Not that long ago, knowledge to make and use explosives was a very limited commodity. However, the growth and ease of publishing and its dissemination opened the floodgates. The internet has since thrown them wide, with information available from an ever-growing list of sites. Some of the information is highly accurate, published by or from military, industrial, or academic sources. Terrorist groups, providing training to their members as well as any other interested reader, openly disseminate information. Many other sites publish a variety of information, plans, formulas, and recipes, their quality varying from excellent to inaccurate collections of hearsay.

Purse strings loosened for the field beginning with President Clinton's issuance of PDD-39, and the purse strings seemed to be cast completely open following the events of September and October 2001. However, times change, and so do funding sources.

The first change was an expected one—a loss of interest by society and changes in government priorities. In public safety, beyond routine, daily needs, most projects look like a rhythm on an oscilloscope. Community policing, driving under the influence (DUI), forensic science support, economic crimes, special victims, etc., have all seen funding reach highs, then drop, sometimes to again rise, sometimes to plateau, sometimes to flat line. This began to affect funding for bomb and WMD response toward the end of the first decade of the twenty-first century.

At the same time, a significant economic downturn seriously impacted the entire American, if not global, society. Not only have private businesses failed or had to cut back, the loss of tax revenue has resulted in government also trimming its services. While some jurisdictions have seen personnel cuts, most often cuts have come to training budgets, equipment budgets, and overtime.

Bomb disposal, as a technical field, must invest heavily in training to maintain currency. When training budgets are cut, the opportunity for attendance at specialized training dwindles. While commanders may remind administrators that accreditation requires each bomb technician to attend 16 h in-service training each month, 40 h of formal training annually, and to recertify at HDS every 36 months, agency heads may ignore such pleas in consideration of the bigger picture.

Commanders and technicians need to consider priorities in training and looking beyond conventional training resources. HDS basic training requires a total of six weeks of a student's time, with all transportation and per diem costs on the agency. Thus, it is important to ensure new or replacement technician positions are adequately funded for attendance. HDS recertification and specialized training at HDS is fully funded, except for salaries, by the FBI, as are specialized training programs at ATF NTC. Here are a variety of top-end programs at a cost as low as it can be imagined.

IABTI training—chapter, regional, and international—requires an obligation to fund attendance. Sometimes meetings may be close enough to permit "day tripping," where the agency's expenditure is salary and transportation. Other times, it may require careful budgeting of time and funds by commander to permit one or two technicians to attend a meeting, representing their agency by their attendance. Indeed, shared rooms will pull down overhead, if vehicle travel is appropriate use of one instead of individual units, and perhaps assigning each tech vendor contacts for researching equipment for future acquisition projects. Also valuable—the IABTI international conferences are filmed and videos are available for sale. Those programs of interest for later viewing as part of in-service training may be purchased, adding to the depth of the team's library.

When economic times are good, it is easy to forget that a professional has a personal obligation to maintain and upgrade knowledge. Techs may, if denied by their agency due to fiscal concerns, be able to attend on their own, possibly even writing off costs as professional development.

Indeed, many techs have turned attendance at IABTI functions into family vacations. Many venues are chosen for their value as tourist destinations; international, regional, and even some chapter conferences provide spousal schedules, providing families day activities while their technicians attend the conference.

It is not out of the question to seek an agency's sharing of costs. Expenses are usually salary, transportation, registration, and per diem. Many agencies will look favorably on sharing costs, and appreciate the professionalism of its officer who is willing to invest in his/her training.

Since the IABTI is a truly international organization, it tends to schedule conferences around the globe. While most are in the United States (as are the majority of members), meetings have been conducted in Australia, Canada, and Romania. While an agency may look upon international travel as extravagant, careful research by commander may show it to be competitive. Early planning may permit booking a flight reservation at rates no greater than cross-country flights. Since the IABTI strives to locate venues that are quality yet reasonable, transportation is the greatest variable facing the technician.

Training is not the only facet of the faces cutbacks due to budget or social parties. Other than criminalistics, bomb disposal is the most equipment heavy aspect of police service (although it may well be considered average or below average in the fire service). The tools of bomb disposal run a wide gamut, from common hand tools to complex robotics to highly specialized transport vessels.

Post 9/11, many agencies took advantage of grants to upgrade their teams, or were the beneficiaries. Thus many medium to large agency teams currently sport custom response vehicles, TCVs, adequate numbers of bomb suits, digital x-ray, and often advanced diagnostics and tools. However, many smaller agency teams were unable to take advantage of the grants. Facing economic difficulties, many agencies are cutting back on not only new acquisitions, but also replacement of worn or obsolete equipment.

A commander must prioritize needs. To maintain national accreditation, a team must have on hand the mandatory safety equipment originally set forth by STB 87-4 and now required through NBSCAB guidelines. Thus while an electronic CBRNE detection meter may be a useful upgrade, replacing obsolete bomb suits is a necessity.

First, recognize some items that cannot be improvised. Today's bomb suits are carefully engineered to maximize protective value. Very few sources even produce x-ray equipment with the level of mobility needed by bomb disposal; rapidly approaching extinction of film, and especially of inexpensive film, dictates digital as being the only viable method of recording radiographs.

Many items may be obtained relatively inexpensively. Tools may be found in the evidence room or obtained locally commercially. While purchasing, it is often a better investment to spend a little more and invest in quality tools, especially from lines with lifetime guarantees. Many items may be locally obtained—breakaway pulleys and other hardware from an industrial supplier, hardware, sporting goods, or other local sources. Here, the highest quality is not an imperative—it will not be supporting a human as would be ropes used by SWAT or rescue. Indeed, any operational user, such as SWAT or fire rescue, discards their rope after any operational use as a safety measure, and may be a source of material.

Although the transport vessel is not mandated under accreditation standards, it is for a team to be classified under DHS regional bomb squad criteria. Although TCV is a wonderful useful tool, it is a very high dollar piece of kit, as well as a much more limited capacity than an open design. A manufactured open-top design can be bought for one-fifth of the price of a TCV; if local capabilities are present, an improvised model for much less than that.

While some agencies equip each technician with a fully equipped van or a SUV, most use a dedicated vehicle to respond their bomb equipment. Custom manufactured units are highly convenient, address many potential working situations, and have an expected life beyond their expected obsolescence. However, they are also very expensive at the outset. Many agencies will continue to improvise, until the opportunity to upgrade comes along.

The improvisation may take many forms—a retired ambulance, a donated delivery truck, or a heavy-duty chassis mated to a commercial, off-the-shelf utility body. While the custom truck, amortized over its potential life, may well have a lower per year cost than the improvised locally built rig, the lower upfront costs of the latter designs make them affordable.

Items such as robots are not a cheap acquisition. Where once retired military units were obtained by teams, the role of EOD in the war on terrorism has stifled many of those actions. However, the multiple capabilities that a robot may perform provide ways to obtain fiscal support. An agency may budget the robot as a support tool for SWAT as well as a bomb squad piece of kit, permitting cost to be expensed across the agency. Similarly, it's capabilities to support fire and hazmat may permit multiple agencies to jointly invest in the acquisition of a UGV.

The previous chapter looked at the role of improvisation and equipping a bomb squad. In tight fiscal times, improvisation takes on greater value. It is easy for many to look upon locally devised as less than professional. Many prefer store-bought equipment to avoid liability. However, locally constructed equipment can provide many benefits. Obviously, it can save valuable funds to be expended on other necessary tools. It may be the only source for items that are not available from commercial sources. As to liability, the greatest avenue of liability faced in this field is not from product design; it is from improper application whether of a tool or technique.

Two outstanding examples come to mind. In the 1990s, the Los Angeles Police Bomb Squad recognized a shortcoming. They needed a robot capable of physically manipulating a vehicle containing explosives. No such tool existed. They designed a radio control system for a large forklift strong enough to lift and remove a small truck from a scene for delivery to a location more capable of withstanding a blast, and freeing up congested urban streets.

Also, in the late 1990s, the FBI funded Philadelphia police bomb technician William Bobridge, permitting him to compile a collection of information on improvised tools and then publish it to the nation's bomb squads via CD. The program recognized the value of locally fabricated tools to the bomb team, and help share ideas from across the country among the many teams who may not have thought of a solution another squad had developed.

Another consideration is future recruitment. For the overwhelming number of American bomb teams, bomb disposal is a collateral duty, with primary duties consuming most if not all assigned work time. Although training and response callouts are compensated, many are not comfortable with the time demands on their personal time, or the constraints in place on off-duty activities and details.

Bomb disposal is also a highly technical aspect of public safety, especially of police work. As our society becomes more of a cyberculture, the kids who played with chemistry kits, built radios, tore down and upgraded auto engines, made their own clothes, cooked, etc., are being replaced by generations highly skilled behind the keyboard but not in its construction beyond part swapping. Thus commanders may find themselves viewing tactical personnel, crime scene investigators (CSI), and others from technical fields for recruitment as bomb technicians.

Because of the role of terrorism, military EOD as a source of recruitment is dwindling. Even Vietnam War era EOD did not have exposure to IEDs as do today's techs. However, many more are often completing a 20- or 30-year career; many viable candidates may opt to fully retire at that time. Further, although some agencies will recruit EOD directly into bomb squads, many require several years of general experience before permitting application to specialized positions. Indeed, considering the investigative nature of the bomb tech's position, it is important to ensure a military recruit is comfortable with that aspect when recruiting a member.

The past 40 years have seen the assimilation of women into public safety, especially police service. Amazingly, few have sought careers with bomb squads. Psychologically, women have strong features for application as bomb technicians: detail-oriented, nimble, and capable of imaginative perception. While the female body does lack upper body strength, the bomb suit, the only truly heavy aspect of the job, is supported by the shoulders, and not a test of upper body strength. Otherwise, weight handling is of little consequence to the technician. The sisterhood of female officers is an untapped, valuable potential.

Many consider the work of the bomb technician as insanely dangerous. While it is a badge of honor to maintain this as a mysterious aspect of the job, it is also important to explain that the bomb tech undertakes a calculated, rather than reckless, risk. Explosives leave no room for reckless behavior; bomb technicians approach their work as highly trained technical specialists. Compared to a traffic stop, a disturbance, an alarm

Figure 11.1 It is important to always remember.

response, or a structure fire, the technician is much safer, being able to apply established procedures steeped in safety to their operations. To recruit future technicians, they must understand that job may be dangerous, as with any other aspect of public safety, but that a knowledgeable practitioner is the safest practitioner.

However, practitioners must recognize that the work has inherent hazards, and that to be successful we must remain cognizance of that. In some quarters there is a concept, a self-deception, that the work can be done with little risk. As the saying goes, if it was easy, anyone could do it. There would be no need for a bomb technician, a risk taker. To be successful, not only render safe but also exploit for as much intelligence and evidence as possible, requires an educated professional who can calculate the risk faced at each individual incident, and determine the safest, most solution to applied to each specific case. Or, as the tagline of one well-respected bomb technician's e-mail states, "You knew the job was dangerous when you took it" (Figure 11.1).

12

Case Study I

Mass Murder

At about 11:00 AM, April 20, 1999, an IED exploded at a rural location of Jefferson County, Colorado. This explosion came to be the initial action that soon involved almost all bomb disposal and investigative resources in the greater Denver, Colorado, region for days.

It was later determined that this bombing was a diversion, to draw public safety resources away from Columbine High School. At about 11:15 AM, Dylan Klebold and Eric Harris, two seniors at Columbine High School, began a rampage through the halls of the school. When finished, both perpetrators, 12 students, and one teacher lay dead, 23 wounded, and 130 others had a variety of injuries due to the panic during evacuation (Figure 12.1).

Columbine High School sent shockwaves to the American law-enforcement field. Previously, training had been given for arriving officers to establish a perimeter until arrival of SWAT personnel on who would enter and pursue. Since then, the concept of active shooter has resulted in responding officers forming teams to immediately engage perpetrators, an attempt to minimize innocent casualties. The events of April 20, 1999 have also affected bomb disposal in many ways, with some aspects even now, 16 years later, still being developed.

Deputies and fire units had just arrived at the diversionary explosion when 911 lines were lighting up with reports of shooting and explosions at Columbine High School. Responding units from a wide variety of city, county, and state agencies evacuated students, staff, and faculty,

Figure 12.1 An aerial FBI photo of Columbine High School. Emergency response vehicles and personnel on the left.

exchanged fire with the perpetrators, and eventually were able to tactically affect a clearance operation of the school, determining the two shooters were dead by their own hand.

The local Jefferson County Sheriff's Office bomb squad had early on realized the conditions would require greater manpower rather than they alone could muster. Soon, they were joined by bomb squads from Arapahoe County Sheriff's Office, Denver Police, and an FBI bomb technician, with a total of 14 technicians. Additionally, Jefferson and Arapahoe County bomb squads had seven apprentice technicians, who were joined by ATF agents in support and search roles. Although the scene was within Jefferson County's jurisdiction, the technicians formed a unified bomb team, and chose Denver's senior technician, who was also the senior and most experienced technician on scene, as its leader. Meanwhile, the Douglas County Sheriff's office bomb squad remained in reserve, available to respond to any incidents coming in from the response region left naked by the necessary response to this massacre.

It was quickly recognized that the scene was littered with unexploded IEDs. Initial surveys and intelligence determined that there were CO_2 cylinder devices, referred to as crickets, one-pound propane bottles with attached crickets as initiation systems, a pipe bomb, and a Molotov cocktail with a cricket initiator. Further, the PBI of the diversionary devices some 3 ½ miles off-campus determined they were fuzed using alarm clocks.

As a death scene, the coroner had jurisdiction until all bodies were removed. At the coroner's direction, bodies could not be removed until the examination was done. As a result, devices in the shooter's pockets were not discovered until the next day, at which time the coroner called for bomb techs to search bodies prior to further examination.

On April 20, as the bomb squads began to search the school building to recover devices (Figures 12.2 and 12.3), ATF agents were searching the parking lot for devices and to identify the suspects' vehicles. Upon locating Klebold's car, the agent immediately saw it contained Molotov cocktails with crickets. When joined by bomb technicians, a timing device was also observed. When Harris's car was located, the backseat contents of his car were found to be concealed by a blanket. As a result, school activities were halted, and attention was focused on rendering safe the contents of the vehicles. Two potato guns, 7 pipe bombs, 11 containers of gasoline, and two 20-pound propane tanks were recovered and rendered safe. Both time devices had been set to explode at noon, but had failed to function. Had the devices functioned as designed, at noon, the area would have been congested with evacuees, police, and rescue personnel, and casualties would be been numerous.

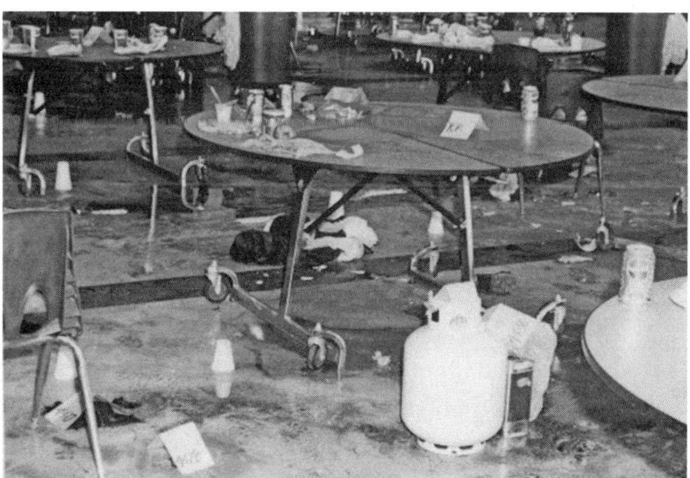

Figure 12.2 Five gallon propane cylinder device recovered unexploded.

Figure 12.3 Pipe bomb recovered embedded in a wall.

The crickets and pipe bombs used "strike anywhere" matches to initiate pyrotechnic fuse; the bomb techs devised a simple method to make these safe, permitting transfer to the Denver bomb trailer pending destruction. However, that first evening, several pipe bombs, not yet rendered safe, initiated while being placed into the vessel resulted in several exploding, and 15 IEDs were blown out of the trailer; this caused a harrowing experience but did not result in any damage or injuries. The devices were then collected and again secured in the trailer.

On the second day, April 21, the team was split into three operating teams; one to continue clearing the school, one to assist with search warrants at Klebold and Harris's homes, and one to conduct RSP and disposal operations at a safe range. However, the presence of explosive canines resulted in their assignment to the school, and reassignment of that bomb team to inspect the parking areas.

As these operations progressed, it began to shift from a tactical bomb response to an evidentiary response. A number of and variety of devices had functioned in the school, and these required PBI, as had the off-site diversionary devices. The search warrants resulted in recovery of additional devices and components. During RSP and disposal operations, devices were documented, lab samples were collected, and other evidence kept secured.

By the third day (April 22), it was felt that the operation had become an evidential and crime scene support one. That was, until the discovery of a second, intact, time-initiated 20-pound propane device, concealed in a pack. Several devices had functioned in this area, including an identical one, during the events of April 20; so the area was contaminated with explosive residue. It was also important to understand that a canine, only trained in search for unweathered explosives, may be confused or overwhelmed when confronted by a postblast scene. To properly function in a postblast scenario requires additional training for the dog to discriminate residue from gross unexploded materials.

As a result, the scene was shut down until this device could be rendered safe. But then another question occurred; if this device was overlooked, could the previous search be trusted? As a result, bomb technicians proceeded to clear 1500 student backpacks and 1900 lockers.

Over a three-day period, a team of 14 technicians, 7 apprentices, and a number of ATF agents handled

- 59 intact IEDs
- 30 explosive devices in the school
- 2 exploded diversionary devices
- 2 vehicle searches
- 2 search warrants
- 1500 backpacks
- 1900 lockers
- 15 body clearances

Additionally, at one time Denver bomb techs had to pull off and respond to suspicious items at a school in their city. Finally, the Douglas County Sheriff's bomb squad had been intentionally omitted from the response; they stayed on mutual aid to handle any responses in the Metropolitan Denver area.

Responding bomb technicians learned a number of valuable lessons.

- Prior to an event, neighboring teams must establish liaison and train jointly
- Need for bomb techs to cross train with SWAT and on active shooter response
- Identify additional mutual aid bomb squads; this incident depleted the area of bomb squads and exhausted the available technician pool

- Have a senior technician in the incident command post as an information pipeline and to aid command's understanding of bomb disposal
- Logistical support of food and water for technicians
- Rest and rehabilitation and mandatory shutdown times to permit sleep for technicians
- Ensure coroner/medical examiner and criminalistics teams understand need for bomb squads to secure the scene for personnel safety before investigative activity
- Use apprentice bomb techs for photo work and evidence logging
- Incorporate ICS/IMS
- Determine jurisdiction and establish a bomb scene commander
- Recognize that canines cannot do everything in regards to search and clearance
- Use available FBI and ATF resources—SABT, CES, NRT, ERT, etc.
- Assign a scribe to log and document for each team
- Prepare with a standby team or standby agency to respond to hoax and panic calls generated in the area stripped of local services by the call

The events of April 20, 1999, ushered in a new era for bomb response operations. To this day, tactics, techniques, and procedures are being developed to provide for successful responses. In the case of Columbine, the bomb squads serving the Metropolitan Denver area successfully confronted a situation with a variety of previously unencountered circumstances. Ninety devices were dealt with as either RSP or PBI, various components were collected and made safe, and most importantly, a major scene was made safe for investigators. Their success speaks to both their previous relationships, and an ability to carefully think through challenges before physically confronting them.

13

Case Study 2

Explosive and Ordnance Cache

While most cases unfold rather expeditiously, occasionally one continues to evolve, or even reappear long after arrests, convictions, and incarceration are complete. In 1990, Federal agents were investigating a smuggling group from Palm Beach County, Florida. When arrested, several defendants, anxious to obtain better terms from federal prosecutors, revealed that they had obtained significant supplies of explosives and ordnance from corrupt members of the military. This aspect of the case was referred to ATF for follow-up, which then brought in the services of the Palm Beach County Sheriff's Office (PBSO) bomb squad. Based on the information investigators gleaned from the cooperating defendants, it was determined that a number of caches have been secreted in various locations. Many had been placed in five-gallon plastic buckets, with lids snapped in place. Some were located buried at a garden nursery; others were recovered from the ground under a child's sandbox in a residential backyard. The total recovery (Figures 13.1 through 13.7) included the following:

- 91 pounds of Mark 35 satchel charges (composition C-4)
- 23 M67 hand grenades
- 3 TH3 incendiary grenades
- 12 pounds of HDX explosive
- An unspecified number of M72 light-weight anti-tank weapon (LAW) rockets

Figure 13.1 Five-gallon bucket containing satchel charges of C-4, 1990. (From USDOJ, ATF.)

No charges were brought; the government honored its agreement with the smuggler defendants. The military was unable to trace the recovered material to any specific bases, and further prosecutions were not possible. The US Army 766th EOD Company took grenades and LAW rockets into custody, while the bulk explosives were turned over to PBSO's bomb squad for its operational use. Fast forwarding to 2008, a PBSO patrol unit, when conducting an auto-theft recovery from a canal outside of West Palm Beach, found a M72 lying on the canal bank. A quick look found a second one, further down the bank, at water's edge. PBSO's bomb squad responded, and, as usual, notified both ATF and FBI of the recovery. The US Air Force 482nd Civil Engineering Squadron EOD Flight responded from Homestead Air Reserve Base to take custody of the rockets. Due to the similarity of lot numbers to those in the 1990 case, thoughts quickly focused on this being an attempt to dispose of some of the materials. As a result, the FBI provided a dive team to search the canal. Nothing was found in the canal. (Note: South Florida canals are muddy, silty, and the water would be dark brown

Figure 13.2 Various grenades recovered in 1990. (From USDOJ, ATF.)

Figure 13.3 Excavation of five-gallon buckets used to protect and conceal cache, 1990. (From USDOJ, ATF.)

Figure 13.4 Recovered rocket from LAW, 1990. (From USDOJ, ATF.)

Figure 13.5 Collection of C-4 recovered from cache, 1990. (Courtesy of Palm Beach County Sheriff's Office.)

Figure 13.6 LAW rockets and satchel charges of C-4 placed on ATF trailer prior to removal to safe storage, 1990. (From USDOJ, ATF.)

Figure 13.7 Plume from disposal shot of LAW rockets on demolition range, 1990. (From USDOJ, ATF.)

with almost zero visibility.) However, an FBI supervisor found detonating cord sticking out of the ground; it was found to lead to a buried Mark 35 C-4 satchel charge. The Miami-Dade Police Department (MDPD) bomb squad was then requested to assist. MDPD has an ARS radio control-modified skid steer loader in its toolkit. This giant robot provided a tool to permit safe remote excavation of the canal banks. No further material was found buried on the banks in this area. With the continued concerns that the canal could contain deteriorating ordnance and high explosives, the FBI next swept the water with side scan sonar. Nothing specific was observed, but unknown hits were later determined to be trash. The FBI then requested the US Navy EOD, all certified divers, detachment from Mayport Naval Air Station, Jacksonville Florida, to conduct another underwater search. This search recovered more C-4 and an additional LAW rocket from the muddy bottom. However, the EOD techs explained they could not certify the area clear of hazards; visibility and silty mud prevented it. The Lake Worth Drainage District, which operates the canal in question, then conducted a dredge of the canal. This resulted in the recovery of C-4 from the silt of the canal bottom. The Lake Worth Drainage District stated that they could dam off the area in question, to permit pumping of that canal segment empty. Once dammed, Palm Beach County Fire Rescue used two canal pumps to drain the canal. Lake Worth Drainage District then carefully excavated canal bottom mud, one scoop at a time; a search team of PBSO and West Palm Beach Police Department bomb techs, plus ATF agents, then sifted the mud, washing it through large plastic field crates from vegetable farms; the crates acted like sifting screens, letting silt flow out while holding larger debris for examination. As a result, one LAW rocket and about 100 pounds of C-4 were recovered. The combined team then transported the deteriorated materials to a disposal site, where they were destroyed by counter charge. Despite the fact that this segment of canal had been cleared, ATF, FBI, and PBSO are not convinced that more deteriorating cachets are not hidden around rural areas of Palm Beach County. Thus the case, while not active, remains on-the-shelf for further reference, whenever military materials are recovered (Figures 13.8 through 13.19).

SUMMARY

This case emphasizes a number of points:

- The need for a close working relationship among various components of the bomb and hazmat response fields: In 1990 and 2008,

ATF, FBI, and PBSO worked shoulder to shoulder; 1990s Army involvement was replaced in 2008 changing DOD assignments to Air Force EOD. 2008 also saw a number of others—Navy EOD for divers/bomb techs, MDPD bomb squad to lend a piece of relatively unique equipment, and bomb technicians from West Palm Beach Police Department, whose presence added knowledgeable personnel to aid in safe search operations. Further, close relations with the Palm Beach County Fire Rescue Special Operations (Hazmat) team provided hazmat on site for support during the hazardous manual searches.

- The need for dive-trained bomb technicians: Evidence trained divers are highly proficient at underwater search, documentation, and evidence recovery; however, they lack the knowledge and confidence to search for and recover deteriorating explosive materials, especially in black water. Since then, PBSO has joined a number of bomb squads with port responsibilities, and has upgraded its techs to be dive trained and equipped.

Figure 13.8 LAW rocket recovered from bank of canal, 2009. (Courtesy of Palm Beach County Sheriff's Office.)

- A working relationship with environmental authorities: PBSO bomb squad has a long history of close cooperation with the Florida Department of Environmental Protection (FDEP), the state's environmental regulatory agency. This was further strengthened when the sheriff's office placed the Environmental Investigations Section under the Bomb and Arson Unit. To shut down the canal requires the authority of, and oversight by, FDEP. The long relationship between the bomb squad and FDEP assured the regulators the operation would be professionally conducted and environmentally responsible.
- Awareness of new technology: The FBI dive team was able to provide access to side scanning sonar; while not fully successful, it did provide targeting of questionable areas on the canal bottom. Familiarity with other teams' capabilities permitted PBSO to know of MDPD's radio control skid steer loader. Use of this tool permitted excavation of canal bank without exposing either search crews or heavy equipment operators to the potential hazards presented by improperly striking buried item.

Figure 13.9 LAW rockets recovered in 2009. Note they were recovered extended, in firing condition. (Courtesy of Palm Beach County Sheriff's Office.)

Figure 13.10 LAW projectile, 2009. (Courtesy of Palm Beach County Sheriff's Office.)

Figure 13.11 LAW rocket recovered in weeds along the edge of canal, 2009. (Courtesy of Palm Beach County Sheriff's Office.)

Figure 13.12 Diver and line tenders during canal search, 2009. (Courtesy of Palm Beach County Sheriff's Office.)

Figure 13.13 LAW recovered from canal waters, 2009. (Courtesy of Palm Beach County Sheriff's Office.)

Figure 13.14 MDPD robotic skid steer loader, preparing to begin excavation of canal bank, 2009. (Courtesy of Palm Beach County Sheriff's Office.)

Figure 13.15 Palm Beach County long-arm dredge used in removing muck from canal bottom, 2009. (Courtesy of Palm Beach County Sheriff's Office.)

Figure 13.16 Dredge removing muck from canal bottom, 2009. (Courtesy of Palm Beach County Sheriff's Office.)

Figure 13.17 Team washes orange grove box of muck removed from canal bottom; this technique located various deteriorated satchel charges of C-4, 2009. (Courtesy of Palm Beach County Sheriff's Office.)

Figure 13.18 Deteriorated C-4 satchel charges and LAW rocket recovered from canal bottom, 2009. (Courtesy of Palm Beach County Sheriff's Office.)

Figure 13.19 Satchel charges prepared for destruction at demolition range, 2009. (Courtesy of Palm Beach County Sheriff's Office.)

14

Case Study 3

Postblast Investigation of a Clandestine Explosives Factory

On the evening of April 16, 2006, the incoming phone lines for the Palm Beach Sheriff's Office communications center lit up with reports of a structure exploding and burning in a suburban area of Lake Worth, Florida (Figures 14.1 and 14.2). As patrol deputies and Palm Beach County Fire Rescue (PBCoFR) arrived, they were greeted by the scene of a large, garage-like structure shattered, remains of a truck frame adjacent to it, acres littered with debris and small fires, with debris hanging from trees and scattered past a canal. PBCoFR established a defensive operation to contain fire from spreading to other structures, and all hunkered down until the PBSO bomb squad arrived.

Arriving bomb techs met with PBCoFR personnel, including their cohorts from the Special Operations Hazmat team. At this time the exact nature of the explosion was unknown; concerns had been raised whether it may be a methamphetamine lab, with additional chemical hazards present. Fires had been knocked down by this time. Special Operations had already begun air monitoring, with no hazards detected. As a result, it was determined that a team of bomb techs, suited up for Level B protection, would reconnoiter the scene to determine its actual nature.

The entry team quickly made two determinations. First, the area was littered with both debris and unexploded pyrotechnic explosive devices

Figure 14.1 Aerial view of scene; debris rained down over the property involved, across a canal, and neighbors on both sides of the canal. (Courtesy of Palm Beach County Sheriff's Office.)

Figure 14.2 Remains of garage/workshop building. (Courtesy of Palm Beach County Sheriff's Office.)

Figure 14.3 Debris—burned tubes and other device-making supplies. (Courtesy of Palm Beach County Sheriff's Office.)

(Figures 14.3 and 14.4). Secondly, badly damaged human remains were found among other debris.

These discoveries initiated a series of decisions. Additional investigative resources, including crime scene investigations, major crime/violent crime detectives, the Office of the Medical Examiner, and ATF were notified of the incident. Due to the late hour and inherent dangers of the scene, activity was suspended until the next morning, with the area secured by patrol deputies and standby firefighters. The following morning, bomb technicians and ATF agents began a sweep of the neighborhood. The sweep had multiple purposes—to document damage to structures through the neighborhood, to document and recover explosive devices scattered throughout the area, and to locate by canvass potential witnesses. Investigation continued at the location of the blast. Unexploded devices were collected and secured. The remains were removed by the MEO; due to body damage, and that at least one body part was recovered separate from the body, a sheriff's office canine, cross trained in cadaver search, was brought in. Through the dog and handler's efforts, other amputated and damaged parts were recovered. By the third day of the search, a team composed of PBSO bomb tech/divers, Fort Lauderdale Police Department

Figure 14.4 Damaged, unexploded device among scattered debris. (Courtesy of Palm Beach County Sheriff's Office.)

(FLPD) bomb tech/divers, and ATF dive qualified personnel conducted an underwater search of an adjacent canal. As a result, a number of intact and also many deteriorated devices were recovered; they were collected and secured for disposal. Meanwhile, the detectives had learned that occupants of the residence involved had given an acquaintance permission to park a motorhome on the property, adjacent to a workshop building. Their understanding was that he needed a place to both park and repair the RV. On the third day, the wife of the RV owner and presumed victim told investigators that her husband had a bay at a large storage facility; she had no idea what he used it for. She provided consent to search, and PBSO bomb squad and ATF agents undertook the search. As a result, cases of completed explosive devices were recovered, plus components (Figures 14.5 through 14.8). After documentation, the explosive materials were taken to a disposal site where they were disposed of by counter charge. To transport, it required PBSO's two TCV trailers, plus their top vent unit to safely move all the materials.

This investigation was ruled accidental; the lead was then transferred to ATF. In their investigation ATF identified a partner to the victim, who was prosecuted federally. An interesting aspect—while it appears the

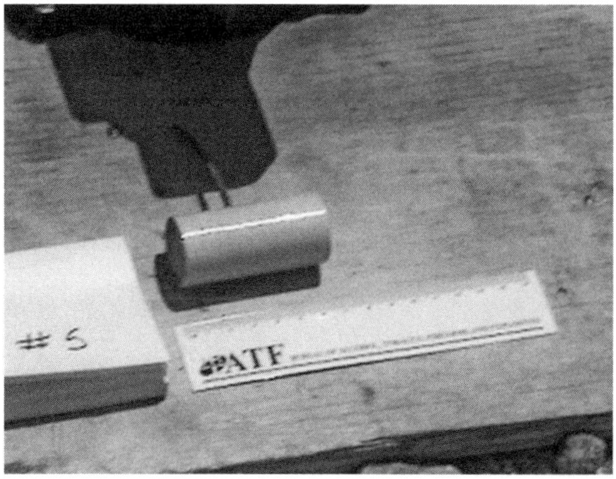

Figure 14.5 Device from among boxes recovered at storage facility. (Courtesy of Palm Beach County Sheriff's Office.)

Figure 14.6 Device being remotely disassembled using improvised cutting device. (Courtesy of Palm Beach County Sheriff's Office.)

Figure 14.7 Stack of boxes filled with devices as recovered at storage facility. (Courtesy of Palm Beach County Sheriff's Office.)

Figure 14.8 Boxes of devices at demolition range, prepared for destruction by countercharging. (Courtesy of Palm Beach County Sheriff's Office.)

individuals were marketing the illegal explosive devices, they also made a video. They had created an entire military set—ground warfare, aerial combat, and an aircraft carrier, using models and toys. Their video showed them using their devices to play war, destroying tanks, soldiers, planes, and ships—an interesting sport for some 40-year-olds!

SUMMARY

- An explosion investigation may be the result of a wide variety of causes. As in this case, actions must be first predicated on determining—safely—the full context of the blast.
- HME sites may be located anywhere—rural, urban, or as in this case, suburban. Especially for the latter two, safety considerations of evacuation or as in this case, shelter in place, must be considered, and implemented appropriately.
- Such an incident will become a multiagency response. Local law enforcement, response bomb techs, fire rescue, ATF, and the medical examiner will of necessity need to mesh. In this case, FLPD bomb squad divers also aided, fleshing out a bomb tech dive team consisting of PBSO bomb squad, ATF, and FLPD, with support from the sheriff's office and fire rescue dive teams.
- Two bomb techs, representing ATF and PBSO, attended the autopsy. They provided the ME with knowledge as bomb investigators, and took into custody fragmentation and other debris collected during the post-mortem examination.
- Transport of recovered energetics required all three transport vessels in the PBSO fleet. Had they needed more, they were familiar with municipal bomb squads, each of which could have provided a unit, plus adjacent counties that could also have lent support. However, if unable, it is valuable to reach back to the early HDS improvised transport vessel—a dump truck loaded with sand—as a safe fall back.
- The bomb squad worked closely with their crime scene unit. Bomb techs collected all energetic materials, while aiding their forensic counterparts in identifying debris or material of evidential value that was collected by CSI.

15

Case Study 4

International Delivery of a Chemical Device

On September 16, 1996, a maintenance man at an apartment complex in Hollywood, Florida, while investigating a tenant complaint, recognized the odor and leakage from the apartment above as human putrefaction. The responding Hollywood police officers entered the second floor dwelling, where they found a decomposing body and signs indicating construction of an IED. They retreated and requested the Broward Sheriff's Office (BSO) Bomb and Arson Squad. As soon as bomb techs arrived, they recognized that the scene was heavily contaminated due to advanced body decomposition. Prior to units being equipped for hazmat response, they requested material support from the BSO crime scene unit, which delivered a variety of blood-borne pathogen protective equipment. Safely dressed out, the bomb techs began their examination of the apartment. Upon entry, the techs took note of the victim, a naked white male with a gunshot wound to the head. It would quickly be determined to be self-inflicted. A video camcorder, on a tripod, aimed at the victim, was soon relieved of its cassette tape; this and a stack of tapes were turned over to Hollywood investigators, who quickly began to review the tapes. As the bomb techs examined the scene, they determined there were no intact devices or current threats. However, they did determine a chemical device had been built. Based upon the scene investigation by the BSO bomb technicians, and video reviews by Hollywood detectives, a disturbing tale unwound. The deceased had been obsessed with Björk, a singer originally from Iceland, then residing in Great Britain (Figure 15.1). His obsession

Figure 15.1 Actress/singer Björk at the 2001 Golden Globe Awards at the Beverly Hilton Hotel, January 2001. (From Shutterstock: Paul Smith/Featureflash.)

took a dark and dangerous turn when he learned she was romantically involved with a black musician. His obsession became a racially motivated, envious hate.

A total of 22 h of videotape had been recovered. Those tapes documented his experimentation and then construction of a chemical release device, designed with the intent of disfiguring his intended victim with an acid spray—all of this work conducted while naked. By carefully researching Björk, he had learned the name of her favorite book. Obtaining a hard copy edition of the book, he carefully hollowed it out. He then constructed a pressurized chemical release system designed to spray into the face of the person opening the book. In building the device, he was careful to make the new contents match the weight of the removed pages, all to prevent suspicion that could undo his plans. However, his plan was undone—by timing. Upon completing the device and packaging it, he dressed and delivered it to a post office, mailing it to her London address. He then returned to his apartment, undressed, turned on the video, and committed suicide. Four days later, decomposition alerted people to his death. As soon as investigators learned from the video of his plan, contact was made with the British authorities. The package was found at a postal facility in the UK, waiting to be delivered. Instead, bomb technicians rendered it safe, preventing tragedy from affecting the singer.

Points:

- Not all devices are explosive. The training, tools, and techniques of the bomb techs make them the only personnel available to safely confront any such device.
- A bomb technician's training in hazardous materials, knowledge of on-scene investigation, and capabilities with standoff operations makes the bomb squad a valuable resource for investigations in chemically contaminated scenes: unlike fire hazmat personnel or environmental emergency response personnel, bomb technicians are criminal investigators, knowledgeable of technical and legal aspects and constraints on these scenes.

16

Case Study 5

1300 Miles of Contract Bombings

At 5:15 AM, Friday, June 7, 1991, Dimitri Callas was passing through the intersection of SW 87th Avenue and SW Miller Road (56th Street), in Miami, Florida, in his brother Enrique "Freddy" Callas's White Chevy Blazer. As he crossed the intersection, where the Miami-Dade County Operation's Center is located, an explosion and fire consumed the vehicle (Figure 16.1). It rolled to a dead stop on the curb, and its occupant, a survivor of the Bay of Pigs invasion and Cuban political prison, was instantly killed.

MDPD homicide detectives and bomb squad personnel and the agents from ATF shut down a four block area to conduct a scene search. Rather than molest the vehicle and its occupant on scene, they wrapped it in plastic, placed it on a flatbed tow truck, and transported it to the Miami-Dade Medical Examiner's Office (MDMEO), where it was placed in the evidence processing garage for secure search and body recovery. Between the PBI at the intersection, the PBI postmortem at MDMEO, and x-ray examination and subsequent evidence recovery on the autopsy table of the victim, debris was located that established a servo motor from a radio control (R/C) model car that had been involved (Figures 16.2 and 16.3). The investigators determined that it was a command detonation bombing; the time, place, and target having been carefully chosen by the bomber.

On September 8, 1991, a device detonated at 12408 SW 18th Terrace, Miami, Florida, the residence of Armaida Quinones, the former girlfriend

Figure 16.1 Vehicle Dimitri Callas was murdered in. (Courtesy of Miami-Dade Police Department.)

of Enrique Callas. The bombing produced no injuries, but considerable damage (Figure 16.4). The PBI by MDPD bomb squad and ATF agents determined that R/C electronics from a model car had been part of the fuzing system (Figure 16.5). Further, chemical analysis of residue determined the presence of an EGDN, an explosive used in dynamites.

Figure 16.2 R/C componentry recovered from victim. (Courtesy of Miami-Dade Police Department.)

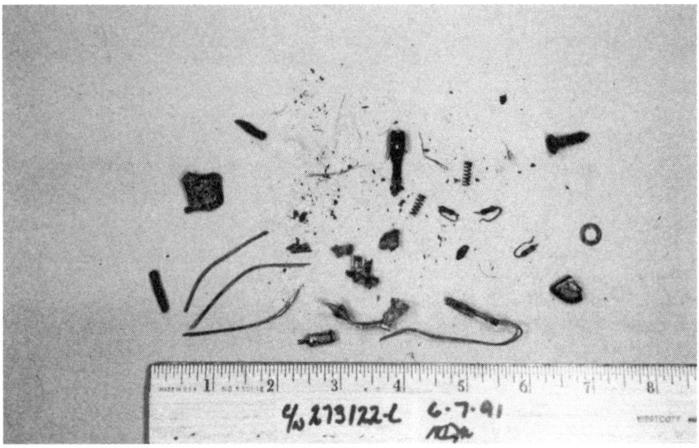

Figure 16.3 R/C componentry recovered from vehicle. (Courtesy of Miami-Dade Police Department.)

In the interim, ATF had assisted in the investigation of a bomb that seriously damaged several rooms at the Lincoln Motel, in North Bergen, New Jersey. During the scene investigation, parts from an RC model car were recovered. Significantly, EGDN was also recovered as residue. Two major facts were also determined. First, another guest, checked in under

Figure 16.4 Scene of associated car bombing in Miami-Dade County. (Courtesy of Miami-Dade Police Department.)

Figure 16.5 Servo motor recovered from scene of second Miami-Dade car bombing. (Courtesy of Miami-Dade Police Department.)

a false name and address, had been seen to enter and leave the room that had been the seat of the blast hours before the explosion. Second, it was determined that the room which was the target was routinely chosen by Enrique Callas for spending a night before returning to Miami as a long-haul truck driver between it and New York City. This bombing led ATF to join NYPD and the FBI in an existing investigation in New York. There, a group had been masquerading as police to conduct drug dealer rip-offs, running a drug organization, and providing contract killings.

The combined investigation force determined

- Enrique Callas had reportedly stolen $5 million from a New York City drug dealer, who threatened the death of Callas's family and associates until repaid within a week. An associate of the group in South Florida saw dynamite and R/C cars at one member's girlfriend's apartment. On the day of Dimitri Callas's murder, this associate saw three members leaving in a red car, to "scope out a house." When he next saw them, one commented about a bombing, and that the wrong guy was injured. Miami witnesses to Callas's bombing saw three men in one small red car and one small white car watching the explosion and scene. Upon arrival of police, they left. The small red car involved was determined to be a rental, rented by a known number of the organization, using a pseudonym. When located by ATF in a rental agency in Orlando, a swab of the trunk revealed the presence of EGDN. When investigation in New York City discovered an apartment that had been rented by the group, a swab of the refrigerator found the presence of EGDN. A search warrant of the bomb maker's apartment resulted in recovery of components for 20 RC model cars, 10 transmitters, and a variety of small hand tools. One of the tools, a pair of needle nose pliers, was identified as having cut wires recovered from the bombing of Dimitri Callas. ATF Explosive Enforcement Officers (EEO) determined all the devices were the work of one bomb maker, or at least, individuals following a single set of plans.

The investigation soon led to indictments of the members of the group and by December 1993, their convictions. Of the five involved in the bombings, three were convicted, one was indicted but unavailable due to serving time for murder in the Dominican Republic, and the last was indicted but not identified until after it was discovered he had been killed in North Carolina.

Post conviction, the bomb maker admitted to his role in the bombings; he stressed he built bombs, but did not place them.

Points:

- Bomb cases often cross jurisdictional lines; it takes cooperation among all concerned to bring a successful solution.
- Minute evidence, debris of an explosion, may be the key to determining construction of a device.
- Signature may tie various cases together, and tie a bomb maker who is not a bomb setter, into the case.
- A specialized explosives laboratory will identify specific explosive products; in this case that provided additional signature.

ADDITIONAL READING AND BOOK RESOURCES

A Field Guide to Germs, Biddle, Wayne, Anchor Books, 1995.
A Fisherman's Guide to Explosive Ordnance, Dunbar, Capt. R.N., UNC Sea Grant College Program, 1981.
A Guide for Explosive and Bomb Scene Investigations, US DOJ NIJ, 2000.
A Handbook on Charcoal Making, American Fireworks News, 2002.
A History of Greek Fire and Gunpowder, Partington, J.R., John Hopkins, 1999.
A Law Enforcement and Security Officer's Guide to Responding to Bomb Threats, Smith, Capt. Jim, C.C. Thomas, 2003.
A Pocket Guide to the Compatibility of Chemicals, Lab Safety Supply.
A Professionals Guide to Pyrotechnics, Donner, John, Paladin Press, 1997.
A Safe Practices Manual for the Manufacture, Transportation, Storage & Use of Explosives, NIOSH, 1978.
A Safe Practices Manual for the Manufacture, Transportation, Storage & Use of Pyrotechnics, NIOSH, 1991.
A Soldier's Handbook, Vol. 1: Explosives Operations, Ledgard, Jared, UVKCHEM, 2007.
Advanced Homemade Fireworks, Barrymore, Blaze C., Butokukai, 1986.
Agricultural Blasting, IME, 1976.
American Engineer Explosives in WW1, Desert Publications, 1977.
American Lightning, Blum, Howard, Crown, 2008.
Antipersonnel Mine M18A1 M18 FM 23-23, US Department of Army, 1966.
Assorted Nasties, Harber, David, Desert Publications, 1993.
ATF Law Enforcement Guide to Explosive Incident Reporting, ATF, 2001.
Basement Nukes, Strauss, Erwin S., Loompanics, 1980.
Basic Digital Electronics, Evans, Alvis J., Radio Shack, 1996.

Basic Electronics, McWhorter, Gene & Evans, Alvis J., Radio Shack, 2000.
Bath Massacre, Bernstein, Arnie, University of Michigan Press, 2009.
Bioterrorism: A Guide for the First Responder, Imaginatics Publishing, 2003
Black Powder Manufacturing Methods & Techniques, Maltitz, Ian Van, American Fireworks News, 1997.
Black Powder Manufacturing, Testing, and Optimization, Maltitz, Ian Van, American Fireworks, 2003.
Blast Damage and Other Structural Cracking, American Insurance Association, 1972.
Blaster's Handbook, ISEE, 2000.
Blasting Cap Recognition and Identification Manual, IACP, 1973.
Blasting Operations, Hemphill, Gary B., McGraw-Hill, 1981.
Blasting Vibrations and Their Effect on Structures, US Department Interior/Bureau of Mines, 1971.
Bomb Security Guide, Knowles, Graham, Security World Publishers, 1976.
Bomb Squad, Esposito, Richard & Gerstein, Ted, Hyperion, 2007.
Bomb Threat and Physical Security Planning, ATF, 1987,
Bomb Threat Management and Policy, Decker, Ronald Ray, Butterworth-Heinemann, 1999.
Bomb Threat Planning, Crouch, James E. (No Publication data)
Bomb Threats, US Department of Army, 1975.
Bombers and Firesetters, MacDonald, John M. MD, C.C. Thomas, 1977.
Bombs and Bombings, 3rd edn., Brodie, Thomas G., C.C. Thomas, 2005.
Bombs: Defusing the Threat, Borbidge, William J. III, UNF/IPTM, 1999.
Boobytraps FM 5-31, US Department of Army, 1965.
Bretherick's Handbook of Reactive Chemical Hazards, 2 Vols., Urben, P.G., Butterworth-Heinemann, 1995.
Buda's Wagon, Davis, Mike, Verso, 2007.
Building Power Supplies, Lines, David, Radio Shack, 1997.
Captains of Bomb Disposal, Reece, T. Dennis, Xlibris Corp., 2005.

Casebook of a Crime Psychiatrist, Brussel, James A., Bernard Geiss Associates, 1969.
Characterization of Non Military Explosives, Liepens, R., Research Triangle Institute, 1974.
Chem-Bio: Frequently Asked Questions, Tempest Publishing, 1998.
Chemical and Biological Warfare, Croddy, Eric, Copernicus Books, 2002.
Chemical/Nuclear Terrorism: A Guide for First Responders, Imaginatics Publishing, 2003.
Chemicals Used for Illegal Purposes, Turkington, Robert, Wiley, 2010.
CIA Field Expedient Methods for Explosives Preparation, Desert Publications, 1977.
CIA Improvised Sabotage Devices, Desert Publications, 1977.
City on Fire, Minutaglio, Bill, Harper Collins, 2003.
Construction Guide for Storage Magazines, IME, 1993.
Control of Communicable Diseases Manual, Berenson, Abram S., APHA, 1995.
Deadly Brew, Lecker, Seymour, Paladin Press, 1987.
Death in the Haymarket, Green, James, Anchor Books, 2006.
Demo Men, Smith, Gary R., Pocket Books, 1997.
Demolition Materials TM 9-1946, US Department of Army, 1955.
Demolition Materials TM 43-0001-38, US Department of Army, 1981.
Designed to Kill, Hughes, Major Arthur, Patrick Stephens, 1987.
Destruction by Demolition, Incendiaries, and Sabotage, USMC, Paladin Press.
Dos and Don'ts, IME, 1978.
Dynamite Stories and Some Interesting Facts about Explosives, Maxim, Hudson, Forgotten Books, 1916.
Electronic Formulas, Symbols, and Circuits, Mims, Forrest M. III, Radio Shack, 2000.
Emergency Care for Hazardous Materials Exposure, Bronstein, Alvin C. & Currance, Phillip L., CV Mosby Co., 1988.
Emergency Characterization of Unknown Materials, Houghton, Rick, CRC Press, 2008.
Emergency Response to Hazardous Materials Incidents, DePol, Dennis R. & Cheremisinoff, Paul N., Technomis Publishing Co., 1984.
Emergency Response to Terrorism Jobs Aid, FEMA/DOJ, 2000.

Encyclopedia of Explosives and Related Items (9 Vols.) (*Picatinny Encyclopedia of Explosives*), Federoff, Basil T., Picatinny Arsenal, 1960.

Enercell Battery Guidebook, 2nd edn., Radio Shack, 1990.

Engineer Field Data FM 5-34, US Department of Army, 1987.

Engineer's Mini Notebook—555 Times IC Circuits, Mims, Forrest M. III, Radio Shack, 1994.

Engineer's Mini Notebook—Classic Semiconductor Circuits, Mims, Forrest M. III, Radio Shack, 1986.

Engineer's Mini Notebook—Digital Logic Circuits, Mims, Forrest M. III, Radio Shack, 1986.

Engineer's Mini Notebook—Magnet and Magnet Sensor Projects, Mims, Forrest M. III, Radio Shack, 1998.

Engineer's Mini Notebook—Optoelectronic Circuits, Mims, Forrest M. III, Radio Shack, 1986.

Engineer's Mini Notebook—Schematic Symbols, Device Packages, Design and Testing, Mims, Forrest M. III, Radio Shack, 1990.

Engineer's Mini Notebook—Science and Communication Circuits & Projects, Mims, Forrest M. III, Radio Shack, 2000.

Engineer's Mini Notebook—Sensor Circuits, Mims, Forrest M. III, Radio Shack, 1986.

Engineers Field Data, US Department of Army, 1987.

EOD FM 90-15, US Department of Army, 1970.

Experimental Design and Evaluation of a Bomb Disposal Unit, IACP.

Explosives and Bomb Disposal Guide, Lenz, Robert R., C.C. Thomas, 1973.

Explosives and Chemical Weapons Identification, Crippin, James B., CRC Press, 2006.

Explosives and Demolitions FM 5-24, US Department of Army, 1986.

Explosives and Demolitions—Subcourse EN0053, Army Correspondence Course, 1994.

Explosives and Homemade Bombs, Stoffel, Joseph Major, C.C. Thomas, 1972.

Explosives and Propellants from Commonly Available Materials, Desert Publications, 1982.

Explosives and Rock Blasting, Atlas Powder Co, 1987.

Explosive and Toxic Hazardous Materials, Meidl, James J., Glencoe Press, 1970.
Explosive Product Guide, ISEE.
Explosive Materials, Wisser, John P., Forgotten Books, 2012.
Explosives, Kohler, Josef & Meyer, Rudolf, VCH Publishers, 1993.
Explosives—History with a Bang, Brown, G.I., The History Press, 1998.
Explosives Data Guide, Hermann, Stephen L., Explosives Research Institute, 1977.
Explosives Tracing Pocket Guide, US Bomb Data Center, ATF, 2005.
Explosives Training Manual, Friend, Robert C., Explosives Training Institute, 1976.
Explosives, Propellants, and Pyrotechnic Safety NOL TR 61-138, Naval Ordnance Laboratory, 1961.
Explosives, Propellants, and Pyrotechnics, Bailey, A & Murray, S.G., Brassey's, 2000.
Field Confirmation Testing For Suspicious Substances, Houghton, Rick, CRC Press, 2009.
Field Engineers No. 30 Part VI Demolitions, The War Office, Groucho Publishing, 1945.
Fire Protection Guide to Hazardous Materials, NFPA, 2002.
Firearms and Explosives Tracing, ATF.
First Responder Chem-Bio Handbook, Tempest Publishing, 1998.
First Responder's Guide to WMD, Adams, Jeffrey A. & Marquette, Stephen, ASIS, 2002.
Forensic Investigation of Clandestine Laboratories, Christian, Donnell R., CRC Press, 2003.
Forensic Investigation of Explosions, 2nd edn., Beveridge, Alexander, CRC Press, 2011.
French Foreign Legion Mines & Booby Traps, Paladin Press, 1985.
Getting Started in Electronics, Mims, Forrest M. III, Radio Shack, 2000.
Glossary of Commercial Explosives Industry Term, IME, 1991.
Glossary of Industry Terms, IME, 1978.
God's Secret Agents, Hogge, Alice, Harper Collins, 2005.
Granddads Wonderful Book of Chemistry, Saxon, Kurt, Atlan Formularies, 1975.

Grenades TM 43-0001-29, US Department of Army, 1994.
Grenades TM 9-1330-200-12, US Department of Army, 1971.
Grenades, Hand & Rifle TM 9-1330-200, US Department of Army, 1966.
Guerilla Arsenal, Harber, David, Paladin Press, 1994.
Gunpowder: Alchemy, Bombards, and Pyrotechnics: The History of the Explosive that Changed the World, Kelly, Jack, Basic Books, 2004.
Handbook for Transportation and Distribution of Explosives, IME, 1997.
Handbook of Chemical and Biological Warfare Agents, Ellison, D. Hank, CRC Press, 1999.
Handbook of Chemistry and Physics, CRC Press, 1985.
Handbook of Poisoning, Dreisbach, Robert H., Lang Medical, 1977.
Handling Telephone Bomb Threats, Mironn, Murray & Reher, Jan R., MTI, 1978.
Hawley's Condensed Chemical Dictionary, Sax, N. Irving & Lewis, Richard Sr., VanNostrand Reinhold, 1987.
Hazardous Chemicals Desk Reference, Sax, N. Irving & Lewis, Richard J. SR., VanNostrand Reinhold, 1987.
Hazardous Materials Field Guide, Bevelacqua, Armando S. & Stilp, Richard, Delmar Publishers, 1998.
Hazardous Materials for Fire and Explosion Investigators, Hildebrand, Michael S. & Noll, Gregory G., Redhat Publishing, 1998.
Hazardous Materials Guide for First Responders, USFA.
Hazardous Materials Handbook, Meidl, James H., Glencoe Press, 1972.
Hazardous Materials Response Handbook, NFPA, 1989.
Heavy Firepower, Kephart, Ryan K., Paladin Press, 1991.
Highly Explosive Pyrotechnic Composites, Schultz, Peder, Paladin Press, 1995.
Home Workshop Explosives, Uncle Fester, Festering Publications, 2002.
Homemade Ignition Thermalite, Ignitercord, Purrington, Gary W., Firefox Enterprises, 2001.
Improvised Explosives, Lecker, Seymour, Paladin Press, 1985.
Improvised Munitions Black Book, V 1 & 2, Desert Publications, 1981.
Improvised Munitions from Ammonium Nitrate, Desert Publications, 1980.

Improvised Munitions Handbook TM-31-210, US Department of Army, 1969.

Improvised Weapons of the American Underground, Desert Publications.

Introduction to Explosives, FBI BDC, 1975.

Introduction to Explosives, Newhouser, C.R., IACP/NBDC.

Introduction to the Technology of Explosives, Cooper, Paul W. & Kurowski, Stanley R., Wiley VCH, 1996.

IRA—The Bombs and The Bullets, Oppenheimer, A.R., Irish Academic Press, 2009.

Janes' Chem-Bio Handbook, Sidell, Frederick P., Patrick, William C. Dr., & Dashiel, Thomas R., Janes Information Group, 1998.

Janes' Unconventional Weapons Handbook, Sullivan, John P., Janes Information Group, 2000.

Kitchen Improvised Plastic Explosives, Lewis, Tim, Information Publishing Co., 1983.

Marijuana Field Booby Traps, Paladin Press, 1992.

Mayday: The History of a Village Holocaust, Parker, Grant, Liberty Press, 1980.

Military Chem-Bio Agents FM 3-11.9, US Army, Eximdyne, 2005.

Military Explosives TM 9-2900, War Department, 1940.

Military Pyrotechnics TM 43-0001-37, US Department of Army, 1994.

Military Pyrotechnics TM 9-1981, US Department of Army, 1951.

Minimanual of the Urban Guerrilla, Marighella, Carlos, 1969.

Modern Explosive Breaching Techniques, Matoon, Steven, Varro Press, 1999.

MTI Bombs Familiarization & Bomb Scene Planning Workbook, Brodie, Thomas G. & Feldstein, Dee, MTI, 1973.

NIOSH Pocket Guide to Chemical Hazards, NIOSH, 2004.

Nitro Explosives: A Practical Treatise, Sanford, P. Gerald, Crosby Lockwood & Son, 1906.

Nitroglycerine & Nitroglycerine Explosives, Naoum, Phukiun & Symmes, E.M., Angriff Press, 1928.

Nuclear Terms Handbook, USDOE, 1996.

PDR Guide to Bio and Chem Warfare Response, Thomson, 2002.

Poisons, Macinnis, Peter, Arcade, 2004.

Police Analysis and Planning for Vehicle Bombs, Ellis, John W., C.C. Thomas, 1999.

Police Guide to Bomb Search Techniques, Moyer, Sgt. Frank A., Paladin Press, 1980.

Poor Man's James Bond, Saxon, Kurt, Atlan Formularies, 1972.

Post-Blast VRT, ATF, 2002.

Practical Bomb Scene Investigation, Thurman, James T., CRC Press, 2006.

Practical Military Ordnance Identification, Gersback, Tom, CRC Press, 2014.

Preparatory Manual of Black Powder and Pyrotechnics, Ledgard, Jared, UVKCHEM, 2007.

Principles of Hazardous Materials Management, Griffin, Rigger D., Lewis Publishers, 1991.

Principles of IEDs, Paladin Press, 1984.

Professional Booby Traps, Lecker, Seymour, Paladin Press, 1993.

Propellant Profiles, Wolfe, Dave, Wolfe Publishing, 1999.

Protection against Bombs and Incendiaries, Pike, Earl A., C.C. Thomas, 1972.

Pyrotechnic Electric Ignition Pyrogens & Construction, Purrington, Gary W., Firefox Enterprises, 1995.

Ragnar's Big Book of Homemade Weapons, Benson, Ragnar, Paladin Press, 1992.

Ragnar's Homemade Detonators, Benson, Ragnar, Paladin Press, 1993.

Rapid Guide to Chemical Incompatibilities, Pohavish, Richard P & Greene, Stanley A., VanNostrand Reinhold, 2000.

Rapid Guide to Hazardous Materials Chemicals in the Workplace, Sax, N. Irving & Lewis, Richard J. SR., VanNostrand Reinhold, 1986.

Recognition of Explosive & Incendiary Devices, Parts 1 & 2, Crockett, Thompson S. & Newhouser, Charles R., IACP.

Recommendations for the Safe Transportation of Detonators in a Vehicle with Certain Other Explosive Materials, IME, 1993.

Rigging TM 5-725, US Department of Army, 1968.

Safety Guide for the Prevention of Radiation Hazards in the Use of Electric Blasting Caps, IME, 1977.

Silent Death, Uncle Fester, Festering Publications, 1997.

Simple Salutes (No Publication Data)

Smart Bombs, Myers, Lawrence W., Paladin Press, 1990.
Solid Propellant Engineering, 2 Vols., Taylor, James, Rocket Science Institute, 1959.
Special Effects with Fire and Smoke, Theatre Effects Inc., 1985.
Suggested Code of Regulation, IME, 1985.
Symbol Seeker, Burns, Paul P., 1994.
Terrorism Handbook, Bevelacqua, Armando S. & Stilp, Richard, Delmar Publishers, 2002.
Terrorism Handbook for Operational Responders, Bevelacqua, Armando S. & Stilp, Richard, Delmar Publishers, 1998.
Terrorist Explosives Handbook, V1—IRA, McPherson, Jack, Paladin Press, 1987.
The American Table of Distances, IME, 1991.
The Best of A.N. Class B Explosives, Hanson, Frank Dr., Self Published, 1995.
The Big Bang, Brown, G.I., Sutton Publishing, 1998.
The Chemistry and Characteristics of Explosive Materials, Cook, James R. Ph.D., Vantage Press, 2001.
The Chemistry of Explosives, Akvahan, Jacqueline, The Royal Society of Chemistry, 1998.
The Chemistry of Powder and Explosives, Davis, Tenny L., Angriff Press, 1943.
The Common Sense Approach to Hazardous Materials, Fire, Frank L., Fire Engineering, 1986.
The Complete Book of Flush Powder, Moran, Paul, Self Published, 1993.
The Confessions and Autobiography of Harry Orchard, Horsley, Albert C., Forgotten Books, 2012.
The Cult at the End of the World, Kaplan, David E, & Marshall, Andrew, Crown Publishers, 1996.
The Day Wall Street Exploded, Gage, Beverly, Oxford, 2009.
The Do It Yourself Gunpowder Cookbook, McLean, Don, Paladin PRESS, 1992.
The Dynamite Fiend, Larrabee, Ann, Palgrave Macmillan, 2005.
The Encyclopedia of Chemistry, Hampel, Clifford & Hawley, Gessner G., VanNostrand Reinhold, 1973.
The Essential Pocket Book of Emergency Chemical Management, Quigley, David P., CRC Press, 1996.

The First Responder's Pocket Guide to Hazardous Materials Emergency Response, 2nd edn., Levy, Jill Meryl, Firebelle Press, 2000.
The Infernal Machine, Carr, Matthew, The New Press, 2006.
The Mad Bomber of New York, Greenburg, Michael M., Union Square, 2011.
The Merck Index, Merck & Co., 1983.
The Official Soviet Hand Grenade Manual, Paladin Press, 1998.
The Poisoner's Handbook, Hutchkinson, Maxwell, Desert Publications, 2000.
The Poor Man's Armorer, V-1, Barrow, Clyde & Saxon, Kurt, 1977.
The Poor Man's James Bond, Saxon, Kurt, Atlan Formularies, 1972.
The Preparation Manual of Explosives: Radical, Extreme Experimental Explosives Chemistry V1, Ledgard, Jared, UVKCHEM, 2010.
The Preparatory Manual of Chemical Warfare Agents, Ledgard, Jared, UVKCHEM, 2012.
The Preparatory Manual of Explosives, 3rd edn., Ledgard, Jared, UVKCHEM, 2007.
The Texas City Disaster 1947, Stephens, Hugh W., University of Texas Press, 1997.
Two Component High Explosive Mixtures and Improvised Shaped Charges, Desert Publications, 1982.
Two Compound High Explosive Materials, Desert Publications, 1982.
Unconventional Warfare Devices and Techniques—Incendiaries TM 31-201-1, US Department of Army, 1966.
Unconventional Warfare Devices and Techniques TM 31-200-1, US Department of Army, 1966.
Understanding Germ Warfare, Warner Books, 2002.
Unexploded Ordnance Procedures FM 21-16, US Department of Army, 1981.
Using Your Meter, Evans, Alvis J., Radio Shack, 1994.
Warnings & Instructions, IME, 1992.
Weapons of Mass Destruction—Emergency Care, DeLorenzo, Robert A. & Porter, Robert S., Brady, 1999.
Weapons of Mass Destruction Awareness Guide, Hughes, Shawn, 1st Books Library, 2003.
Weapons of Mass Destruction Response and Investigation, Drielak, Steven C. and Brandon, Thomas R., C.C. Thomas, 2000.

ADDITIONAL ELECTRONIC/DIGITAL RESOURCES

A Guide to Industrial Explosion Protection, Fenwal Safety Systems.
Afghanistan Ordnance Identification Guide, Crittendan Schmitt Archives.
ATF Detonator Recognition and Identification Database, ATF.
ATF Law Enforcement Ordata II, US DoD.
Bomb Countermeasures for Security Professionals, Palladium Media, Field Manuals FM-200, Military Media Productions, 2000.
Bomb Data Center General Information Bulletins, FBI, 1999.
Bomb Data Center Investigators Bulletins, FBI, 1999.
Bomb Data Center Special Technicians Bulletins, FBI, 2000.
Bomb Threat Response Planning Tool, ATF, 2002.
Bombings: Injury Patterns and Care, CDC, 2008.
Explosives Disposal Safety, ATF, 2001.
IED Incident Management, FBI/TSWG.
Improvised Bomb Disposal Tools, FBI, 1999.
Investigating Terrorism and Criminal Extremism, DOJ BJA, 2008.
Islamic Extremist Ops/Training, Intelcenter.com, 2003.
Kurt Saxon's CD ROM Library, 1997.
Military Demolitions Plus, ArchAngel Software.
MineFacts, US DoD, 1997.
Post-Blast VRT, ATF, 2002.
SLATT Reference Material CD, DOJ BJA, 2008.
Sleuth 2011 Bombs, www.vwtapes.com, 2011.
Technical & Field Manuals EOD, Military Media Productions, 1999.
Tox Profiles, HHS ATSDR.
With Deadly Intent, USPIS, 2006.

GLOSSARY

American table of distances: The quantity–distance table, prepared and approved by IME, for storage of explosive materials to determine safe distances from inhabited buildings, public highways, passenger railways, and other stored explosive materials

Ammonium nitrate fuel oil mixture (ANFO): A blasting agent composed of ammonium nitrate and liquid hydrocarbons. Mixing fertilizer (33% nitrate based) and fuel oil can make an improvised mixture

Amperage (amps): Impedance, or quantity of electrical energy

ANAL: Ammonium Nitrate and Aluminum

ANIS: Ammonium Nitrate and Icing Sugar

Armed: In munitions, the condition of being ready to function

Arming delay: The pyrotechnic, electrical, chemical, or mechanical action that provides a time delay between the initiating action and complete alignment of all firing components. Usually installed in improvised explosive devices to allow the perpetrator to distance himself from the bomb

ATA (ATAP): Anti-Terrorism Assistance Program, an international police training program of the US Department of State

ATF: Bureau of Alcohol, Tobacco, Firearms, and Explosives

BATS: Bomb and Arson Tracking System

BDC: Bomb Data Center

Binary explosive: A two-component explosive that does not become explosive until the two components are mixed

Black powder: A mechanical mixture of potassium nitrate (75%), sulfur (10%), and charcoal (15%). Black Powder deflagrates rather than detonates; it is thus classified as a "low" explosive. Black powder is sensitive to heat, shock, and friction

Blasting agent: A relatively low-sensitive explosive, usually based on ammonium nitrate, which is insensitive to detonators and does not contain any high explosives such as nitroglycerine or TNT

Blasting cap (detonator): Any device containing any initiating or primary explosive that is used for initiating detonation

Blasting galvanometer (galvanometer): A device used for testing electrical continuity of firing lines and electrical initiators

Blasting machine: An electrical or electromechanical device that provides energy for the purpose of energizing detonators in an electric blasting circuit

Blasting multimeter: A multimeter specifically designed for testing electrical continuity of firing lines and electrical initiators

Blasting ohmmeter: An ohmmeter specifically designed for testing electrical continuity of firing lines and electrical initiators

BLEVE: Boiling Liquid, Expanding Vapor Explosion

Bomb threat plan: An organizational plan of response upon receipt of a bomb threat

Booby trap: A contrived device, explosive or nonexplosive, designed to be initiated by the unsuspecting actions of a person

Booster: An explosive used to ensure the initiation of a less sensitive explosive. A booster can be a cap-sensitive cartridge or press molded cylinder for the initiation of noncap-sensitive charges, such as blasting agents

Bridge wire: An incandescent bridge made of thin resistance wire, which is made to glow by application of an electric pulse. This heated wire is the igniter for the initiating charge in an electric detonator

Brisance: The shattering power of an explosive material as distinguished from its total work capacity. The relevant parameters are the detonation rate and the loading density (compactness) of the explosive, as well as the gas yield and the heat of the explosion

Cap crimper: A nonsparking tool used to measure and cut safety fuse, and for crimping detonators to safety fuse

Cast explosive: An explosive substance that is liquefied and poured into a mold for hardening. An example would be TNT melted and poured into a casing for hardening

CBR (CBRNe): Chemical Biological Radiological Nuclear Explosive

CFR: Code of Federal Regulations

Chemical explosion: The extremely rapid conversion of a substance, solid or liquid, into gases

Circuit: A completed path for conveying electrical current

Combustion: Simple burning. An example would be the burning of a log in a fireplace

Command initiation: An explosive device which is initiated by a command sent by wire, radio, or other direct connection; provides maximum control over initiation of the device

Commercial explosives: Those explosive materials legally manufactured for industrial purposes

Composition C-4: Military plastic explosive, consisting of Cyclonite (RDX) and a plasticizer. American composition, part of the composition explosives family

Composition explosives: A variety of explosives (Compositions A, B, C) designed by American military scientists

Confinement: Enclosure, as by a container. Typically used with low-explosive devices such as pipe bombs

Connecting wire: The wire that carries the electrical current from the power source to the electric detonator and back to the power source; also see leg wires

Consumer fireworks: Small fireworks designed to produce audible effects, ground devices containing 50 mg or less of flash powder, and aerial devices containing 130 mg or less of flash powder. Their manufacture is regulated by ATF; they are defined under the Consumer Product Safety Code (CPSC)

Continuity (electrical): The property of an electrical circuit indicating that there is a continuous and relatively low resistance path for the flow of electric current

Cook off time: See wait time

Counter charge: The placing of one explosive charge against another for purposes of detonating the charges. Used as a render-safe procedure or to destroy a misfire

Crater: Effects of an explosion when detonated on a surface. The crater configuration is a function of the surface material, surroundings, and geometric placement of the explosive material. Often used synonymously with terms seat of the explosion or epicenter

Crimping: The act of securing a fuse cap to a section of safety fuse by compressing the metal shell of the cap against the fuse by means of a cap crimper

Date-shift code: A code, required by CFRs through ATF, applied by manufacturers to the outside containers and in many cases the immediate packaging of explosive materials to aid in their identification and tracing

Deflagration: An explosive reaction such as a rapid combustion that moves through an explosive material at a velocity less than the speed of sound in the material

Delay device: A device attached to the firing system that allows the person initiating the explosive to move to a safe distance before the bomb arms or detonates

Delay detonator: An electric or nonelectric detonator used to introduce a predetermined lapse of time between the application of a firing signal and detonation

Demolition: The act of demolishing, as in destruction by explosives

Datasheet: See sheet explosive

Detonate (detonation): An instantaneous form of combustion. A high explosive is said to detonate. Detonation is the chemical reaction that takes place when a solid or liquid material (explosive) instantly changes to its gaseous form. Detonation velocities lie in the range of approximately 5000 to 30,000 feet per second (1500–9000 m per second)

Detonating cord (det cord): Detonating cords consist of a PETN core with wound hemp or jute threads and a plastic coating. The cord is initiated by a detonator, and its detonation velocity is about 21,000 feet per second (7000 m per second)

Detonation velocity: The speed of the reaction front (shock front) in a detonation. Typical velocities of detonation range from approximately 5000 to 30,000 feet per second (1500 m per second to 9000 m per second)

DHS: Department of Homeland Security

Diode: Any of a wide variety of devices that display the characteristic of permitting an electric current to flow in only one direction through their structures

Display fireworks: Large fireworks used in fireworks display shows designed primarily to produce visible or audible effects by combustion, deflagration, or detonation. They include, but are not limited to, salutes containing more than 2 grains (130 mg) of flash powder, aerial shells containing more than 40 g of pyrotechnic compositions (including any break charge and visible/audible effect composition but exclusive of lift charge), and other display pieces that exceed the limits of explosive materials for classification as "consumer fireworks." They also include fused set pieces containing components which together exceed 50 mg of flash powder

Disruptor: Mechanical device designed to project a column of water or a frangible round into a suspected bomb and "disrupt" or disarm the bomb

Double-base propellant: A commonly used propellant that uses nitrocellulose and nitroglycerine as the main ingredients. Designed as a low explosive, but may be functioned as a high explosive

Dud: The failure of a munition or improvised explosive device to function as intended

Dynamic pressure: The pressure resulting from the high wind velocity and increased density of air behind the blast shock wave; similar to incident pressure

Dynamite: Dynamite was the first trade name introduced for a commercial explosive by Alfred Nobel. Generally modern dynamites are variations in the concentration of nitroglycerine by the addition of EGDN, and binder material

E-cell: An electronic timer that relies on a very small current to plate or deplate an electrode

Electric firing system: An explosive device initiation system utilizing electricity as the power source

Electric match: A device used to cause the ignition of pyrotechnic or low-explosive materials

EOD: Explosive Ordnance Disposal. Military bomb and explosives disposal, trained in the wide variety of ordnance fuzzing systems as well as improvised explosive devices

Ethyleneglycol dinitrate (EGDN): An explosive with properties and performance characteristics almost identical to nitroglycerine. It is used in mixtures with nitroglycerine since it markedly depresses the freezing temperature of the latter compound

Exploding bridgewire detonator (EBW): An electric detonator with no primary explosive, which requires a very high electric current to function

Explosion: The sudden conversion of potential energy (chemical or mechanical) into kinetic energy with the production and release of gases under pressure. These high pressure gases then do mechanical work such as moving, changing, or shattering nearby materials. Tongue in cheek—A sudden movement from one place to another, accompanied by release of large quantities of heat, light, and pressure (Thomas G. Brodie)

Explosive compound: An explosive in which the chemicals making up the explosive have been blended molecularly. All high explosives are compounds

Explosive cutting tape (ECT): A commercially manufactured linear (flexible) shape charge with an adhesive strip attached

Explosive firing train (firing train): A series of explosions specifically arranged to produce a desired outcome, usually the most effective detonation or explosion of a particular explosive

Explosive jet: The jet of burning gases that is formed during the detonation of a shaped explosive charge, which focuses on the majority of the blast energy. Most often being associated with shaped charges (Munroe effect)

Explosive mixture: A mixture in which the chemicals (fuel and oxidizer) making up the explosive have been mixed mechanically. An example would be black powder

Explosive residue: By-products of an explosive material identifiable through laboratory examination

Exudation: The condition under storage by which the oily components ooze from explosives. An example is nitroglycerine exuding from dynamite. This condition is usually accelerated by high temperature

FBI: Federal Bureau of Investigation

Fire in the hole: Traditional warning used by American-based blasters immediately prior to initiating an explosive charge. Used to warn persons in the immediate area of impending explosive shot

Firing line: The wire that carries the electrical current from the power source to the electric detonator and back to the power source; also see leg wires. Also referred to as connecting wire

Flechette: A small dart-like metal projectile used as shrapnel in anti-personnel bombs and shells

Flex-x: See sheet explosive

Flexible linear-shaped charge: Malleable, light-weight charges that permit a directional explosive cutting force to be applied in a generally straight line against many types of hardened targets

Focusing: The effect that occurs when a blast pressure wave is directed in a specific direction

FPS: Feet per second

Fragmentation: The fast moving solid pieces created by an explosion. Primary fragmentation is that of the explosive container itself; secondary fragmentation is that of the target shattered by an explosion

Fragmentation flight path: Path or direction of travel taken by fragmentation projected away from the blast seat

Friction igniter: A pull-friction-type igniter, which, when activated, causes a spark to ignite a piece of time fuse that is abutted to the sparking source in the igniter

Fuel: Anything combustible or acting as a chemical reducing agent

Function: To operate; to explode; to cause to operate; to dispose of by functioning

Fuse: A tube or wick filled with combustible material for initiating an explosive charge

Fuse lighter: An igniter device that causes a spark to ignite a piece of time fuse that is abutted to the sparking source in the igniter

Fuze: A mechanical, electrical, or chemical igniting device for initiating an explosive

Fuzing system: A device with explosive or pyrotechnic components designed to initiate an explosive

Gels: A dynamite substitute, generally less sensitive than dynamite; may be classified as an explosive or blasting agent; also called water gels or slurries

Grains: Avoirdupois measurement of weight; one grain = .0648 grams; 7000 grains = one pound

Hazmat: Hazardous materials

HDS: Hazardous Devices School, American public safety bomb technician training center operated by FBI and US Army at Redstone Arsenal, Huntsville, AL

High explosive: High explosives detonate, which has been described as instantaneous combustion. A material that is capable of sustaining a reaction front that moves through the unreacted material at a speed equal to or greater than the speed of sound (typically 3300 fps or 1000 mps)

High order: The complete combustion of an explosive at its designed velocity with complete consumption of the explosive material

Hoax bomb: A fake bomb designed to give the appearance of an explosive bomb

Homemade explosives (HME): The use of readily available materials and/or simple chemical compounds that, when mixed together in the correct manner, form an explosive material. Also referred to as Improvised Explosives

Hygroscopic: The property of a material that absorbs and retains moisture from the air

Hypergolic: Self-igniting chemicals or compounds that, when mixed, are capable of spontaneous ignition on contact

Hypergolic compounds: Certain chemical compounds that spontaneously ignite upon contact with other chemical compounds, especially improvised pyrotechnic mixtures

IAP: Incident Action Plan

IED: Improvised explosive device

IME: Institute of Makers of Explosives, a trade organization for explosives manufactures. They produce guides for the safe handling of explosives

Incendiary: Designed to cause fires

Incident pressure: This is the pressure that travels at right angles (90°) to the direction of travel of the blast shock front

Inert: Having no explosive charge (i.e., nonfunctional)

Initiation: The action of initiating an explosive or explosive device

Insulators: Materials that inhibit or slow down the flow of electricity

Integrated circuit (IC): Technology that allows a complete circuit of as many as several hundred circuit elements, to be created on a tiny chip of silicon

Kick-outs: Unconsumed explosives or other live items not destroyed by a blast originally designed to do so, that get "kicked out" to random distances from the point of initiation

Lead azide: An excellent initiating agent for high explosives that is used extensively as the intermediate charge in detonators

Lead styphinate: An excellent initiating agent for high explosives that is used extensively as the intermediate charge in detonators

Leg wires: Wires built into an electric blasting cap, designed to tie into the firing circuit

Linear-shaped charge: A charge specifically designed to focus on the blast. Used for cutting through solid targets

Low explosive: Any material designed to function by deflagration. A material designed to deflagrate (burn) rather than detonate (explode) having a reaction front that moves through the unreacted material at a speed less than the speed of sound (typically lower than 3300 fps or 1000 mps)

Low order: The incomplete combustion of an explosive or one that has detonated at less than its maximum velocity

LVBIED: Large Vehicle-Borne IED, a type of device incorporating a vehicle as a container for transport and camouflage of a device. Contains a significant quantity of explosives, designed to target and destroy entire buildings

Magazine: Any building, structure, or container, other than the explosives manufacturing building, approved for the storage of explosive material

Mechanical explosion: The result of bursting pressure on a container. An example would be a steam boiler bursting

Mercury fulminate: A primary high explosive that was used in detonators prior to the change to Lead Azide

Military dynamite: Not a true dynamite, in that it is manufactured of 75% RDX, 15% TNT, 5% motor oil, and 5% guar flour. It was used as a substitute for commercial dynamite in military construction. It is no longer manufactured in the United States

Military explosives: Those explosive materials legally manufactured for military or combat purposes. Generally much less sensitive to initiation, and generally more powerful than commercial explosives

Misfire: Failure of an explosive to detonate as expected at the completion of a normal firing procedure; should be approached and rectified with great caution; approved waiting period must be observed

Molotov cocktail: An improvised pyrotechnic device consisting of a bottle containing a flammable liquid, such as gasoline, with a cloth stuffed in the bottleneck. The cloth is ignited and the bottle is thrown at the target

MSHA: Mine Safety and Health Administration

Munroe effect: The jetting effect of a shape charge

Negative pressure: Pressure that follows the positive pressure phase, forming a partial vacuum

NEW: Net Explosive Weight

NFPA: National Fire Protection Association

Nonelectric detonator: A time fuse-initiated detonator of explosive charges; consists of a cylindrical copper or aluminum capsule containing a mixture of initiating explosive

Nonsparking: Will not produce sparks or flame; associated with explosive ordnance disposal tools

Normally closed (NC) contact: A switch, which permits electrical current flow unless it is disturbed by applied pressure or released pressure, that causes flow to stop

Normally open (NO) contact: A switch, which does not permit electrical current flow unless it is disturbed by applied pressure or released pressure, that causes current to flow

Nuclear explosion: A nuclear explosion may be induced in two ways: fission, which is the splitting of the nucleus of atoms, or fusion, which is the joining together of the nuclei of atoms under great force

Ohm: The unit measure of electrical resistance

Ohm meter: An electronic measuring instrument used to measure electrical resistance. Traditional Ohm meters or VOM meters are never used in conjunction with explosive circuits for safety reasons

Open circuit: An electric circuit in which there is no continuous path through which an electric current can flow

Ordnance: Any and all explosive munitions including weapons and chemical/biological munitions

Oxidizer: Oxygen-rich, ionically bonded chemicals that decompose at a moderate temperature. When these chemicals decompose, they release oxygen which is then able to combine with fuels

Parallel circuit: A type of electric circuit in which the current from a power source divides to pass through a number of individual devices, after which the individual currents are brought together and flow back to the power source. Thus, any of the circuit elements can be removed from the circuit without disconnecting the other elements

PBI: Postblast Investigation

Percussion primer: Shotgun, rifle, or pistol ammunition primers which serve as initiators in some bomb and explosive assemblies, particularly those with heat or spark-sensitive explosives or nonelectric detonators

Permissible explosives: Explosives that are permitted for use in gassy and dusty atmospheres and that are approved by MSHA

PETN: Pentaerythritol Tetranitrate; used as a booster and as a filler for detonating cord; can also be used as a major main charge explosive

Photocell: A device that allows an electric current flow when exposed to light

Photodiodes: Diodes designed specifically to allow current to flow when exposed to light

Pipe bomb: An improvised explosive device in which explosives are contained in a section of metal or PVC pipe

Plosophoric: Describing any of several nonexplosive materials that become explosive when mixed

PLX: Picatinny Liquid Explosive; made by mixing nitromethane and ethylenediamine; originated at Picatinny Arsenal

Positive pressure: Pressure wave formed at the instant of detonation which compresses the surrounding atmosphere

PPE: Personal Protective Equipment

Premature ignition: A situation where a device functions before its intended time

Pressure impulse: The duration of the pressure wave

Pressure wave: Instantaneous violent movement of air that radiates outward from an explosion with high speed and great force

Primacord™: A specific brand name of detonating cord, often used as a generic term for detonating cord

Primary evidence: Fragments or parts of the actual IED and its container

Primary high explosive: Explosive compounds that are extremely sensitive to heat, shock, friction, and static electricity; typically found in detonators and used as initiators for other explosives

Primer: Synonym for booster

Printed circuit (PC): A modern method of manufacturing electronic circuitry which uses a thin insulating board to which a thin sheet of copper metal has been laminated

Projectiles: Generally those munitions associated with artillery, rockets, and mortars

Propagation: The continuous action within a mass of energetic material whereby one portion of material causes other portions to similarly react

PSI: Pounds Per Square Inch

Radio controlled (RC) device: An explosive device that uses a radio transmitter and receiver to communicate a firing signal

Radio frequency (RF) hazards: Potential hazard of radio frequency energy causing the unintentional initiation of explosive devices

RDX: Research Division Formula X, also called Cyclonite. It is used in several commercial primers and boosters, as well as C-4 plastic explosive

Rectifier: See Diode

Reflected pressure: An enhanced pressure wave created when the shock front strikes any surface or barrier in its path and reflects off the surface

Relative effectiveness (RE) factor: A number used to relate power among explosives where TNT is set as 1. For example, TATP rated .8, black powder .55, and C-4 1.34.

Relay: An electro-magnetic switch

Remote removal: The moving of a suspected bomb from one location to another utilizing ropes, hooks, lines, pulleys, and other mechanical contrivances so as to safely distance the technician from the suspected package

Render-safe procedure: The means by which a bomb or improvised explosive device is disarmed

Rigging: Use of line, rope, pulleys, etc. to move an item remotely over distance

Robot: A wheeled or tracked remotely operated vehicle used by an explosive ordnance disposal technician

Safe: Not armed

Safety: A device used to prevent arming; a positive blocking mechanism

Safety fuse: A flexible cord containing an internal burning medium by which fire or flame is conveyed at a continuous and uniform rate from the point of ignition to the point of use, usually a fuse detonator

SCR: Silicon Controlled Rectifier (semi-conductor switch)

Seat of explosion: The area of most intense physical damage caused by explosive pressures and shock waves in the vicinity of the explosive material, such as a crater

Secondary device: An explosive device designed to detonate by time delay, command, or action subsequent to an initial device. This device typically targets first responders and/or investigators

Secondary evidence: Parts, fragments, or samples of an object, structure, or location that was close to the explosion and device

Secondary high explosive: Explosives that are generally less sensitive to heat, shock, friction, and static electricity than primary high explosives

Semi-conductors: Man-made crystals, which may, under certain conditions, act either as a conductor or as an insulator

Semtex™: A high explosive manufactured in Semtin, Czechoslovakia; composed of a mixture of RDX and PETN of varying percentages and a plasticizer

Sensitivity: A physical characteristic of an explosive material classifying its ability to be initiated upon receiving an external impulse such as impact, shock, flame, friction or other influences that can cause explosive decomposition

Series circuit: An electrical circuit that allows electrical current to flow through more than one component in succession

Series-parallel: A combination of one or more series circuits and parallel circuits

Servo switch: A type of magneto-electrical switch

Shaped charge: An explosive with a cavity, either conical or linear, used to focus the energy of a detonation. See also Munroe effect

Sheet explosive: Ribbon or rectangular sheet-shaped flexible explosive consisting of PETN and binders. Synonyms Flex-X, Datasheet

Shock front: The leading edge of the pressure wave

Shock tube initiating system: A nonelectric initiating system utilizing a flexible tubing containing small amounts of high explosive to transmit a shock to a detonator. Referred to as "shock tube" or "Nonel"™

Shock wave: A transient pressure pulse that propagates at supersonic velocity

Shrapnel: Fragmentation included as a component of the bomb for the specific purpose of personnel and material damage

Shunt: A plastic, metal, or other material used to connect the loose ends of initiator wires and provide a short circuit for safety

Shunting: The connecting together of the ends of the leg wires of an electric detonator to prevent extraneous electrical energy from entering the circuit

Signature: Those characteristics of a device that are consistent with being manufactured by the same person or group

Silicon controlled rectifier (SCR): A semiconductor switching device that acts in a somewhat analogous fashion to a trap door. The application of a small electrical signal to the SCRs gate electrode turns the device on, permitting a substantial current flow between the anode and the cathode terminals

Single-base propellant: A commonly used propellant that uses nitrocellulose as the main ingredient. A low explosive

Slurries (explosive): Saturated aqueous solutions of ammonium nitrate and a fuel such as aluminum powder. Generally not detonator sensitive, but can be sensitized with the addition of additives, such as TNT or PETN

Smokeless powder: A pyrotechnic material containing nitrocellulose, and often nitroglycerine. It is used in small arms ammunition, military ammunition, and propellant actuated power devices. See also double-base and single-base propellants

Solid state: A term used generally to describe a class of electronic components in which current flow and its control take place within a solid material

Squib: An electrical device used to initiate low explosives where a burning action is desired; not to be confused with electric detonators. Similar to electric matches

Stand-off distance: The distance between an explosive charge and the target

Switch: Any wide variety of devices designed to establish, interrupt, divert, transfer, or otherwise control the flow of an electrical current or signal

Sympathetic detonation: The explosion of a second charge or device caused by nearby detonation of another charge or device without any physical connection

Tamp: To cover an explosive so as to direct the explosive energy. An example would be to place an explosive charge in a hole in the ground and cover it with a quantity of soil, thus directing the force (energy) of the explosive downward

TCV: Total Containment Vessel

Thermal effects: Effects of heat produced by an explosion relative to both the length of time and intensity of the temperature produced

TNT: Trinitrotoluene, a secondary high explosive; the standard by which all other explosives are measured

Trip wire: A hidden or camouflaged wire placed to trigger an explosion when tripped

TSWG: Technical Scientific Working Group, a US Department of Defense IED research organization

USC: United States Code

UXB/UXO: Unexploded Bomb/Unexploded Ordnance

VBIED: Vehicle Borne IED, a type of device incorporating a vehicle as a container for transport and camouflage of a device

Venting: Occurs when blast pressure is able to escape a confined space

VOD: Velocity of Detonation

Voltage: Electrical pressure

Wait time: The amount of time recommended to wait at a safe distance for misfired, low ordered, or potentially hazardous ordnance, devices, or explosives to function. Synonym of cool off time

Water cannon: See Disruptor

WMD: Weapons of Mass Destruction

APPENDIX A: LISTING OF EXPLOSIVES—MANUFACTURED AND IMPROVISED

Explosive Common Name/Synonym	Synonym 1	Synonym 2	Synonym 3	Synonym 4
Amatex				
Amatol				
Ammonal				
Ammonium nitrate explosive mixtures (cap sensitive)				
Ammonium nitrate explosive mixtures (noncap sensitive)				
Ammonium perchlorate explosive mixtures				
Ammonium picrate	Picrate of ammonia	Explosive D		
ANFO [ammonium nitrate-fuel oil]				
ANAL				
ANIS				
Azide explosives				
Baranol				
Baratol				
Black powder substitutes				
Black powder				
Blasting agents	Nitro-carbo-nitrates			
Blasting caps/ nitro-carbo-nitrates				

(*Continued*)

Explosive Common Name/Synonym	Synonym 1	Synonym 2	Synonym 3	Synonym 4
Blasting gelatin				
Blasting powder				
Bulk salutes				
Chlorate explosive mixtures				
Composition A and variations				
Composition B and variations				
Composition C and variations				
Cyclotol				
DATB [diaminotrinitrobenzene]				
DDNP [diazodinitrophenol]				
DEGDN [diethyleneglycol dinitrate]				
Detonating cord				
Detonators				
Dinitroglycerine [glycerol dinitrate]				
Display fireworks				
Dynamite				
EGDN/ethylene glycol dinitrate, nitroglycvol	Nitroglycol	Ethylene glycol dinitrate		
Erythritol tetranitrate explosives				
Flash powder				
Fulminate of mercury				
Fulminate of silver				
Fulminating gold				
Fulminating mercury				
Fulminating platinum				
Fulminating silver				
Guncotton				
Hexolites				

(*Continued*)

Explosive Common Name/Synonym	Synonym 1	Synonym 2	Synonym 3	Synonym 4
HMTD [hexamethylenetriperoxidediamine]				
HMX [cyclo-1,3,5,7-tetramethylene 2,4,6,8-tetranitramine]	High Melt Explosive	Her Majesty's Explosive	Octogen	
Igniter cord				
Igniters				
Initiating tube systems				
Lead azide				
Lead styphnate/lead trinitroresorcinate, styphnate of lead	Lead trinitroresorcinate	Styphnate of lead		
Mercuric fulminate				
Minol-2 [40% TNT, 40% ammonium nitrate, 20% aluminum]				
Nitrocellulose explosive				
Nitrogen tri-iodide/ammonium tri-iodide	Ammonium tri-iodide			
Nitroglycerine/glyceryl trinitrate, trinitroglycerine	Glyceryl trinitrate	Trinitroglycerine		
Nitroguanidine explosives				
Nitroparaffins Explosive Grade and ammonium nitrate mixtures				
Nitrostarch				
Nitrourea				
Octol [75% HMX, 25% TNT]				
PBX [plastic bonded explosives]				
Pentolite				
Perchlorate explosive mixtures				

(*Continued*)

Explosive Common Name/Synonym	Synonym 1	Synonym 2	Synonym 3	Synonym 4
PETN [nitropentaerythrite, pentaerythrite tetranitrate, pentaerythritol tetranitrate]				
Picrate explosives				
Picratol				
Picric acid (manufactured as an explosive)				
PLX [95% nitromethane, 5% ethylenediamine]				
Potassium nitrate explosive mixtures				
Pyrotechnic compositions				
PYX [2,6-bis(picrylamino)] 3,5-dinitropyridine				
RDX	Cyclonite	Hexogen		
Safety fuse				
Salutes (bulk)				
Silver azide				
Silver fulminate				
Slurried explosive mixtures of water, inorganic oxidizing salt, gelling agent, fuel, and sensitizer (cap sensitive)				
Smokeless powder				
Sodium azide explosive mixture				
Special fireworks				
Squibs				
TATB [triaminotrinitrobenzene]				
TATP [triacetonetriperoxide]	Acetone Peroxide	Mother of Satan		

(Continued)

Explosive Common Name/Synonym	Synonym 1	Synonym 2	Synonym 3	Synonym 4
TEGDN [triethylene glycol dinitrate]				
Tetrazene [tetracene, tetrazine, 1(5-tetrazolyl)-4-guanyl tetrazene hydrate]				
Tetryl [2,4,6 tetranitro-N-methylaniline]				
TMETN [trimethylolethane trinitrate]				
TNEF [trinitroethyl formal]				
TNEOC [trinitroethylortho-carbonate]				
TNEOF [trinitroethylorthoformate]				
TNT	Triton trinitro-toluene	Trotyl	Trilite	Triton
Torpex				
Urea nitrate				
Water-in-oil emulsion explosive compositions				

APPENDIX B: EXPLOSIVE PRECURSORS

1H-Tetrazole
5-Nitrobenzotriazol
Acetone
Aluminum (powder)
Ammonium nitrate
Ammonium perchlorate
Ammonium picrate
Barium azide
Calcium ammonium nitrate
Calcium nitrate
Carbohydrates (e.g., spices) in bulk
Citric acid
Diazodinitrophenol
Diethyleneglycol dinitrate
Dinitroglycoluril (Dingu)
Dinitrophenol
Dinitroresorcinol
Dipicryl sulfide
Guanyl nitrosaminoguanylidene hydrazine
Hexafluoroacetone
Hexamine
Hexanitrodiphenylamine (Dipicrylamine [or] Hexyl)
Hexanitrostilbene
Hexolite
Hydrazine
Hydrochloric acid
Hydrogen peroxide
Lead azide
Lead styphnate (Lead trinitroresorcinate)
Magnesium (powder)
Mercury fulminate
Methanol
Methyl ethyl ketone

Nitric acid
Nitrobenzene
Nitrocellulose
Nitroguanadine
Nitromannite (Mannitol hexanitrate)
Nitromethane
Nitrostarch
Nitrotriazolone
Petroleum jelly
Phosphorus
Potassium chlorate
Potassium nitrate
Potassium perchlorate
Potassium permanganate
Sodium azide
Sodium chlorate
Sodium nitrate
Sodium perchlorate
Sugar (including heavily sugar-based products)
Sulfur
Sulfuric acid
Tetranitroaniline
Tetrazene
Trinitrophenol (Picric acid)
Urea

INDEX

F

G

H

O

P

T